Networking in
Multinational Enterprises

CRITICAL ISSUES FACING
THE MULTINATIONAL ENTERPRISE

Brian Toyne, Series Editor

*Multinationals and
Canada—United States Free Trade*
by Alan M. Rugman

*International Business
and Governments:
Issues and Institutions*
by Jack N. Behrman and Robert E. Grosse

*Entrepreneurship in Training:
The Multinational Corporation
in Mexico and Canada*
by Michael A. DiConti

*Networking in Multinational
Enterprises: The Importance
of Strategic Alliances*
by Bernard Michael Gilroy

Networking in Multinational Enterprises
The Importance
of Strategic Alliances

by BERNARD MICHAEL GILROY

University of South Carolina Press

Copyright © 1993 University of South Carolina

Published in Columbia, South Carolina, by the
University of South Carolina Press

Manufactured in the United States of America

Library of Congress Cataloging-in-Publication Data

Gilroy, Bernard Michael, 1956–
   Networking in multinational enterprises : the importance of
strategic alliances / by Bernard Michael Gilroy.
      p.   cm. — (Critical issues facing the multinational
enterprise)
   Includes bibliographical references and index.
   ISBN 0–87249–845–X (alk. paper)
   1. Strategic alliances (Business) 2. International business
enterprises. I. Title. II. Series.
HD69.S8G55 1993
338.8'8—dc20   92–27434

For my parents and network peers at home
Martina, Patrick, and Niklas

Contents

Illustrations

Tables

Series Editor's Preface

The purpose of this series is to explore the multifaceted relationship of multinational enterprises (MNEs) with their global environment. Essentially, each book in the series is written by an expert, and addresses a single issue of recognizable concern to MNEs. Thus, the aim of each book is to draw together and present the views of the various groups interested in the issue in a way that presents constructive suggestions for multinationals, irrespective of their nationality and inherent interests. Toward this end, each issue is placed in its historical setting and explored from the perspective of the MNEs, their home countries, and the host countries in which they operate—where they agree and where they disagree, and why. Of particular concern are the differences that have emerged, or are emerging, by region (even by country when necessary) and among multinationals from different parts of the world.

Thoughtful practitioners will find the series helpful in developing a better understanding of the organizations they work for, and interact or compete with. They will also gain a much better appreciation of the extent of the MNE's social, economic and political influence. Specifically, the series is designed to provide a "library" of the many views taken toward the multinational by the governments, labor organizations, and societies in which they operate or intend to operate, and the reasons for these differing views.

Educators will also find the series of value as a supplemental set of readers for topics in business administration, economics, international relations, and political science courses. Because of the scope of the series, and its historical perspective, students will eventually have access to an extensive and thorough analysis of the MNE, the role it plays, the influence it has on the global economic and political order, and thus the way it is viewed by other societal organizations.

The topic of *Networking in Multinational Enterprises: The Importance of Strategic Alliances* by Bernard Michael Gilroy is both timely and important. The network concept has captured the interest of academics, government policy makers, and practioners alike. More specifically, this book focuses on the importance of a multinational network to the multinational enterprise and its economic opportunities. The main advantage of the multinational enterprise, as differentiated from a national enterprise, lies in its ability to transfer resources through a global network comprised of other multinational enterprises, international organizations, and governments. These resources range from information and influence to the use of advanced technology and capital in cooperative ventures. The concept of networking calls for the development of a theoretical framework and specific examples of network activity on a global scale. Dr. Gilroy provides them in this study. Thus, the book should be of interest to specialists in international business and economic policy and practice.

Brian Toyne
Series Editor

Preface

Recent literature on the phenomenon of multinational enterprises has emphasized the applications of so-called new forms of internationalization which include foreign involvement other than 100 percent equity ownership. Recent implementation of these transactional regimes in multinational enterprise is, however, not new at all. Scholars of international business have well recognized their importance (e.g., Richard Robinson's article about nonequity forms of foreign involvement that appeared in the *Columbia Journal of World Business* in 1958). What is new is the idea of examining the multinational enterprise from a network perspective as an explicitly chosen business strategy. Conceptually, the network approach is founded upon the value-added chain of microeconomics and flows of information, which emphasizes the role played by a high degree of flexibility (central decentralization) as the relevant determinant of multinational international competitiveness.

Nonequity and equity transactional relationships, or networks of strategic alliances, are found upon complementary firm-specific assets which permit the existence of quasi-rents in network partnerships and collaborative arrangements. Traditional theorizing on multinational enterprise maintains that firm-specific assets are internalized due to transaction cost economizing. Along these lines of thought, the rapid expansion of multinational enterprises is founded upon internalization strategies. This approach stresses the relative triviality of marginal intraenterprise transaction costs compared to those of spot markets. Within the network approach to multinationality presented here, it is also postulated that enterprises possess important complementary functions embedded in their interdependent transactional environments. The establishment of global networks of strategic alliances among enterprises, as well as among enterprise employees and among nations, is in itself a firm-specific asset which also creates an economic quasi-rent increasing long-run enterprise (i.e. network) profitability. Given these observed linkages, the central focus of the study is to examine the multinational enterprise from the perspective of networking on a broad scope, as opposed to the now common internalization approach toward multinationality. A broad approach is employed, in order to make the material commonly accessible to economists, managers, and politicians.

Applying the concept of networking in writing this book, I have gone beyond my own boundaries of wisdom and borrowed heavily where necessary from the thinking of others. A long list of people share credit for casting my thinking (both through personal contact and from the literature) about networks of multinational enterprise. Without any attempt at completeness, I do wish to mention Udo Broll, Peter Buckley, Pascal Burkard, John Cantwell, Mark Casson, Richard Caves, Jens Cordes, John Dunning, Wilfred Ethier, Suman-tra Ghoshal, Heinz Hauser, Elhahan Helpman, Hans-Joachim Heine-mann, Heinz Kaplanek, Dietmar Knies, Paul Krugman, Robert Leu, Robert D. Pearce, Norbert Reetz, Norimasa Satoh, Bernd Schips, Jonathan B. Tucker, Brian Toyne, and Joachim Wagner. Finally, helpful detailed comments were also received from an anonymous reader at the University of South Carolina Press. The usual disclaimer applies. In addition to those mentioned above, I would like to thank Yngve Abrahamsen, Leslie Bocanegra, and Guido Boller for their PC-assistance. Christine Baer, Juergen Florschutz, and Karoline Jostes of the library at the University of St. Gallen also were very helpful in supplying me with the necessary literature given a tight time constraint. A special note of thanks goes to the Forschungsstelle fuer empirische Wirtschaftsforschung (FEW), University of St. Gall, Switzerland, and the Department of Economics, University of Reading, England, for providing a creative and enjoyable working atmosphere while working on this book.

Networking in
Multinational Enterprises

CHAPTER 1

The General Setting

> Now that the global village is truly upon us, it looks more like a global industrial park. We live in an expansive new world of economic interconnections where business roars through borders and time zones. —*Fortune,* July 30, 1990

The economic and management consequences of analyzing the multinational enterprise from the perspective of networking on a broad scope are the focus of this book. Recent developments in the field of international business are changing our picture of the multinational enterprise of the early 1970s and 80s. It is no longer appropriate to classify multinational enterprises as simple headquarter–subsidiary relationships. Instead, new organizational forms and operating procedures are evolving.

The management of network structures and the competitive advantages that arise from the potential scope economies of such network structures are now the key issues to be identified. Industrial transformation processes are occurring rapidly at the boundaries of enterprises, rather than at their core. Postwar growth of international trade and production of the manufacturing firms of the industrialized countries can be viewed as an accumulation of technology and capital within multinational enterprises, and in international networks of production and trade (Cantwell 1989).

Competition in international markets has led to an increasing awareness among management that many of today's international business success stories are based upon cooperative behavior among enterprises. Recent authors on international business[1] have recognized the need to develop a theoretical framework to study both aspects of enterprise behavior (cooperative and competitive) as compatible, complementary aspects of a unique reality—i.e., networking and strategic alliances. Furthermore, it is becoming increasingly evident that the cooperative relationships of multinational enterprises can contribute significantly to an enterprise's competitive strength and strategic value.

---

1. Notably Fennema (1982), Mueller (1986), Thorelli (1986), Dunning (1988a, b), Jarillo (1988, 1989), Bartlett and Ghoshal (1988, 1989), Robinson (1988), Johanson and Mattson (1987, 1988), Walker (1988), Forsgren (1989), Marcati (1989), Ghoshal and Bartlett (1990), Hagedoorn and Schakenraad (1990), Auster (1990), Casson (1990), Business International (1990), Larson (1991), and Ohmae (1990).

Major multinational enterprises such as General Motors–Toyota–Hitachi–Isuzu–Suzuki–Daewoo, Chrysler–Mitsubishi, Ford–Mazda–Nissan–Volkswagen, Daimler-Benz–Mitsubishi, Volvo–Renault, General Electric–Samsung–Societé National d'Etude de Construction de Moteurs d'Aviation S.A. (SNECMA), AT&T–Olivetti–NEC–Mitsubishi, Corning Incorporated–CIBA-GEIGY, Fuji–Xerox, Nippon–Otis, Canon–Eastman Kodak, Thomson–JVC–Siemans, Motorola–Toshiba, Honeywell–Ericsson, Siemans–IBM, and Texas Instruments–Hitachi, to name just a few, have teamed up with former rivals in order to take on the challenge of future economic prospects in the interdependent 1990s. Given such observations, the basic point of this book is to emphasize that multinational enterprises are not necessarily entirely "internalized" entities, but rather that the activities necessary for the production of a given good or service can be carried out either by an integrated firm or by a network of firms (Jarillo 1988, 39). More specifically, however, all enterprises are embedded in a network environment. A multinational enterprise consists of an internal network of internationally dispersed and goal disparate organizations that includes their headquarters and their foreign affiliates. Such an entity is also embedded in an external network consisting of all other organizations such as customers, suppliers, regulators, and so on (Ghoshal and Bartlett 1990). Networks are strategic industrial governance structures based upon the formation of intra-enterprise and inter-enterprise long term cooperative relationships that enhance both static and dynamic resource allocation efficiency culminating in superior enterprise competitiveness.

If an enterprise is successful in creating strategic alliances among the most efficient suppliers of intermediate goods and services along the value chain toward the end product, and managers are successful in positioning their enterprises upon the frontier of superiority due to comparative advantage of some core asset, transaction costs will be reduced and an economically efficient strategic network system of multinationality evolves. The network mode of organization that emerges permits multinational enterprises to reap the economic efficiency benefits of the properties of markets and some of the properties of hierarchies simultaneously.

Current analysis of multinational enterprises along the lines of the now common internalization or hierarchical approach overemphasizes the structural dimensions of internationalization. The analysis is commonly static (in the sense of placing emphasis upon the structural elements of plant location and the elimination of transaction costs at a discrete point in time). A theory of foreign direct investment based solely upon hierarchical structures inadequately captures the exciting nature of multinationality and observed patterns of internationalization. A network perspective of multinational enterprises offers a more realistic explanation of the observed operational, organizational flexibility and externalities present in international investment patterns. Although networks do not necessarily replace hierarchical structures of multinational enterprises, they may make existent hierarchical structures more effective.

At one time multinational enterprises may have been simply the providers of technology and finance for foreign direct investment. Recently they have become global organizers of economic networks, including systems for strategic allied technological development. Globalizing markets are dramatically reshaping organizational methods of production. The boundaries of industries are being redefined through the power of information and bargaining technologies and investments in mutual trust capital. As noted by Williamson (1991), a consensus is emerging that the theory of the firm must be more fully developed in "management respects" (see further Coase 1988, 38; Demsetz 1988, 155; Williamson and Winter 1991).

GENERAL MANAGEMENT NEEDS FOR THE 1990S

In a recent survey on strategic management (Lyles 1990), the respondents were asked to indicate the topics that will have the most relevance to practicing general managers in the next ten years. Seventy-eight items were listed, with the average respondent listing 2.7 items. Table 1.1 summarizes these results.

Across the board, globalization seems to be the most important area for a future research agenda. Over 18 percent of the suggestions focused on the topic of international and global competition, and a frequency of 15 suggests that 50 percent of the respondents listed it. Globalization is seen as clearly the most important topic for practicing managers in the 1990s. Two other topics that will be of increasing importance to practicing managers and theorists of multinational enterprise in the future are technology, innovation, information, and strategic alliances. Globalization, technology, innovation, information, and strategic alliances are all at the very heart of the preeminent network structures of multinational enterprises.

Managing changing organizations, transformation, and implementing strategy now consistently ranks high in many of the articles in recent business and economic journals.[2] Contrary to common static

---

2. See, e.g., the recent special issues: *The Columbia Journal of World Business* 22 (Summer 1987), Focus: International Corporate Linkages; *Management International*

Table 1.1:   **Topics Most Relevant To Practising**

General Managers In Next 10 Years

Topic	Frequency	Percentage
International/global competition	15	18.29
Technology, innovation, information	10	12.20
Strategic alliances	9	10.97
General management	9	10.97
Strategy implementation	8	9.76
Strategic change and flexibility	8	9.76
Industry/environmental analysis	5	6.10
Strategic competitive advantages	4	4.88
Mergers, takeovers, crises	4	4.88
Strategic decision-making	3	3.66
Diversification	3	3.66
Other	4	4.88
Total	82	100.00

Source: Lyles (1990), page 369.

Review 28 (1988); *The Swiss Review of International Economic Relations (Aussen-wirtschaft)* 1.2 (June 1988): Technology and Public Policy; *Administrative Science Quarterly* 35 (March, 1990): Technology, Organizations, and Innovation; and *Organizational Dynamics* (Winter 1991), devoted entirely to international cooperative ventures. Further consult the conference volume Contractor and Lorange (1988a), and Business International (1990) as well as various issues of *Japan Economic Journal*.

economic belief, as Cantwell (1989) has stressed, these developments have very little to do with any failure or malfunctioning of the markets for technology, innovation, or information. Instead they are illustrative of the close connection between the generation and the utilization of a characteristic kind of technology within each enterprise. Through the extension of networks each enterprise extends the use of its own unique line of technological development, and by extending it into new environments it increases the complexity of this development. The expansion of international production thereby brings cumulative gains to the enterprise as a whole, as the experience gained from adapting its technology under new conditions feeds back new ideas for development within the rest of the enterprise network. For this reason, once they have achieved a sufficient level of technological strength in their own right, multinational enterprises are particularly keen to produce in the geographical areas from which their major international rivals have emanated, which offer them access to alternative sources of complementary innovation.

Local entrepreneurial competitiveness attracts global competitors, resulting in the clustering of multinational enterprises as global networks with higher levels of inward direct investment in entrepreneurially competitive countries. For empirical evidence with regard to the clustering of the American, British, German, and Japanese 200 top enterprises see Chandler (1987, 59–67, Tables 3.1–4). Axelrod and Hamilton (1981, 1394) have found that clustering is a mechanism that can get cooperation started when participating parties of a noncooperative game situation find themselves locked into the "defect-defect" subcell of their corresponding payoff matrix. Another possible explanation of clustering is that such behavior is based upon the objective of developing "insider" market advantages; for example, Japanese regional investments in the automobile and consumer electronics industries are such clustered investments (Morrison, Ricks, and Roth 1991, 25).

In order to explain why multinational enterprises have expanded so rapidly, it is necessary to understand the alternative modes of mediating international transactions (foreign direct investment, equity and nonequity forms of internationalization) as well as the strategic scope of their application by multinational enterprises.

The main advantage of the multinational enterprise, as differentiated from a national corporation, lies in its flexibility to transfer resources internationally through a globally maximizing network.

There is a division of labor in a network that means that enterprises are dependent on each other. Their activities need to be coordinated. Coordination takes place through interaction among enterprises in the network, in which price is just one of several influencing conditions.

Enterprises maintain a complex set of external ties with customers and competitors. These external ties lead to a corresponding set of internal ties that link the various parts of the enterprise and are necessary in performing transactions with customers. This network of ties adapts rapidly to changing market conditions and customer needs.

The internationalization of production has given rise to modern industrialism, reducing the independence of the individual producer while simultaneously increasing the total product available through cooperative effort. Enterprise organizational structure involves not only important issues of control such as span of responsibility and authority (stressed commonly in the transaction cost approach associated with Oliver Williamson) but also even more important relational issues pertaining to the key linkages that need to be maintained to conduct business in a dynamic and flexible enterprise network system.

Rugman (1980a, 23) characterizes internationalization as the process of expanding abroad at a slow and cautious pace. Foreign markets are penetrated by appropriate entry strategies such as exporting, licensing and establishing local warehouses, direct local sales, assembly and packaging facilities. Other strategies include joint venture formation or, ultimately, foreign direct investment in the form of full-scale local production and marketing by a wholly owned subsidiary. Thus, globalization of production is a very broad concept including all the business linkages that arise on an international basis.

The forces of globalization have arisen in response to fundamental structural changes that have transformed production methods in world markets. Worldwide sourcing strategies of multinational enterprises reflect the new international division of labor, that is, the movement from simple commodity exchange to international production and cooperative inter-enterprise arrangements.

The global strategies of multinational enterprises and the internationalization of national economies are due to the rising levels of interdependence among the world's nations. To a large extent, the rapid growth in intrafirm trade has enhanced international specialization along the lines of comparative advantage at the firm level (Gilroy 1989; Rugman 1990). Intrafirm trade reflects strategic attempts to diversify over broad ranges of industries, allowing for specialization along product lines or according to processes within industries rather than the traditional interindustry specialization. The upshot of this is relative ease in adjusting to structural change (UNIDO 1981; Preusse 1985).

Figure 1.1 briefly lists those factors that have promoted the extension of a *novel* division of labor and the international specialization of production.[3] A direct consequence of these developments is that the welfare of most nations is becoming increasingly and more inextricably linked to the foreign trade sector and international production (Gilroy 1989).

The division of labor has become increasingly complex, involving higher degrees of specialization and transactional involvement at the level of the firm within international trade flows. As suggested by Shachar and Zuscovitch (1990, 136), "The basic threat to the stability of the division of labor between markets and hierarchies is the development of information technologies."

INFORMATION CREATION, DIFFUSION, AND CONTROL

Previous analyses concerning the incorporation of multinational enterprise have stressed the so-called internalization hypothesis (discussed below in chapter 2) when explaining the phenomenon multinational enterprise. Multinational enterprises were regarded as self-contained and internally controlled administrative systems. Global firms were thought to optimize the control of fully owned affiliates.

The casual assumption that control via ownership in the parent-subsidiary relationship is more complete and easily enforceable than control via contract, as Robinson (1988, 165) has stressed, requires further examination.[4] "In the international case, where markets may be disorganized, prices far removed from representing true scarcity values, and national values and priorities at wide variance, governments intervene in many ways. In so doing, they impinge heavily on ownership-based control. I would argue the point in that assets located on the other side of an international border from the owners are *never* subject to the same degree of control by the owners as in the purely domestic case, even if those assets are 100 percent-owned" (Robinson 1988, 166, 175).

Masten, Meehan, and Snyder (1989) have also pointed out that ownership of physical assets does not necessarily require that production be governed within the enterprise. A buyer may own the physical assets specific to production of a component but purchase the

---

3. For an interesting detailed discussion of these developments see Casson et al. (1986, chaps. 2, 3); OECD 1987a.
4. See the discussion in Ghoshal and Bartlett (1990, 607).

Figure 1.1:
Factors Promoting the Extension of the Division of Labor and
the International Specialization of Production

Affecting the division of labor in general:

    (1) Advances in product design, especially the redesign of
         products as multicomponent goods

    (2) Skills in promoting the division of labor through
         standardization and quality control

    (3) Changes in tastes, and higher incomes, promoting the demand
         for mass-produced consumer durables

Affecting international specialization in particular:

    (4) Rural-urban migration in NIC's

    (5) Better management education in developed countries

    (6) Improved communications: jet travel for executives, satellite
         links in telecommunications, etc.

    (7) Development of skills in organizing commercial intelligence

    (8) Improved transport systems: motorways, enlarged ports,
         containers, roll on/off systems, etc.

    (9) Creation of customs areas, free trade areas, export processing
         zones, etc.

    (10) Development of new greenfield production sites

Source: Casson et. al. (1986, page 3)

component from an outside supplier. As an illustration of this practice
they note that the U.S. automobile industry manufacturers commonly
own specialized tooling whether or not they decide to internalize
production. Hence the decision to internalize production—e.g.,
through vertical integration—can be separated from the question of
ownership of physical assets.

Monteverdi and Teece (1982) have argued that retaining ownership title to specialized physical capital required for input supply, and
thus the right to transfer those assets to another supplier if necessary,
may be sufficient to deter supplier opportunism.

Models of foreign direct investment have stressed the motivational and structural reasons for going abroad based on locational
factors and market imperfections (e.g., the appropriability risk problems of proprietary knowledge, industrial structures, and product
differentiation). While recognizing the importance of internalizing
such transactions on an international basis, this book stresses an externalization hypothesis, as observed through the recent high-level
usage of equity and nonequity forms of internationalization without
complete control and their economic foundation in the principles of
networking and strategic alliances. Managing international networks
of multinational enterprises is not simply a problem of control. It is
rather a problem of deployment and allocation of resources within
internal and external networks to take advantage of country poten-
tials and of establishing the right transfer mechanisms to move resources globally where they achieve the best strategic organizational
fit (Marcati 1989).

Centralized decisions cannot adjust as flexibly to the special circumstances of cases in global markets as decentralized decisions can.
Agents within a hierarchical system possess private information that
should affect decisions but which, for various reasons, is not available
to the central authority. Hayek (1945) first realized the existence
of such informational problems. According to Hayek, the Walrasian
"decentralization" notion is incorrect since one must postulate that
the central auctioneer collects all the economy's necessary information and processes it, thereby setting the market-clearing prices.
However, as Hayek points out, true decentralization consists of dele-
gating decisions to those who possess the most relevant information.
Or, in his own words, "The problem is precisely how to extend the
span of our utilization of resources beyond the span of the control of
any one mind [or enterprise]" (p. 527). Hayek argued further that
"economic problems arise always and only in consequence of change.
The economic problem of society is mainly one of rapid adaptation
in the particular circumstances of time and place" (pp. 523–24). Johanson and Mattson (1987) have also emphasized that in networks
the exchange process serves to permit transacting parties to test how
well they fit each other. The process is simultaneously a learning
process and an adaptation process.

The creation and diffusion of information is essential to any firm strategy. Formal channels of information diffusion in multinational enterprises are often distorted, and informal information flows are becoming more and more relevant. Networks have the advantageous feature that "they do not have a top person or a central power elite. In a sense, every networker is at the center of the net" (Barham 1990, 2).

As Hayek has pointed out elsewhere, the process of competition has the function of being a method of discovering new techniques of production and new products and services (Hayek 1968). The important advantage of the market coordination mechanism is hence the dynamic functions it carries out, rather than the simple static perspective of allocative efficiency given unrealistic assumptions. In this vein new forms of multinational organization through networking and strategic alliances may be viewed as the result of interactions between rational economic agents in the market for entrepreneurial functions.

Technological change has also greatly affected the amount of externalization of services formerly internal to multinational enterprises (Sylos-Labini 1984). In December 1988 the first transatlantic fiber-optic cable was completed. This was rapidly followed by the first transpacific fiber-optic cable linking California to Japan in December 1989. The deployment of such advanced global telecommunications infrastructures permits the transmission of information at the speed of light. Location is becoming irrelevant for a growing number of enterprise activities (Davidson 1991, 10). The full potential of these technological developments has only begun to be realized by enterprise management.

Multinational enterprise networks have expanded the contractual route of transferring and sharing firm-specific assets throughout the world as well as nonequity forms of international business.[5] The term "nonequity forms of investment" is defined as international investments in which foreign investors do *not* hold a controlling interest via equity participation—i.e., nonmajority ownership investment.

Specifically, nonequity forms of investment refer to: (a) joint international business ventures in which foreign-held equity does not exceed 50 percent; (b) international contractual arrangements which involve at least an element of investment from the foreign enterprise's viewpoint but which may involve no equity participation by that enterprise whatsoever, as is often the case with licensing ar-

---

    5. See Buckley (1983, 1987), Oman (1984), Borner (1986), and United Nations Centre on Transnational Corporations (1987).

rangements, management, service, production-sharing contracts, and, occasionally, subcontracting and turnkey operations (Oman 1984, 12).

Networking is a continuously changing dynamic process. As Buckley (1988, 183) comments,

> Industrial structure to some degree represents industrial archaeology. For instance, multinationals are increasingly foregoing control of production in favour of control of distribution (see, for instance, Rugman and McIlveen 1985). . . . These issues are bound up in the evolution of a new international division of labour in which a hierarchy of functions is emerging (Hymer's 1971 article was prophetic here). Multinational firms' dominance is no longer through ownership of production but through a network of contracts appropriate to the strategy of the firms and entailing tight control only of key core functions.

WHAT IS NETWORKING?

Imai (1989, 124) appropriately defines networking as follows:

> In "network industrial organization" analysis, the basic unit is not the firm or other economic agents acting in isolation but a relation among various economic agents. The network view is basically a process view, in which dynamic changes in the interconnected network of market decisions are emphasized. The focus is on the dynamism of multi-structured connections rather than the static and orderly alignment of firms such as that sometimes presumed in the traditional industrial organization analysis.

Networking lies somewhere between the spectrum of spot-market (arm's length) transactions and organizational hierarchies (see Figure 1.2, Thorelli 1986, and Ireland 1990). Markets and hierarchies represent the common mechanism by which an optimal allocation of scarce resources is achieved in economic theory.

The basic proposition of networking, as Imai points out, is that resource allocation in the market area is not only through the market principle but also, to a great extent, by the organization principle. The allocation of resources within an enterprise is also based upon the market principle and organization principle. As Ireland (1990, 107) notes, "A market, in its broadest sense, is nothing more than an informationally integrated network within which individuals transact

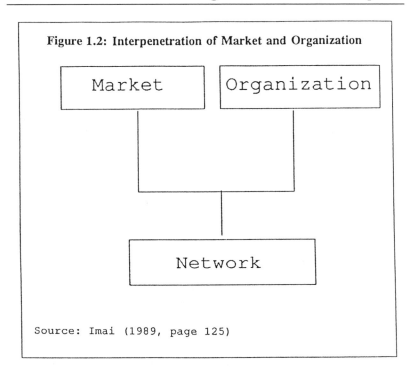

Figure 1.2: Interpenetration of Market and Organization

Source: Imai (1989, page 125)

with each other and consider alternative individuals with whom to transact in the future."

Textbooks usually presume that enterprises have one goal according to the market principle: profit maximization. They have one strategy: price competition, and one organization principle: cost minimization. As Richardson (1972) earlier pointed out, however, enterprises are mutually related units located in linked positions rather than standing as completely independent units, which leads to networks. Imai and Itami (1984) have termed this the "interpenetration of market and organization." Being a combination of markets and hierarchies, a network is thus an intermediate form of resource allocation. Behind the concept of networking is an economic theory of cooperation as an alternative to competition and integration. If one wishes to maintain a hierarchical view of multinational enterprises, then it may be assumed that networks create a hierarchy of corporate membership within the network group, "one based on considerations of long-term economic promise and financial viability" (Lei and Slocum 1991, 60).

The goal of absolute efficiency (cost minimization) in production of goods and services is not universal but contingent. Enterprises with the lowest cost of production may or may not win in the market, contingent upon their market competitors' strategies. Enterprises must evaluate their relative strengths and weaknesses as compared with competitors. Since the environment is in flux, the form of competition continually shifts. The organization principle along the lines of networking promotes potential success, much like it does for teams in sports contests (Best 1990, 139).

In recent years one observes the fact that multinational enterprises or even government research programs appear to be increasingly incapable of internalizing required resources to produce and commercialize new technologies (Mytelka 1987; Mytelka and Delapierre 1987; Shachar and Zuscovitch 1990; Traxler and Unger 1990).

Given that enterprises often cannot afford the cost or risks of internalizing required resources, they must rely on one of the two remaining options: the market or some form of network collaboration. The market option may be suboptimal. Furthermore, the cost aspects play a large role in deciding which option to take. It now costs, for example, approximately four billion dollars to produce a new automobile model and 5 billion dollars to create a new jet aircraft. Each new generation of mainframe computers requires enormous financial research and development investments, while the product life cycle has been reduced to less than four years (Badaracco 1988).

Networks of inter-enterprise cooperative agreements (strategic alliances) in complementary knowledge production activities function as a means of minimizing the costs, risks, and uncertainties associated with technology-based modes of production (exchange of information). Market risks are externalized throughout the network, instead of being internalized (Traxler and Unger 1990). Enterprises desiring to increase their working technological base, thereby increasing their flexibility, may seek to appropriate new skills and capacities through subcontracting; linkages between universities, research institutes, and firms; and inter-enterprise agreements in research and development, production, and marketing. This results in an added strategic enterprise value. The key to networking is the creation of new information instead of simply executing predetermined tasks in an efficient manner (Imai 1989, 124). In this process of information generation new relationships and linkages emerge, redefining the network.

Networking is often quite complicated. Because of the specific internal and external market constellations, several types of infra-

structures have to coexist at a given point in time. This makes good
and economically efficient network management both essential and
at the same time very difficult to achieve.

Networks are not necessarily hierarchical. Authority and control
are not tightly centralized, and the group is not dependent on any
single individual or enterprise for its survival. Participation by members of the network is voluntary, and members treat each other often
as equals rather than as superior or subordinate (Sonnenberg 1990).
A network of strategic alliances is a combination of elements intended
to act together to accomplish an objective: survival and excellence in
global markets. According to Barham (1990, 1) "Networking is the
ability of the international company to exploit informal networks of
opportunity between its managers. The informality of networks is
vital because formal hierarchical structures are no longer capable of
handling an ever more complex and fast-moving international environment."

Since nothing in nature can be completely isolated from every-
thing else, we see that our selection of the boundaries of enterprise
system depends on the purpose and the limitations of our study.
Economists interested only in analyzing an enterprise's overall performance would not have the need nor the time to study in detail the
organizational design of the enterprise. Given the information that
enterprises maximize profits,[6] we tend to consider enterprises as a
black box—a term used to convey the fact that the organizational
details are not important to the study (or at least constitute a luxury
we cannot afford).

The black-box concept is essential to what has been called the
"systems approach" to problem solving. With this approach each ele-

---

6. Microeconomic price theory assumes that the enterprise's objective is profit
maximization. Hart (1985, 106–07) has observed, however, that "in a competitive
framework, this is usually accepted without question as the right objective for a firm.
Under imperfect competition matters are more complicated, a point noted a long time
ago by Marshall (1940, 402) and emphasized recently by Gabszewicz and Vial (1972).
The reason is that the owners of the firm are not interested in monetary profits per
se, but rather in what this profit can buy. Given that a monopolistically competitive
firm can influence prices, the owners may prefer low monetary profit but favorable
prices for consumption goods to high monetary profit and unfavorable prices.

"This argument suggests that we should substitute owner utility maximization for
profit maximization as the firm's goal. Unfortunately, things are not that simple. If
owners have different tastes, they will have different trade-offs concerning high monetary profits versus favourable consumption goods prices. That is, each owner will have
his own private objective function which he would like the firm to pursue, and the
problem then is how to aggregate these into an overall objective function."

Other scholars have also commented on this problem (e.g., Cornwall 1977, Bonanno 1990, 301), but to date no satisfactory alternative hypothesis has been effectively established.

ment in the system is treated as a black box, and the analysis focuses on how connections between the elements influence the overall behavior of the system. Its viewpoint implies a legitimate willingness to accept a less detailed description of the operation of the individual elements in order to achieve an overall understanding. The behavior of a black-box element is specified by its given input–output relation (i.e., the production function). An input is a cause, an output is an effect due to the input. Thus, the input–output relation expresses the cause and effect behavior of an element.

The conscious implementation and development of increasingly complex organizational and bargaining technologies through networks of strategic alliances are challenging our traditional black-box concept of what enterprises really are and how they function. Teece among others (e.g., Langlois 1989) has emphasized that conclusions regarding the appropriate boundaries of the enterprise cannot be derived by simply studying the nature of the underlying cost structure. The cost function summarizes all economically relevant information about the production technology of the enterprise. The traditional usage of the cost function does not, however, summarize the enterprise's organizational technology. "To assert otherwise would involve assuming rather than deducing the conditions for efficient multiproduct organization" (Teece 1980, 225).

Closer relationships between suppliers and customers blur the operational distinctions between legally separate organizations. New workplace realities and work force demographics are changing the implicit contract about what employers and employees owe to each other. Harrigan and Newman (1990, 420) have applied the term "internal venturing" to describe such implicit contract phenomena. Managers recognize that entrepreneurial ideas of their employees may not effectively be getting to the marketplace. The enterprise thus creates an internal venturing unit. However, entrepreneurial employees often want equity in the ideas they develop, and enterprises may find they must enter into joint ventures with their employees.

Changes are taking place on the boundaries of enterprises rather than at their core, where traditional business economists have commonly concentrated their analysis. The dependence of business on an adequate supply of natural and human resources puts external environmental, educational, and even family restrictions on the enterprise's internal agenda (Badaracco 1988).

Common Coasian theorizing about the nature of firms presupposes that boundaries of some sort separate them from their markets or, more broadly, their environments. Arm's-length, explicitly contractual, market-based relations with other organizations define an enterprise's boundaries, within which managers exercise authority and deploy assets that the enterprise owns or controls. Recently, however, managers have been blurring these boundaries with networks of cooperative arrangements with other enterprises, labor unions, universities, and government bodies.

It is becoming increasingly evident that in order to capture these effects it is necessary to shift our attention away from the more traditional static industrial organization approach and toward that of industrial dynamics (Carlsson 1987; Cantwell 1989). We must readjust our emphasis away from the structure of an industry at a given point in time and toward its cumulative evolution as a process over time at the international, national, and firm level. In this context the main issue is no longer the question "Why do multinational enterprises exist?" but rather, more importantly, "Will the firms in a given country and industry, when faced by global competition, possess the capacity to generate technological and allied advantages of their own that enable them to respond effectively, and in so doing to establish international networks of their own?" (Cantwell 1989, 3).[7]

WHAT ARE STRATEGIC ALLIANCES?

In international markets characterized by high risk, formal and informal commercial collaborations between legally separate enterprises serve as "transition mechanisms that propel the partner's strategy forward in a turbulent environment" (Lei and Slocum 1991, 44).[8] Business International (1990, 27) defines alliances as follows: "A corporate alliance is a formal and mutually agreed commercial collaboration between companies. The partners pool, exchange or integrate specified business resources for mutual gain. Yet the partners remain separate businesses." Such commercial collaborations are on the rise. In the literature partnerships are often classified as collaborative agreements, consortiums, or strategic alliances. The Business International definition given above includes a wide spectrum of possible formations of international partnerships. General discussions on the variety and distinctions of international collaborative agreements are well documented in Robinson (1988) and Contractor and Lorange (1988).

Common to all strategic alliances is that they represent the

---

7. See further the discussion in Porter 1990a, 84–85.
8. See further Hamel, Doz, and Prahalad (1989).

mechanism by which enterprises decide how far to go along the inter-corporate integration spectrum from simple spot-market exchanges of assets to full-fledged integration in their "make or buy" procurement strategies.

Figure 1.3: The Assets In Play

Alliance builders are trying to capture business assets by linking with other companies. Whether they are trying to fill gaps or create new businesses, the assets in play are the same. Some of the assets are easily visible ("above the waterline"); some are hidden within the company ("below the waterline").

Above the Waterline	Below the Waterline
■ Distribution networks	■ R & D capacity
■ Market acceptance	■ Process skills
■ Manufacturing capacity	■ Technology
■ The needed product	■ Organizational skills
■ Cash and convertibles	■ Market knowledge
■ Buying power	■ Tutored suppliers

Source: Business International (1990, page 28)

Figure 1.3 illustrates the palette of assets commonly involved in international partnerships. Strategic alliances may be distinguished according to those based on asset exchange and those based on asset integration (Business International 1990). Alliances based upon asset exchange are basically "trading alliances." The cooperation linkages may be weak.

Problems of integration do not arise since transactions occur at arm's length. Alliances involving asset integration may be regarded as "functional alliances." Close cooperative linkages may evolve as partners execute functions collectively. The quality of strategic alli-ances may be categorized either as passive (e.g., arm's-length trading alliances) or dynamic (e.g., functional alliances). The degree of integration and strategic dynamism present in a strategic alliance environment results in a "hierarchy of alliances," as proposed in Figure 1.4.

Figure 1.4 : The Hierarchy of Alliances

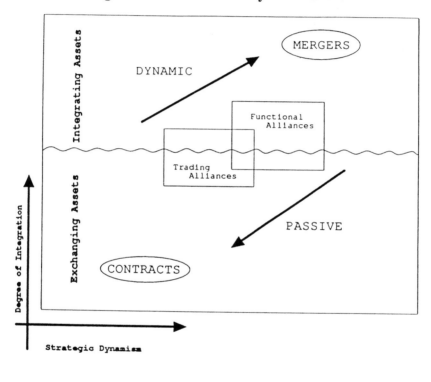

Source: Business International
(1990, page 29)

For example, consider the strategic alliance conceptualized in Figure 1.5. Partners retain cost control and access to product marketing. The network of external suppliers assume their normal role of providing goods and services to the partners. Exchanges of personnel take place at the department level. Given this constellation, the partners have agreed to delegate authority, personnel, and financial control to a joint management team that carries out the terms of the agreement. A partnership marketing entity may be legally instituted in both partners' countries or in third countries. Revenues are distributed through the management team, back to the partners via terms of the original agreement.

THE "PROBLEM" OF CONCEPTUALIZING THE REALITIES OF NETWORKS

According to Jarillo (1988), the concept of networking is often not studied for the simple reason that it is hard to harmonize with the basic postulates of competitive behavior. He suggests that this avoidance of conceptualizing the realities of networks has probably been aggravated by the preeminence of models of strategy based on microeconomic theory (see Porter 1981). Since the construct of networks is difficult to fit within the basic paradigm of competitive strategy, one simply neglects the significance of networks.

In a somewhat different context Casson (1987, 40) has noted that "in the neoclassical world, the invisible hand of the market does practically all the managing that is required. One cannot have an economic theory of the multinational enterprise that includes both the neoclassical theory of location and a realistic theory of management." Teece (1981, 2) has also remarked that "modern production and exchange theory, useful as it is for many purposes, is erected in a fashion which deflects attention from many important organizational issues. In particular, the boundaries of the firm are taken as datum. However, a useful theory of industrial organization must derive rather than assume the boundaries of the firm. This requires an analysis of the nature of exchange processes at the level of the individual transaction—that is, a study of markets in microcosm."

In order to illustrate networking at a simple conceptual level let us consider the brain-teaser in Figure 1.6, found in Gray (1989, 237–40) and more recently in the editorial column of the *Harvard Business Review* (Nov./Dec. 1990). Nine dots are arranged in three rows and three columns. Try to connect all the dots with straight four lines.

If you stay within the boundaries defined by the dots, as our neoclassical theory of the firm assumes one must, the task cannot be completed. A solution is found only by going outside the apparent boundaries as presented in Figure 1.7.

Now try using just three lines to connect the dots. Impossible, you say? Not if you challenge another apparent constraint. Enlarge the dots enough, and the puzzle is solved, as seen in Figure 1.8.

Integrative thinking—that is, thinking across boundaries—is the ultimate entrepreneurial act. Entrepreneurial talent requires the ability to rethink categories and transcend boundaries. Today suc-

Figure 1.5 International Partnership (or Strategic Alliance)

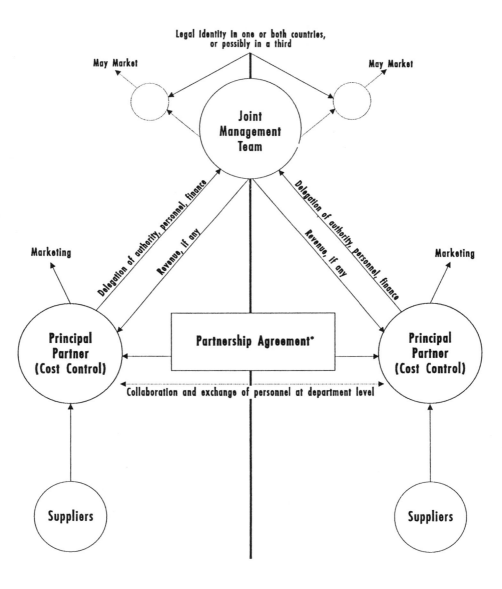

*Defines purpose, management, duration, division of work,
division of revenues (if and when received), a renegotiation
process, liability, access to the other firm, investment

Source: Robinson 1988, 171

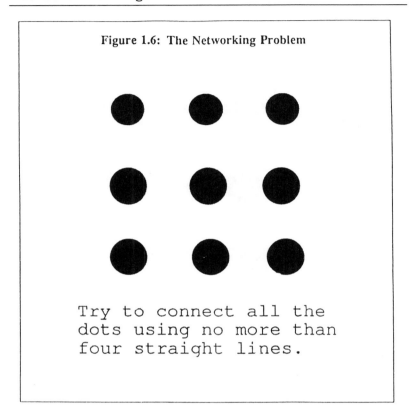

Figure 1.6: The Networking Problem

Try to connect all the
dots using no more than
four straight lines.

cessful multinational enterprises are currently leapfrogging over boundaries as they generate new ideas and innovations. As Shachar and Zuscovitch (1990, 148) have written, "In the long run it is the intangible capital of knowhow which determines the competitive strength of the firm rather than the book value of its physical goods."

Networking is the most common method that entrepreneurs apply to get access to external resources. Hence, awareness of the importance of networking, as well as an understanding of the required skills for effective networking strategies, are two of the most important entrepreneurial skills that need to be taught and developed in international business (Jarillo 1988).

Unfortunately, today's management is commonly characterized by "compartmentalization" (Barham 1990). Managers have become closely acquainted with comfortable day-to-day routines within the fields of their specializations such as design, production, or marketing.

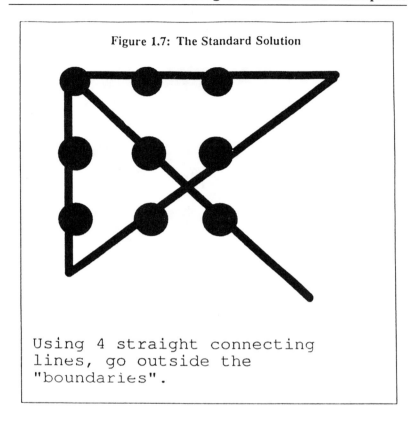

Figure 1.7: The Standard Solution

Using 4 straight connecting lines, go outside the "boundaries".

The "competitive edge" challenge is to implement a management culture open for networking, that is, to get them to break out of their compartmentalized problem-solving thinking and to look beyond the boundaries of their enterprise. It is not simply a matter of maximizing profits and organizational method, but rather a continuous search process for a competitive edge based upon prolonged upgrading strategies of products, processes, and organizational forms. According to Best (1990, 144), "The New Competitor is a business organization that pursues a strategy of continuous improvement by integrating thinking and doing."

RESEARCH EVIDENCE ON THE SPREADING OF NETWORKS: TRENDS IN COOPERATION

Johnston and Lawrence (1988, 98) recognize that cooperative networks are not really a new phenomenon at all. The international construction industry, for example, has been operated like a value-

Figure 1.8: The Entrepreneurial Solution

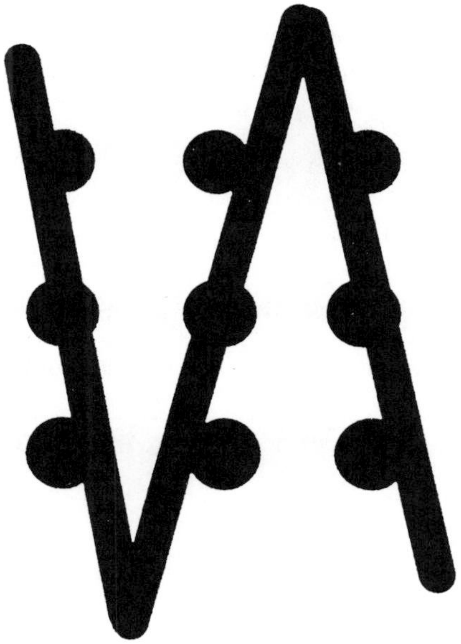

Enlarge the dots and use
3 straight lines.

adding partnership since the time of the Roman Empire (see further Casson 1987, ch. 6). General contractors subcontract the main share of work for a specific construction job, soliciting bids from a selected set of subcontractors ("network peers") they trust. Finally, they contract with "partners" who offer reasonable prices but not necessarily the cheapest.

Brown (1984) has argued that in addition to the widely acknowledged marketlike behavior in firms, there also exists firmlike behavior in markets through administered marketing channels arising from nonpecuniary influences of one channel partner on another (see also Buckley 1987, 38). Von Hippel (1985, 1986) has further demonstrated how a close relationship with suppliers and customers provides enterprises with the most important source of innovation.

Vernon (1979, 233–35) has observed the transformation in industries such as chemicals, electronics, machinery, and transportation equipment in which innovations tend to be especially prominent (see Table 1.2). He points out that enterprises with well-developed multinational networks of manufacturing units typically account for more than half the global output in their respective product lines.

The scope of the dramatic increase in overseas subsidiary networks of a group of the world's largest enterprises in 1950 with the networks of those same firms in the 1970s is well documented in Table 1.2.

Table 1.2: Networks of Foreign Manufacturing Subsidiaries of 315 Multinational Companies 1950 and 1970s

Number of enterprises with networks including	180 US-based MNCs		135 MNCs based in UK and Europe	
	1950	1975	1950	1970
Fewer than 6 countries	138	9	116	31
6 to 20 countries	43	128	16	75
More than 20 countries	0	44	3	29

Source: Harvard Multinational Enterprise Project, cited in Vernon (1979, page 258).

In a further study (Vernon and Davidson 1979), it was found that the spreading of networks of subsidiaries followed reasonably well-defined patterns. According to data on 180 U.S. multinational enterprises, the spreading of subsidiary networks was consistent and stable throughout the postwar period. American enterprises began the spreading of their subsidiary networks in geographical areas with which they were well acquainted, such as Canada and the United

Kingdom. Thereafter, foreign direct investments spread to areas that were not as familiar, such as Asia and Africa. Similar subsidiary network investment patterns have also been observed for Canadian multinational enterprises (Niosi 1985) and European multinational enterprises (Franko 1976).

The elapse of time, as well as "learning by doing," brought about an increase in the propensity to network as geographical areas became less and less unfamiliar. Vernon (1979, 259) elaborates on these developments as follows:

> For product lines introduced abroad by the 180 firms before 1946, the probability that a Canadian location would come earlier than an Asian location was 79 percent; but for product lines that were introduced abroad after 1960, the probability that Canada would take precedence over Asia had dropped to only 59 percent. The consequences of this steady shift in preference could be seen in a corresponding shift in the geographical distribution of the foreign subsidiaries of the 180 firms. Before 1946, about 23 percent of the subsidiaries had been located in Canada; but by 1975, the proportion was only about 13 percent, with the offsetting gains recorded principally in Asia, Africa, and the Middle East.

Vernon (1979, 235) concludes that "it seems reasonable to assume that we confront a basic change in the institutional structure of the MNCs concerned."

Robinson (1988, 175) has noted that a study performed by Albert Bressard, director of Promethee, Paris, based on a survey of 974 agreements between enterprises in industrialized nations between 1982 and the first quarter of 1984, found that 60 percent of recently formed international business relationships involved no purchase of equity. According to the study, "National Semiconductor is selling Hitachi computers, RCA is selling Hitachi PBX equipment and Matsushita's VCRs, and Honeywell is selling Ericsson telephone switching gear. This new phenomenon is changing how companies will compete in the future."

Another study from Harvard University found that 70 percent of the alliances entered into by American consumer electronics with Japanese enterprises involved mutual commitments to distribute and sell each other's products. Often common were commitments for joint development. One such case was the NMB Semiconductor Company, an affiliate of the Japanese Minebea Company, who linked to National Semiconductor of the United States for the joint development of very large scale integrated circuits. A five-year agreement was enacted for joint development at a Japanese plant. Subsequently National Semiconductor was to introduce the jointly developed products into its worldwide marketing network (Robinson 1988, 176).

In the semiconductor industry all the world's leading enterprises have multiple cross-arrangements which emphasize the two-way exchange of complementary technical expertise. Semiconductors constitute the prime example of a globally oligopolistic industry dominated by a small set of enterprises, where no enterprise has a controlling influence, and where competition is accordingly acute with rapid technological change (O'Brien and Tullis 1989). Haklisch (1986) has found in her study on the semiconductor industry that U.S. enterprises have been rather active in cooperative agreements. United States–Japanese agreements dominate at approximately 50 percent of the total, followed by 35 percent for United States–European agreements.

Contractor and Lorange (1988b) state that negotiated arrangements outnumber fully owned foreign subsidiaries by a factor of at least four to one for U.S.–based enterprises. For European– and Japanese–based enterprises the ratio is most likely higher, since it is believed that enterprise in these countries has a higher propensity than U.S. enterprises to engage in international joint ventures and contractual arrangements.

According to *Fortune* magazine, U.S.–based enterprises engaged in some 2,000 alliances with European enterprises during the 1980s. The United Nations Centre on Transnational Corporations identified more than 850 interfirm technology arrangements entered into by enterprises from France, West Germany, Italy, Japan, the United States, the United Kingdom, and the Benelux countries between 1984 and 1986 (Cascio and Serapio 1991, 64).

A recent study by the Centre d'Etudes et de Recherches sur les Entreprises Multinationales (CEREM), surveying 497 agreements regarding the aerospace, biotechnology, information technology, and materials industries, found that only one-quarter of the contracts involving an enterprise based in the European Community were made with other European Community enterprises. In more than half of the instances the European enterprise's partner was an American company (LAREA/CEREM 1986b, 14).

Similarly, Futuro Organizzazione Risoise (FOR), a Rome-based private research group, found that intra-European Community agreements constituted only 29 percent of the 468 agreements they identified in the aerospace, information technology, scientific instrumentation, and pharmaceutical industries during the period 1982–85. Contracts between European Community and American enterprises constituted 54 percent of that total (Mytelka and Delapierre 1987; 231; see further OECD 1986, 24).

	Table 1.3: Distribution of Inter-Firm Agreements[a] by Function				
Year	Knowledge	Production	Commercialization	Global[b]	Total
1980	11	12	6	2	12
1981	15	13	10	10	31
1982	17	16	15	24	58
1983	24	25	31	41	97
1984	36	37	36	57	131
1985	47	39	51	58	149
Total	150	142	149	192	481
%	31.2	29.5	31.0	39.9	100

[a]Includes only agreements to which at least one European-based firm is party.

[b]Agreements which involve two or more of the preceeding functions.

Source: LAREA/CEREM (1986, page 8). Cited according to:

Mytelka/Delapierre (1987, page 235).

Data from the CEREM survey of agreements provide evidence of the rising importance of inter-enterprise network cooperation for European-based multinational enterprises. In Table 1.3 the data are classified by functions into agreements which involve knowledge production in a broad sense (choice of research priorities, joint precompetitive research, joint engineering or development activities), goods production (including licensing, subcontracting, and joint ventures), and the commercialization of goods or services whether jointly pro-

duced or not. The fourth category covers those agreements that were
global in nature involving at least two of the above functions. Over
the period 1980–85 the share of knowledge production agreements
increased from a low of 2.3 percent in 1980 to 9.8 percent in 1985.

Such strategic alliances appear to be the magical success formula
for international business in the 1990s. While during the ten years
between 1976 and 1986 the analysts of the international auditing
company KPMG Peat Marwick McLintock registered only 1,000
strategic alliances (Rubner 1990, 61), in the last quarter of the year
1989 alone they registered some 670 corporate partnerships, as illustrated in Figure 1.9. Not surprisingly, due to the new open door
policy, the USSR led with 179 strategic alliances with Western
partners.

NETWORKS OF LEADING MULTINATIONAL ENTERPRISES

Among the most well-documented cases of networking is the rise
of suppliers by Japanese manufacturing enterprises.[9] Manufacturing
in business groups is a way of life in Japan. The dissolution of the
prewar "headless" zaibatsu (literally "financial clique") combines created a competitive market system in Japan. However, the ties and
linkages remained largely intact in a weaker form, the keiretsu.
Keiretsu, broken into its component parts, is *kei* meaning "lineage,
faction, group" and *retsu* meaning "arranged in order" (Hadley 1970).
Keiretsu members commonly agree not to sell their holdings, protecting them against hostile takeovers.

Community-level networks such as the kinyu keiretsu (financial
linkages) or kigyo shudan (enterprise group) have been common
within Japan throughout its history (Gerlach 1987; Auster 1990; Best
1990). Similar developments of community-level forms of networks
between the United States and Japan and within the United States
are evolving, although at an admittedly slow pace. The Boeing, Mitsubishi, Fuji, and Japanese government network which is building
and improving the Boeing 767 (Roehl and Truitt 1987; Auster 1990)
and the Texas Instruments, Motorola, and Hitachi network developing the next-generation chips exemplify international networks
between the United States and Japan.

Since U.S. and European consortia networks are a relatively
new phenomenon,[10] little information is currently available on their

---

9. E.g., Yasumuro (1979), Imai, Nonaka, and Takeuchi (1985), Buckley (1985),
Imai (1989), Best (1990), Dolles and Jung (1990), Ferguson (1990).

10. The term "consortia" is applied broadly to include large, interlocking relationships between business entities of a corporate family (Robinson 1988).

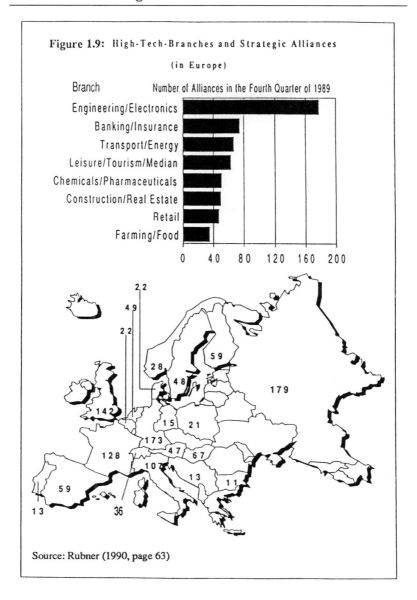

Figure 1.9: High-Tech-Branches and Strategic Alliances (in Europe)

Source: Rubner (1990, page 63)

structure and performance. However, the formation of consortia networks in the United States and Europe to meet the new competitive challenges has not been especially successful to date. American attempts to establish cross-industry consortia such as MCC, Sematech, and U.S. Memories in the electronics and computer branches have largely failed due to the difficulties involved in getting enterprises to pool their resources into integrative networks (Lei and Slocum 1991).

Korean industrial enterprises are also organized in groups, or chaebols (the major industrial concerns). Korean chaebols produce a wide range of diverse products and services. The similarity to the Japanese zaibatsu is high, but substantial differences do remain (Tung 1991). South Korean chaebols are usually dominated by founding families. Blood relationships dominate the pattern of wealth distribution and management across the chaebol. Chaebols rely more strongly than the Japanese keiretsu on the government for capital. Lucky Goldstar, Samsung, Daewoo, and Sunkyong belong to the largest chaebols (Yoo and Lee 1987; Steers, Shin, and Ungson 1989).

Multinational Japanese trading companies (sogo shosha) arrange for the buying and selling of goods at every stage of the value-added chain internationally, without ever getting directly involved in actual manufacturing (e.g., Young 1979; Yasumuro 1979). Buckley (1988, 188) interestingly suggests that the rise of confidential specialized information by sogo shosha reflects the parallel development of international merchant banks in Western economies. Along such lines, an interesting study of interlocking directorates and other organizational ties between Western enterprises and international networks of banks is to be found in Fennema (1982).

Japanese enterprises commonly specialize in a single sector. MITI, the Japanese governmental Ministry of International Trade and Industry, directly promotes networking, as indicated by the amount of resources devoted to tracking interdependencies of enterprises. The Japanese External Trade Organization, a branch of the Ministry of International Trade and Industry, periodically collects all forms of linkages announced publicly. MITI actively attempts to create appropriate conditions for the competitiveness of Japanese multinational enterprises in the long run. Japanese enterprises also possess in-house tracking and monitoring of interorganizational linkages in their industry (Auster 1990; Isaak 1991).

Japanese enterprises belonging to a single sector often build networks for collective learning and joint power, or one strong enterprise is incorporated into a zaibatsu, which is centered around large banks and linked to non-zaibatsu groups. Although such zaibatsu groupings were officially dismantled after World War II, the sogo shosha remained intact along traditional organizational forms. The five largest (Mitsubishi, Mitsui, C. Itoh, Marubeni, and Sumitomo) of the nine major sogo shosha are not just simple trading enterprises but follow a strategy aimed at securing sources of basic raw materials and maintaining world market shares (Isaak 1991, 165).

The sogo shosha eliminates entry barriers for small member enterprises into new foreign markets. The strength of the sogo shosha's world networks is to be found in its activities of gathering global marketing intelligence, then sifting through the information, targeting it for the right enterprise at the right location at the right time (Isaak 1991, 165).

Japan's largest industrial group, Mitsubishi, is illustrative of the network linkages among Japanese enterprises.[11] Twenty-eight core members of the Mitsubishi group are woven tightly together by networks of cross-ownership and other financial linkages, interlocking directorates, as well as social and historical ties. Figure 1.10 illustrates the Mitsubishi network. Located at the center of the network are the Mitsubishi Corporation (the trading company), Mitsubishi Bank (the group's bank), and Mitsubishi Heavy Industries (the leading manufacturer). In addition to these three core flagship members, hundreds of other Mitsubishi-related companies are linked together. Figure 1.10 sketches these linkages in a simple manner. Percentages refer to the shares of each enterprise held by other members of the group.

The Mitsubishi trading company is one of Japan's largest trading firms, handling 25,000 items from missiles to instant ramekin. It earned ¥16.6 trillion ($120 billion) in sales in 1989, roughly one-quarter the value of Japan's national budget (Katayama 1991). The Mitsubishi trading company employs some 60,000 market analysts around the world whose main activity is to filter and feed market information to the parent corporation. Although such an extensive information-gathering network requires enormous amounts of resources, the returns can be highly critical to business performance. The new electronic information networks have facilitated the flow of information on an incremental basis as field personnel forward relevant information as needed. Mitsubishi's ability to develop and maintain a global information network has become an efficient core skill necessary for the identification of potential strategic alliances or criti-

---

11. See further the recent cover story entitled "Mighty Mitsubishi" in *International Business Week* Sept. 24, 1990, and Imai (1989).

Figure 1.10 The Heart of the Mitsubishi Group

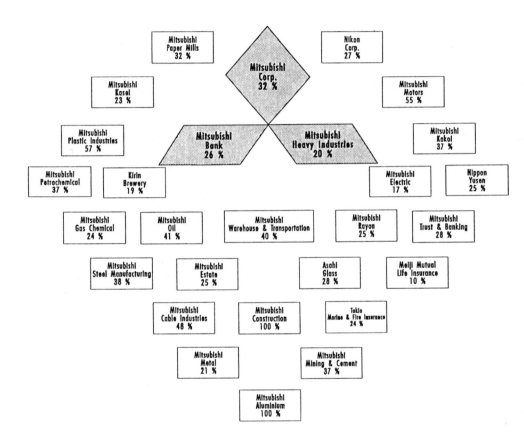

Source: International Business Week, Sept. 24, 1990: 39

cal business relationships (Davidson 1991, 14). Mitsubishi has effectively demonstrated that it is possible to develop an optimal network
position in the increasingly global business environment.

To further enforce the capabilities of suppliers most Japanese
parent enterprises have founded kyoryokukai, or formal associations
of cooperative parent and supplier firms. Such formal or informal

associations are a means of transferring organizational innovations among members. They serve to create "shared network norms." Imai et al. (1985, 273) have studied the kyoryokukai and found that:

> Written contracts are unheard of. But if the lead manufac-
> turer delivers, a trusting relationship begins to develop. In
> the long run, this kind of relationship leads the subcontractors
> as a group to accept the lead manufacturer as the legitimate
> leader and establish a strong cooperative system in support
> of it. A set of "shared network norms" is established over
> time, laying out a basic understanding of how business should
> be conducted within the network. Such a norm may tolerate
> an unreasonable demand made by the lead manufacturer dur-
> ing times of competitive crisis.

The Japanese systems of networked supplier relations have been extremely successful in meeting the challenges of rapid technological change. Many manufactured products today contain thousands of component parts; an automobile, for example, is composed of some 20,000 parts. It is virtually impossible for one enterprise to stay on top of technological developments in all intermediate inputs. A flexible supplier-parent relationship creates efficient network structures which enhance allocative efficiency given rapid technological change.

Network structures must not necessarily follow the Japanese or Korean systems. Networking does not offer a single institutional configuration that may simply be copied with success.

Best's (1990) study of the "Third Italy," a rapidly growing region located in the north central part of Italy, offers substantial evidence which provides an interesting contrast to Asian network structures. The Third Italy is characterized by internationally competitive independent small firms, strong unions, leftist political parties, and an active local citizenry. Through the organization of interfirm collective service associations with governmental-like powers and industrial policy agencies of local government, small firms cooperate to provide services with substantial economies of scale. As a consequence of this "industrial district" institutional configuration, small firms maintain their independence in production without being reduced to the status of simple subcontractors for products designed in the central office of a large multinational enterprise. Networked groups of small firms with a quasi-public status have been highly successful in global markets. Such a strategy could possibly be applied in developing countries.

Ghoshal and Bartlett (1990, 695) have recently graphed the organizational units and some of the interlinkages within N.V. Philips, a multinational enterprise headquartered in the Netherlands. Philips is the largest manufacturer of electronic components in Europe and one of the largest in the world. Philips of Eindhoven alone has formed over 800 strategic alliances worldwide, has 350 wholly or jointly owned affiliates, and is characterized by thousands of licensing or technical servicing agreements with international customers and subcontracting arrangements with their suppliers (Dunning 1988b, 330, 342). As Figure 1.11 demonstrates, Philips operates in some sixty countries. Philips exhibits a wide range of subsidiary organizational size as well as product diversity. It is especially active in the information technology industry.

Ghoshal and Bartlett (1990, 3) correctly assert that the operating environment of today's multinational enterprises demands more than efficient central management and flexible local operations. "It requires companies to link their diverse organizational perspectives and resources in a way that would allow them to leverage their capabilities for achieving global coordination and national flexibility simultaneously. In response to this need, a few companies have evolved beyond the simpler multinational or global approach to international business and developed what we term a *transnational* capability—an ability to manage across boundaries." Philips is a good example of such an enterprise.

Along similar lines Hagedoorn and Schakenraad (1990) have studied the strategic partnering and technological cooperation of 45 enterprises in the information technology and biotechnology industries. Applying a nonmetric multidimensional scaling technique (Kruskal and Wish 1978), they derived Figure 1.12, illuminating the network of cooperation in information technology.

The process of multidimensional scaling is a method of data reduction that is similar to principal components analysis and other methods of factor analysis. Multidimensional scaling algorithms offer scaling of a similarity or dissimilarity matrix into points lying in an X-dimensional space. Multidimensional scaling provides coordinates for these points such that the distances between pairs of points fit as closely as possible to the observed (dis)similarities. Figure 1.12 has two dimensions. The second dimension represents a stress value indicative of the goodness-of-fit of the configuration.

In their study Hagedoorn and Schakenraad regarded the total number of cooperative agreements (joint ventures, research corporations, technology exchange agreements, cross-licensing, second-sourcing, minority stakes, and research and development contracts)

Figure 1.11 Organizational Units and some of the Interlinkages within N.V. Philips

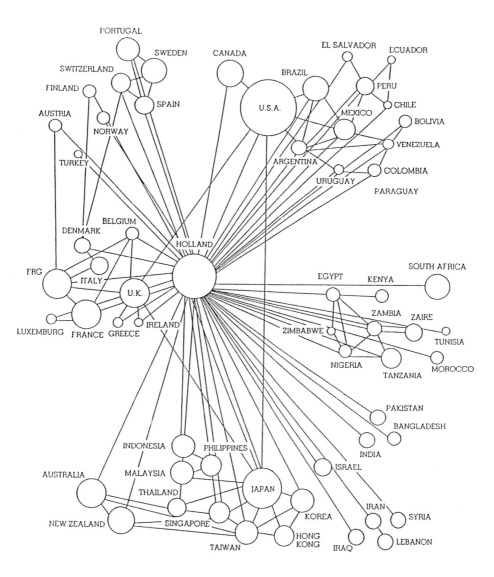

Figure 1.12:
The Network of Co-Operation in Information Technology

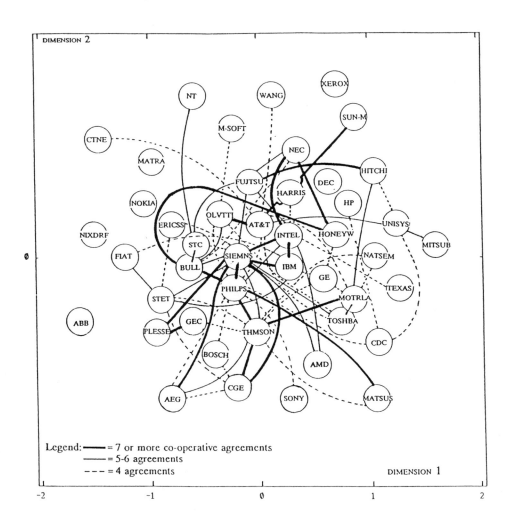

Source: Hagedoorn and Schakenraad (1990, page 183)

between two enterprises as a measure of similarity between intensive cooperation.

For information technology the intensity and structure of cooperation is demonstrated in Figure 1.12. The stress value amounts to 0.15, which is a fair goodness-of-fit value. The first dimension accounts for the largest part of the observed (dis)similarities. Figure 1.12 suggests that many U.S. and Japanese enterprises cooperate both within and between their regions since they are found at the right hand side of dimension 1.

Viewing the left hand side of dimension 1 one observes a concentration of intra-European cooperation. Enterprises such as GEC, AEG, Fiat, Plessey, CGE, STET, Ericsson, Bull, STC, and Bosch collaborate. Enterprises in the center of both dimensions 1 and 2 possess the largest number of international cooperative agreements. Especially the enterprises Philips, Siemans, Olivetti, AT&T, Intel, Fujitsu, Thomsen, IBM, and Harris are characterized by a high degree of international cooperative agreements.

Structure may also be observed in Figure 1.12 by means of neighborhood interpretation. Small distances in the configuration signify large similarity. The application of clustering techniques—e.g., drawing lines between enterprises where proximity exceeds some threshold value—further emphasizes networking. Thick solid lines indicate very strong cooperation (7 cooperative agreements or more), thin solid lines reflect strong cooperation (5 or 6 agreements), while broken lines represent moderate cooperation (4 agreements). Enterprises having three or less agreements with another enterprise have not been connected, although they still play a significant role in the network.

As Figure 1.12 suggests, all large enterprises in information technology are basically involved in tightly knit networks of cooperation. Siemans has agreements with Philips, Intel, IBM, Plessey, AEG, CGE, Fujitsu, Toshiba, Thomson, Ericsson, and STC. Philips actively collaborates with Bull of France, Siemens, Thomson, Matsushita, Intel, AEG, Bosch, CDC, Sony, Olivetti, STC, and AT&T. AT&T also engages in strategic partnering with Olivetti, Sun-Microsystems, Unisys, Wang, CTNE, Philips, and Toshiba.

The networks of cooperation in biotechnology are illustrated in Figure 1.13. Applying the same multidimensional scaling analysis, Hagedoorn and Schakenraad derive a stress value of 0.07, which is generally accepted as a good fit. Inspection of Figure 1.13 shows no clearly emerging network pattern. Intra-American cooperation is less pervasive than expected, considering the fact that some 34 percent of all cooperative agreements are intra-U.S. Hagedoorn and Schaken-raad attribute the lack of pattern to the fact that their data pool included only 45 enterprises. In addition, they argue that biotechnology is at an earlier industry life cycle phase of development than information technology, which could explain why the "weaving" pattern of network building has not reached the levels of those patterns in information technology.

Figure 1.13 offers once again evidence that it is the large and more advanced enterprises engaging in the biotechnology network of cooperations according to the limited data. As in Figure 1.12, the intensity of cooperation is illustrated by line graphing between enterprises. A number of U.S. enterprises are aligned strategically. European enterprises such as Merck and Ciba-Geigy, Boehringer and Genentech, Bayer and Bristol Meyers, Gist-Brocades and Shell, Shell and Cetus, and Abbott and Amgen are networking.

OUTLINE OF THIS BOOK

Despite daily business press announcements of the formation of new international alliances, research on international networks of multinational enterprises is still in its infancy. The purpose of this book is to come to terms with the current extent and development of networking phenomena and begin to trace an economic explanation of them. In so doing the analysis will hopefully raise more questions than give definitive answers, thereby serving to direct future research into the field of multinational networking structures.

As chapter 1 has stressed, escalating costs and risks in technology-intensive industries "are making simultaneous partners out of competitors" (Lei and Slocum 1991, 51). The driving forces behind the trend of establishing dense cooperative networks of multinational enterprise are rapid technological developments and the globalization of markets, products, services, and processes.

A wide range of strategic alliances and network structures are evolving because international partners need to:

- collaborate in order to spread and lower the development costs of high-risk, technology-intensive production;
- obtain global economies of scale and scope in value-adding activities;
- learn about a partner's technology and proprietary processes or seek access to new distribution channels;
- participate in shaping the evolution of competitive activity in the industry;

Figure 1.13:
The Network of Co-operation in Biotechnology

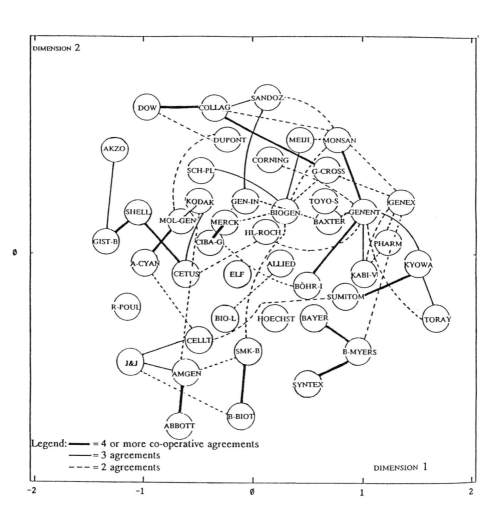

Source: Hagedoorn and· Schakenraad (1990, page 184)

- collaborate in order to meet consumer demands for high variety and low cost.

Given the above objectives, chapter 2 selectively surveys theories of multinational enterprise. The economic analysis of the multinational enterprise as a network is presented in chapter 3. The role of networks in the entrepreneurial process from the practical viewpoint of management implementation is then discussed. Chapter 5 focuses on cooperative strategies in developing countries. The role of public policy aspects of industrial policy networking is the topic of chapter 6. The final section reemphasizes the undeniable realities of networking as a model of international business competitive strategy and suggests areas for future research.

CHAPTER 2

The Search for a Paradigm

> The multinational of the 1970s is obsolete. Global companies must be more than just a bunch of overseas subsidiaries that execute decisions made at headquarters. Instead, a new type of company is evolving. —*Business Week*, May 14, 1990

This chapter selectively reviews theories of multinational enterprise. Emphasis is placed on the more dynamic aspects of multinationality as a process of evolving products and technologies. An understanding of these theories will aid us in formulating a network perspective of multinational enterprise to be presented in chapter 3. We first take a quick look at some examples of multinational enterprises and the nature of multinational enterprises. Next, the standard neoclassical capital arbitrage hypothesis of multinationality (MacDougall 1960) is discussed. Then, when the concepts of the product life cycle (Vernon 1966) and technology gaps (Posner 1961) are applied, the significance of technological change as a proximate determinant of trade and multinational enterprise is examined. Current mainstream thinking concerning the structural dimensions of multinational enterprise along the lines of the internalization theory (McManus 1972; Buckley and Casson 1991), the transaction cost view (Teece 1986; Hennart 1989a, b), and the competitive advantage view (Porter 1980, 1985, 1990a; Grosse and Kujawa 1988) are briefly reviewed. The chapter concludes with Dunning's (1981a) eclectic theory.

The original studies of multinational enterprise, searching for an explanation of the phenomena, are Penrose (1956, 1959), Dunning (1958), and Behrman (1962). Economic theorists continue to search for an appropriate theoretical framework explaining the level and composition of foreign direct investment at the enterprise, industry, and country levels.

Many excellent studies have surveyed the literature on the theory of multinational enterprise (e.g., Buckley and Casson 1991; Hood and Young 1979; Dunning 1981a, 1988b; Rugman 1981; Calvet 1981; Caves 1982; Clegg 1988). To date, however, there exists no firmly established theory of multinational enterprises per se. Due to the multifaceted dimensions of multinational enterprises, this will probably remain so for some time.

Several branches of economic theory have been applied in ex-

41

plaining the existence of multinational enterprises. Caves (1971a), Dunning (1974a, b), and others have argued that there is basically no need for a special theory of multinational enterprises, because the establishment and operation of such firms, as well as the effects of their activities, can be adequately explained by the existing body of economic theory (Koutsoyiannis 1982, 312). The causes and effects of foreign direct investment can be analyzed in the framework of the general theory of the firm, the theory of investment, the theory of location, the theory of industrial organization, and the theory of international trade. To date, however, there does not exist a network theory of the firm either at a domestic or international level.

Multinational enterprises have been defined in many ways (see, e.g., Aharoni 1971). Stopford and Dunning (1982) define multinationality according to three criteria: (1) at least 25 percent of consolidated sales or assets from foreign direct investment, (2) at least 25 percent of the voting equity in at least three foreign countries, and (3) at least $75 million in sales from foreign operations.

Vernon and Wells (1981) offer a broader definition. They view multinational enterprises as

> clusters of affiliated firms [that], although in different countries, nevertheless share distinguishing characteristics as follows:
> 1. They are linked by ties of common ownership.
> 2. They draw on a common pool of resources, such as money and credit, information systems, trade names and patents.
> 3. They respond to some common strategy.

As Grosse and Kujawa (1988, 24) note, this is a useful functional definition of the multinational enterprise regarded as an international contractor. It focuses on the functioning of the enterprise and not only on its ownership structure or other characteristics. As emphasized throughout this book, direct ownership structures are increasingly playing a less important role in various areas of international business. For our purposes, therefore, multinational enterprises are defined simply as organizations that engage in the production of goods and services in three or more nations such that it adds value in more than one national economy (Dunning 1974, 13; Casson 1985, 31).

The main difference between a multinational enterprise as differentiated from domestic firms is hence its flexibility to transfer resources internationally through a strategic global network. Basically, "multinational enterprises consist of a number of linked business establishments, which are planned and operated together to achieve established objectives. Multinational enterprises must be regarded as integrated business systems in order to analyse their behavior" (Hood and Young 1979, 3).

EXAMPLES OF MULTINATIONAL ENTERPRISES

Much theorizing on multinational enterprises is still dominated by the idea of extremely large structures of enterprises achieved during the "American era" of the first quarter-century after World War II. One should, however, recognize that, while multinational enterprises are the most important actor in international business, carrying out the bulk of the value of transactions in international business, they do not necessarily undertake the largest number of transactions. Many small firms are involved, especially in exports and imports (Grosse and Kujawa 1988, 22).[1]

Table 2.1 illustrates that the United States still does lead all countries, according to the annual ranking of *Fortune's* International 500 list for 1990 of the world's largest industrial corporations (as ranked by sales), with 167 enterprises. Americans are No. 1 in 14 of the 25 industries on the *Fortune* list, including aerospace (Boeing, No. 45), computers (IBM, No. 5), and electronics (General Electric, No. 7). The main competition in aerospace comes from France, which has 4 enterprises, compared with the United States's 11. In computers, the United States has 10 enterprises to Japan's 3.

Today, however, global market structures and global competition are rapidly changing due to the altered nature of the environment in which multinational enterprises must compete. The U.S. dominance as exhibited in Table 2.1 is slowly giving way to foreign rivals. Let us look at a few examples. In 1980, *Fortune's* International 500 list registered 23 U.S. enterprises that made the top 50, compared with only 5 Japanese. In 1989 (see Table 2.2) they registered 17 American and 10 Japanese enterprises. Two of the largest enterprises, Samsung (No. 20) and Daewoo (No. 47), are South Korean. The electronics

---

1. Along these lines, Jarillo (1989) supports the emerging concept of networks of multinationality. He finds that entrepreneurial enterprises make more use of external resources, i.e., are less integrated. He finds an even stronger effect for small ($20–100 million in sales) firms. Birley (1985) has offered some evidence in a domestic context, however, that small entrepreneurs may not perceive the full potential of developing a dense network structure, but rather rely upon networks of personal relationships to obtain advice, financing, "insider" sales, etc. These factors have also been emphasized by Mueller (1986). This may be an even more relevant aspect in an international small firm context. See also the discussion of international cooperative ventures of small firms from newly industrializing countries by Tallman and Shenkar (1990).

TABLE 2.1: COUNTRIES WITH THE BIGGEST COMPANIES ACCORDING TO FORTUNE'S "INTERNATIONAL 500"		
COUNTRY	COMPANIES ON THE LIST	LARGEST COMPANY
UNITED STATES	167	GENERAL MOTORS
JAPAN	111	TOYOTA MOTOR
BRITAIN	43	BRITISH PETROLEUM
GERMANY	32	DAIMLER-BENZ
FRANCE	29	RENAULT
SWEDEN	15	VOLVO
CANADA	13	CANADIAN PACIFIC
SOUTH KOREA	11	SAMSUNG
AUSTRALIA	10	ELDERS IXL
SWITZERLAND	10	NESTLE

Source: Fortune, July 30, 1990, page 43

industry especially is characterized by this trend. Of the 46 enterprises in this category, the United States has 16 and Japan 15. But after General Electric, 5 of the top 10 are Japanese, and the rest are from South Korea, Germany, the Netherlands, and France.

As Table 2.3 illustrates, 14 U.S. enterprises are among the biggest companies by industry. In 6 industries the leader is a Japanese enterprise. Asea Brown Boveri of Switzerland is the largest producer of industrial and farm equipment. Italy and Spain follow in the metals, mining, and crude oil production industries respectively with a leading enterprise.

The global-spanning activities of multinational enterprises is reaching new heights. The apparent supremacy of U.S. enterprises illustrated in Tables 2.1–3 has been recently questioned in an *International Business Week* (May 14, 1990) cover story entitled "The Stateless Corporation."

The trend toward "stateless" enterprises is unmistakable. A wave of mergers, acquisitions, and strategic alliances suggests that European, Japanese, and American multinational enterprises are going through a learning process of how to juggle multiple identities and multiple loyalties. In this new phase of multinational expansion, according to *International Business Week,* American enterprises are Johnny-come-latelies in the stateless game compared with many of their European and Japanese competitors (see Table 2.4). For example, the United States's share of world GNP declined from 33 percent in 1960 to 22 percent in 1980, with the downward tendency progressing. Japan, on the other hand, has increased its share of World GNP threefold, from 3 percent in 1960 to 10 percent in 1980.

THE NATURE OF MULTINATIONAL ENTERPRISE

Regarding the nature of multinational enterprises, the following basic working hypotheses may be listed (Niosi 1985):

- Capital travels primarily among countries where it is plentiful rather than to regions where it is scarce. Postwar international foreign direct investment flows are not consistent with the capital arbitrage theory that capital moves from capital-abundant locations to capital-scarce locations. Capital not only flows in the "wrong" direction, but also substantial amounts of capital move between two countries in both directions simultaneously (Buckley and Casson 1991).
- Some industries breed multinational enterprises more prolifically than others. One finds multinational enterprises often in markets that are highly concentrated. Research and development and technological barriers play a major role in such markets.
- Multinational enterprises are most often the largest firm in each industry, the "leader" of the branches in which multinationalization has occurred. The degree of multinationality tends to be larger the larger the firm.
- As a general rule, they have a "special asset" which is often a technological advantage (new products or processes) but can also be an organizational advantage. It is the existence and variety of such advantages that

TABLE 2.2:
THE WORLD'S 50 BIGGEST CORPORATIONS
ACCORDING TO FORTUNE'S "INTERNATIONAL 500"

1989	ENTERPRISE Country	SALES $ Millions	PROFITS $ Millions	Rank	ASSETS $ Millions	Rank
1	GENERAL MOTORS U.S.	126,974.3	4,224.3	2	173,297.1	1
2	FORD MOTOR U.S.	96,932.6	3,835.0	4	160,893.3	7
3	EXXON U.S.	86,656.0	3,510.0	7	83,219.0	4
4	ROYAL DUTCH/SHELL GROUP BRITAIN/NETHERLANDS	85,527.9	6,482.7	1	91,011.0	4
5	INT'L BUSINESS MACHINES U.S.	63,438.0	3,758.0	5	77,734.0	6
6	TOYOTA MOTOR JAPAN	60,443.6	2,631.1	12	49,672.8	10
7	GENERAL ELECTRIC U.S.	55,264.0	3,939.0	3	128,344.0	3
8	MOBIL U.S.	50,976.0	1,809.0	20	39,080.0	15
9	HITACHI JAPAN	50,894.0	1,446.7	33	52,253.2	7
10	BRITISH PETROLEUM BRITAIN	49,484.4	3,498.8	8	51,042.4	8
11	IRI ITALY	49,077.2	1,177.7	38	N.A.	

Rank	Company / Country					
12	MATSUSHITA ELECTRIC INDUSTRIAL JAPAN	43,086.0	1,664.0	26	48,217.9	11
13	DAIMLER BENZ GERMANY	40,616.0	3,584.6	6	37,133.5	17
14	PHILIP MORRIS U.S.	39,069.0	2,946.0	9	38,528.0	16
15	FIAT ITALY	36,740.8	2,410.8	16	46,355.2	12
16	CHRYSLER U.S.	36,156.0	359.0	169	51,038.0	9
17	NISSAN MOTOR JAPAN	36,078.4	889.7	64	35,713.4	19
18	UNILEVER BRITAIN/NETHERLANDS	35,284.4	1,729.7	24	20,804.4	47
19	E.I. DU PONT DE NEMOURS U.S.	35,209.0	2,480.0	14	34,715.0	20
20	SAMSUNG SOUTH KOREA	35,189.1	515.1	119	28,415.6	32
21	VOLKSWAGEN GERMANY	34,746.4	523.2	116	33,661.7	23
22	SIEMENS GERMANY	32,659.6	786.8	71	34,390.5	21
23	TEXACO U.S.	32,416.0	2,413.0	15	25,636.0	34
24	TOSHIBA JAPAN	29,469.3	930.8	58	31,676.8	25

TABLE 2.2:
THE WORLD'S 50 BIGGEST CORPORATIONS
ACCORDING TO FORTUNE'S "INTERNATIONAL 500"

1989	ENTERPRISE Country	SALES $ Millions	PROFITS $ Millions	Rank	ASSETS $ Millions	Rank
25	CHEVRON U.S.	29,443.0	251.0	235	33,884.0	22
26	NESTLE SWITZERLAND	29,364.8	1,474.5	31	22,976.0	41
27	RENAULT FRANCE	27,456.9	1,457.3	32	21,143.1	46
28	ENI ITALY	27,119.3	1,125.9	40	41,479.1	14
29	PHILIPS' GLOEILAMPEN-FABRIEKEN NETHERLANDS	26,992.5	648.1	93	28,807.4	31
30	HONDA MOTOR JAPAN	26,484.3	758.5	74	17,206.1	63
31	BASF GERMANY	25,317.0	1,071.3	47	20,791.1	48
32	NEC JAPAN	24,594.8	502.6	123	25,204.6	35
33	HOECHST GERMANY	24,403.0	1,025.6	49	19,737.8	54
34	AMOCO U.S.	24,214.0	1,610.0	28	30,430.0	28
35	PEUGEOT FRANCE	24,090.5	1,616.1	27	18,584.2	56

36	BAT INDUSTRIES BRITAIN	23,528.9	2,123.2	17	18,655.5	55
37	ELF AQUITAINE FRANCE	23,501.4	1,132.4	39	33,261.9	24
38	BAYER GERMANY	23,021.2	1,107.5	42	21,388.6	45
39	CIE GENERALE D'ELECTRICITE FRANCE	22,575.0	774.5	72	31,018.2	27
40	IMPERIAL CHEMICAL INDUSTRIES BRITAIN	21,889.4	1,733.0	23	18,197.0	57
41	PROCTOR & GAMBLE U.S	21,689.0	1,206.0	36	16,351.0	68
42	MITSUBISHI ELECTRIC JAPAN	21,213.3	415.0	146	20,380.6	50
43	ASEA BROWN BOVERI SWITZERLAND	21,209.0	589.0	102	24,156.0	38
44	NIPPON STEEL JAPAN	20,767.0	607.9	98	26,143.7	33
45	BOEING U.S.	20,276.0	937.0	51	13,278.0	92
46	OCCIDENTAL PETROLEUM U.S.	20,068.0	285.0	206	20,741.0	49
47	DAEWOO SOUTH KOREA	19,981.4	114.5	306	28,986.2	30
48	UNITED TECHNOLOGIES U.S.	19,765.5	702.1	84	14,598.2	80

TABLE 2.2:
THE WORLD'S 50 BIGGEST CORPORATIONS
ACCORDING TO FORTUNE'S "INTERNATIONAL 500"

1989	ENTERPRISE Country	SALES $ Millions	PROFITS $ Millions	Rank	ASSETS $ Millions	Rank
49	FUJITSU JAPAN	18,734.1	541.1	110	19,770.5	53
50	EASTMAN KODAK U.S.	18,546.0	529.0	112	23,652.0	39

Source: Fortune, July 30, 1990, page 47.

explains cross-investment in the same industry in
advanced countries.
- The firm-specific "core asset" advantages of multinational
  enterprises are subject to erosion.
- Products manufactured by multinational enterprises
  follow a natural product cycle.

The relevance of these basic working hypotheses in searching for a
theory of multinational enterprises is the task to which we turn our
attention in the following sections.

CAPITAL ARBITRAGE APPROACH

Within the neoclassical framework, analysis of foreign direct investment was carried on in terms of a theory of the impact of international capital flows. Economists did not consider the multinational
enterprise or foreign direct investment as a distinctive phenomenon
(Teece 1986). The simplest possible model was applied: two factors
(capital and labor), one homogeneous good, full employment, perfect
competition, and constant returns to scale. The relative rates of return on investments of various countries were examined in order to
assess the impact of foreign direct investment upon a host country in
terms of marginal productivity of capital. Capital is assumed to be
internationally mobile in response to relative returns such that a
tendency toward international factor price equalization arises. Capital moves from countries where it is abundant, and hence interest
rates are low, to countries where it is scarce and interest rates are
high. Capital continues to move until interest rates are equalized in
both countries. Caves (1960, ch. 5) has surveyed the earlier literature
on this point.

In the more recent literature the equalization of rates of return
among countries is often included in the market disequilibrium theories of foreign direct investment category (Calvet 1981; Boddewyn
1985).

Applying neoclassical analysis, MacDougall (1960) and Kemp
(1964) examined the circumstances under which a capital-receiving
country would gain or lose from a foreign direct investment inflow.
The main point arising from this analysis was that a gain is likely,
given that profits are taxed by the government of the foreign direct
investment country (Corden 1974, 193).

This analysis was extended along the lines of the standard optimum tariff argument applied to capital imports and exports. From a
domestic viewpoint (given no retaliation), a capital-importing nation

TABLE 2.3: THE BIGGEST COMPANIES BY INDUSTRY
ACCORDING TO FORTUNE'S "INTERNATIONAL 500" (1989)

INDUSTRY	COMPANY	COUNTRY	SALES $ millions
AEROSPACE	BOEING	U.S.	$20,276
APPAREL	LEVI STRAUSS ASSOCIATES	U.S.	$3,628
BEVERAGES	PEPSICO	U.S.	$15,420
BUILDING MATERIALS	HANSON	BRITAIN	$11,833
CHEMICALS	E.I. DU PONT DE NEMOURS	U.S.	$35,209
COMPUTERS (INCLUDES OFFICE EQUIPMENT)	IBM	U.S.	$63,438
ELECTRONICS	GENERAL ELECTRIC	U.S.	$55,264
FOOD	PHILIP MORRIS	U.S.	$39,069
FOREST PRODUCTS	INTERNATIONAL PAPER	U.S.	$11,378
FURNITURE	JOHNSON CONTROLS	U.S.	$3,690
INDUSTRIAL AND FARM EQUIPMENT	ASEA BROWN BOVERI	SWITZERLAND	$21,209
METAL PRODUCTS	NKK	JAPAN	$10,926
METALS	IRI	ITALY	$49,077
MINING, CRUDE OIL PRODUCTION	INI	SPAIN	$15,277
MOTOR VEHICLES AND PARTS	GENERAL MOTORS	U.S.	$126,974
PETROLEUM REFINING	EXXON	U.S.	$86,656
PHARMACEUTICALS	JOHNSON & JOHNSON	U.S.	$9,844
PUBLISHING, PRINTING	DAI NIPPON PRINTING	JAPAN	$7,892
RUBBER AND PLASTIC PRODUCTS	BRIDGESTONE	JAPAN	$12,379
SCIENTIFIC AND PHOTOGRAPHIC EQUIPMENT	EASTMAN KODAK	U.S.	$18,546
SOAPS AND COSMETICS	PROCTOR & GAMBLE	U.S.	$21,689
TEXTILES	ASAHI CHEMICAL INDUSTRY	JAPAN	$7,992
TOBACCO	BAT INDUSTRIES	BRITAIN	$23,529
TOYS, SPORTING GOODS	YAMAHA	JAPAN	$3,794
TRANSPORTATION EQUIPMENT	KAWASAKI HEAVY INDUSTRY	JAPAN	$6,906

Source: Fortune, July 30, 1990, page 44.

TABLE 2.4: THE "STATELESS" WORLD OF MANUFACTURING

This is a sampling of manufacturing companies with a minimum $ billion in annual sales that derive at least 40% of those sales from countries other than their home country. It does not include state-owned companies or holdings.

Company	Home Country	1989 Total Sales Billions	Sales Outside Home Country	Assets Outside Home Country	Shares Held Outside Home Country	Management Approach
NESTLE	SWITZERLAND	$32.9*	98.0%*	95.0%	Few	CEO is German. Has 10 general managers of whom five are not Swiss
SANDOZ	SWITZERLAND	8.6*	96.0	94.0	5.0%	All Swiss at top, more conservative in style than other Swiss companies
SKF	SWEDEN	4.1	96.0	90.0	20.0	Foreigners have cracked board and top management group
HOFFMANN-LA ROCHE	SWITZERLAND	6.7*	96.0	60.0	0.0	All-Swiss board, but next level of managers mixed
PHILIPS	NETHERLANDS	30.0	94.0	85.0*	46.0	Solidly Dutch company, but number of senior foreign managers is increasing

TABLE 2.4: THE "STATELESS" WORLD OF MANUFACTURING

This is a sampling of manufacturing companies with a minimum $ billion in annual sales that derive at least 40% of those sales from countries other than their home country. It does not include state-owned companies or holdings.

Company	Home Country	1989 Total Sales Billions	Sales Outside Home Country	Assets Outside Home Country	Shares Held Outside Home Country	Management Approach
SMITHKLINE BEECHAM.	BRITAIN	7.0	89.0	75.0	46.0	Joint US-British management at all levels
ABB	SWEDEN	20.6	85.0*	NA	50.0	Moved headquarters to Switzerland; managers are Swedish, Swiss, German
ELECTROLUX	SWEDEN	13.8	83.0	80.0	20.0	Of 50 top managers outside Sweden, only five are Swedish
VOLVO	SWEDEN	14.8	80.0	30.0	10.0	Solidly Swedish at all top levels
ICI	BRITAIN	22.1	78.0	50.0	16.0	40% of top 170 executives are not British; top ranks include four other nationalities

MICHELIN	FRANCE	9.4	78.0	NA	0.0	Secretive, centralized, with top management almost entirely French
HOECHST	W.GERMANY	27.3	77.0	NA	42.0	No foreigners on board, but most foreign operations are run by locals
UNILEVER	BRITAIN/NETH.	35.3	75.0*	70.0*	27.0	Five nationalities on board, thoroughly state less management
AIR LIQUIDE	FRANCE	5.0	70.0	66.0	6.0	English is official language, but it considers itself thoroughly French
CANON	JAPAN	9.4	69.0	32.0	14.0	Foreigners run many sales subsidiaries, but none in top ranks
NORTHERN TELECOM	CANADA	6.1	67.1	70.5	16.0	Thoroughly Canadian, but assumed U.S. identity
SONY	JAPAN	16.3	66.0	NA	13.6	Only major Japanese manufacturer with foreigners on board

TABLE 2.4: THE "STATELESS" WORLD OF MANUFACTURING

This is a sampling of manufacturing companies with a minimum $ billion in annual sales that derive at least 40% of those sales from countries other than their home country. It does not include state-owned companies or holdings.

Company	Home Country	1989 Total Sales Billions	Sales Outside Home Country	Assets Outside Home Country	Shares Held Outside Home Country	Management Approach
BAYER	W.GERMANY	25.8	65.4	NA	48.0	No foreigners on board, but six of 25 business groups run by foreigners
BASF	W.GERMANY	13.3	65.0	NA	NA	Relies on local managers to run foreign operations, but none in top ranks
GILLETTE	U.S.	3.8	65.0	63.0	10.0*	Three foreigners among 21 officers
COLGATE	U.S.	5.0	64.0	47.0	10.0*	CEO, other top execs have had several foreign posts; many multilingual
HONDA	JAPAN	26.4	63.0	35.7	6.9	Foreigners running offshore plants, but none at top levels at home
DAIMLER BENZ	W.GERMANY	45.5	61.0	NA	25.0*	Similar to other German giants

IBM	U.S.	62.7	59.0	NA	NA	Relies on locals to manage non-U.S. operations; increasing number of foreigners in ranks
NCR	U.S.	6.0	58.9	40.5	NA	Nationals run foreign operations, but none in top ranks
CPC INTERNATIONAL	U.S.	5.1	56.0	62.0	5.0*	One third of officers are foreign nationals
COCA-COLA	U.S.	9.0	54.0	45.0	0.0	Thoroughly multinational management group making big international push
DIGITAL	U.S.	12.7	54.0	44.0	NA	Five of 37 top officers are foreign; most foreign operations run by locals
DOW CHEMICAL	U.S.	17.6	54.0	45.0	5.0	Out of top 25 managers, 20 have experience outside U.S.
SAINT-GOBAIN	FRANCE	11.6	54.0	50.0	13.0	Of 25 top managers, only two are not French

TABLE 2.4: THE "STATELESS" WORLD OF MANUFACTURING

This is a sampling of manufacturing companies with a minimum $ billion in annual sales that derive at least 40% of those sales from countries other than their home country. It does not include state-owned companies or holdings.

Company	Home Country	1989 Total Sales Billions	Sales Outside Home Country	Assets Outside Home Country	Shares Held Outside Home Country	Management Approach
XEROX	U.S.	12.4	54.0	51.8	0.0	Major joint ventures with Rank; Fuji have shaped top management thinking
CATERPILLAR	U.S.	11.1	53.0	NA	NA	Of top five executives, four have foreign experience, including CEO-elect
HEWLETT-PACKARD	U.S.	11.9	53.0	38.6	8.0	Five of top 25 officers not U.S. citizens; many units managed offshore
SIEMANS	W.GERMANY	36.3	51.0	NA	44.0	Some business groups managed from outside Germany by non-Germans but none on management board
CORNING	U.S.	3.1*	50.0*	45.0*	NA	Company is leader in use of joint ventures to penetrate markets
JOHNSON & JOHNSON	U.S.	9.8	50.0	48.0	NA	First foreign national on board 1989; senior managers include foreign-born

UNITED TECHNOLOGIES	U.S.	19.8	49.7	26.7	NA	Because of U.S. defense business, few foreigners at top
UNISYS	U.S.	10.1	49.0	31.0	10.0	Aside from Japanese joint venture, management is largely American
MERCK	U.S.	6.0	47.0	NA	NA	Top management is American, but foreign nationals run overseas operations
NISSAN	JAPAN	36.5	47.0	20.0	2.9	Foreign operations managed by locals; completely Japanese at headquarters
3M	U.S.	12.0	46.0	42.0	15.0	CEO pushing to raise foreign sales to 50% of total by 1992
DU PONT	U.S.	35.5	44.0	20	24.0	Has two foreign directors, both Canadians, but top management is heavily American
MATSUSHITA	JAPAN	41.7	42.0	NA	7.0	American named no. 2 for North America, but no foreigners in top ranks
HEINZ	U.S.	6.0	40.0	41.0	0.6	CEO is Irish citizen, management thoroughly mixed
P & G	U.S.	21.4	40.0	32.0	NA	International operations chief recently named CEO

NA = not available   DATA: COMPANY REPORTS, * Business Week Estimates

Source: International Business Week, May 14, 1990, page 57

can exploit its monopsony power (or a capital-exporting country its monopoly power) by imposing a tax on the import or export of capital. Kemp (1966), Jones (1967), and Cordon (1967) further developed this theory of optimum tax on capital inflow or outflow integrated with the theory of the optimum tariff. Effective or potential increases in trade barriers offer a necessary incentive for enterprises to establish a subsidiary inside the protected market, rather than export to it.

Based upon factor endowments in a pure exchange model, Kennan and Riezman (1988) have extended the theoretical discussion by demonstrating the possibility that a large country may gain from a tariff war despite retaliation. Their model provides a potentially important explanation for the persistence of tariffs.

EVIDENCE ON THE CAPITAL ARBITRAGE APPROACH

Empirically, it has been difficult to find any correlation of capital interest rate differentials with foreign direct investment in time-series analysis (Ruffin and Rassekh 1986, 1126). However, Haynes (1988) has also analyzed the empirical difficulties involved regarding the traditional paradigm outcome that capital movements respond to differences in interest rates between countries and simultaneously reduce interest rate differentials. Haynes argues that the correlation relationship may be demonstrated empirically by specifying a simultaneous model in which dynamics of adjustment and data interval are adequately specified. Using U.S. and Canadian data from the 1960s, he finds that monthly data strongly support this view, whereas no significant relationship is obtained if quarterly observations are used. The basis of Haynes's argument is that regarding the relationship between capital flows and interest rates, lead-lag information between price and quantity may be of use in understanding dynamic adjustment in the conventional paradigm of arbitrage between national capital markets that are traditionally thought to be underidentified.

In summary, this type of macroeconomic-oriented comparative cost view of foreign direct investment emphasizes supply-side considerations. It commonly focuses on the commercial policy constraints on exports and foreign direct investment (which may be related in a substitutive or complementary nature), emphasizing production costs rather than distribution costs (Boddewyn 1985, 59; Ruffin 1984). Most researchers, however, now stress that the key ingredient of foreign direct investment is *not* foreign investment (the transfer of capital per se). Summaries of the literature by Caves (1982, 31–36) and Borner (1983; 1985, 104ff.) further discuss the various arguments against a strict application of the capital arbitrage approach. As Caves points out in his summary, Hufbauer (1975, 261–63) has shown formally that foreign investment depends on demand elasticities and production-function parameters, not just capital-cost differences.

SPECIFIC ADVANTAGES AND MULTINATIONAL ENTERPRISES

The pioneering work in the modern theory of the multinational enterprise is Hymer's 1960 doctoral dissertation, written under Kindleberger's supervision at Massachusetts Institute of Technology. Hymer's research, however, remained unpublished until 1976. His specific advantage hypothesis was popularized by the summary of it in Kindleberger (1969, 1970) and Caves (1974a, b, c) and rendered dynamic by Vernon (1966).

Hymer argued that interest rates alone, as proposed by the capital arbitrage hypothesis, do not adequately describe observed capital movements. Capital moves normally from one capital-abundant country to another capital-abundant country. In addition to cross-movements of capital, he observed that enterprises that invest outside their countries of origin commonly finance a large portion of their capital through borrowing in the host countries. Hymer further observed that almost all foreign direct investment is accounted for by enterprises based in some ten countries in Europe, North America, and Japan. Hence, he suggested that there must be something inherent in the industrial structure of these countries which promotes foreign expansion. An enterprise that successfully becomes a multinational enterprise must therefore, according to Hymer, possess some technological, organizational, or other advantage.

The specific advantage hypothesis is that a multinational enterprise must have some nonmarketable advantage over foreign domestic firms that is sufficient to overcome the natural obstacles of operating in some distant foreign market. The relevance of Hymer's work is found in essentially every study of multinational enterprise. The insights of Hymer's analysis laid the foundation for a completely new paradigm of multinational enterprise, one embedded in industrial organization theory rather than international trade and finance (Teece 1986).

Caves (1974b) has classified the sources of firm-specific advantages in three main categories:

(1) Technological advantage in products or processes. Multinational enterprises are assumed to possess some specific asset in the

form of a patented differentiated product or a patented new method of production. Being profit maximizers, they open foreign subsidiaries if they can gain greater profits through foreign direct investment than by exporting or licensing. Caves stresses product differentiation as the main source of technological advantage.

(2) Entrepreneurial excess capacity. Underutilized resources of the firm may cause foreign direct investment. Multinational expansion occurs in order to give full employment to a firm's stock of managerial talent. Unique management skills possess a higher efficiency relative to foreign enterprises. Helpman and Krugman (1985), for example, explain the expansion of multinationals along similar lines applying the concept of managerial headquarter services in connection with product differentiation, market structures, and factor cost differences.

(3) Multiplant economies. Multiplant economies are advantages that arise due to the single ownership of two or more production plants over and above the outcome achievable given independent ownership of the same kind of production facilities among more than one party. Domestic plants may rapidly exhaust possible economies within single plants. Further cost reductions may be obtained through becoming multiplant producers both domestically and at an international level. Marketing economies, managing service economies, advertising economies, capital market and other financial economies, administrative economies from coordination of input procurement or output distribution, or economies from spreading research and development over larger outputs may arise (Markusen and Melvin 1984; 1988, 306–08).

EVIDENCE ON THE SPECIFIC ADVANTAGE HYPOTHESIS

Affirmative empirical evidence on the specific advantage hypothesis is now well documented (e.g., Caves 1982). The specific advantage of multinational enterprises commonly rests in the presence of some intangible asset. Such assets deny direct measurement. Most empirical studies therefore examine the outlays that enterprises make for the purpose of producing such assets. Traditionally, economists have studied the outlays for advertising and research and development as indicators of the specific advantages of multinational enterprises. However, as Buckley (1988, 187) has formulated "The search for the secret ingredient (firm-specific advantage) rather begs the question. There is also an element of post hoc, propter hoc in these explanations."

THE PRODUCT CYCLE HYPOTHESIS

In many sectors the major factors determining competitiveness are still strongly related to relative abundance of factors, especially where specialization among countries takes place at the industry level and where trade possesses a strong interindustry character. Such trade is still largely the basis of trade between industrial and newly industrializing countries and with less developed countries (Casson et al. 1986). On the other hand, an increasing portion of trade under the auspices of multinational enterprises has evolved between countries with similar factor abundancies. These trade flows have a pronounced intraindustry character. Under these circumstances economies of scale and product differentiation, as well as technology gaps created by research and development (R & D), are important.

Several authors (e.g., Arndt and Bouton 1987; Best 1990) have recently pointed out two major developments in the postwar era that have fundamentally altered the competitive game to the disadvantage of the established and mature industrial economies in Europe and North America. First is the emergence of new and highly aggressive competitors, beginning with Japan and continuing with the newly industrializing countries of Asia and Latin America. Second is the quickening pace of international communication and the more rapid diffusion of information and technical knowledge it has engendered. These developments have resulted in the shrinking length of the technology gap and the contraction of the product cycle and an increase in competitive pressures. The shortening product cycle and the rapid pace of global competition require new strategies and greater flexibility than were needed in the more tranquil past.

It is often assumed in economic theory that the state of technology is unchanging. Of course economists are well aware that technology changes. A technical change may be expressed in improved manufacturing methods of existing products or in the production of entirely new goods. Normally this process will affect the pattern of comparative advantage, hence also effecting investment and trade strategies of multinational enterprises. Economists have not entirely disregarded aspects of technological change; however, they have commonly assumed that the economic effects of technological innovation may be entirely captured through its consequences for increased productivity—that is, through a change in production costs.

Businessmen and business schools, on the other hand, began to consider the fact that products may go through a natural life cycle. Throughout a product life cycle forecastable changes were thought to occur in product characteristics, which led to changes in the production technique and production location. Also, the nature of the market was considered to possess a natural life cycle, including changes in the degree of competition and in the character of demand (Vernon 1987a, 987).

The product cycle hypothesis postulates that a new product will, as a rule, follow a natural life cycle. Products come into existence, change in character (standardization and upgrading), and eventually disappear. The duration of the life cycle varies from industry to industry. The longest life cycles are observed in extractive industries and industries producing intermediate standardized products. The shortest life cycles are observed in consumers' "fashion goods." There has been a significant trend toward a shortening of the life cycles of products due to refined technological progress and deliberate action of firms. To the questions "why" and "where," the product life cycle model adds the dimension "when" to the theory of multinational enterprise investment in a dynamic context.

The original product life cycle concept was first applied as a marketing management tool (Levitt 1965). Robinson and Pearce (1986) and Gardner (1987) have illuminated the discussion of the marketing strategy aspects of the product cycle model from a business perspective. Vernon (1966), Hufbauer (1966), and Hirsch (1967, 1975) first utilized the concept for international trade. The product life cycle model was applied to the theory of international trade, including technological and production considerations. These aspects supplement the earlier studies of Linder (1961), Kravis (1956), and Keesing (1966), who emphasized domestic demand and availability considerations as the determining variables for trade.

Vernon suggested that the theory of comparative advantage of international trade and explanations of foreign direct investment flows do not provide an adequate explanation of trade and international investment. Vernon's theory places less emphasis upon the comparative cost doctrine of international trade theory and more upon the timing of innovation.

Enterprises located in the rich developed countries, according to Vernon's product cycle hypothesis, have a strong incentive to acquire a technological advantage over producers in less developed markets. While other theorists assume that multinationals have a specific advantage, Vernon attempts to explain theoretically how this advantage is achieved (Koutsoyiannis 1982, 323).

Multinational enterprises in developed countries create a technologically superior product or method of production through their large expenditures on research and development. Operating in markets with high per capita incomes, multinational enterprises respond quickly to the consumer needs for new products. Hence, large funds are invested in producing new, higher quality and upgrading old products and processes. Proximity of enterprises is a powerful determinant of research and development expenditures. On the other hand, developed economies have in general high labor unit costs and an abundant supply of capital, making labor-intensive production methods relatively expensive. Therefore, an incentive exists to develop products and processes that are relatively more capital intensive.

Investment in the development of new products is a function of spatial proximity. Enterprises that operate in developed economies are the first normally to perceive an opportunity for high-income markets for labor-saving new products and processes. The specific advantage in the form of a new product or process thus depends on the proximity of enterprises to high-income markets or markets in need of labor-saving products or processes (Koutsoyiannis 1982, 324).

The product cycle model is founded upon four basic assumptions (Buckley 1981, 75): (1) products undergo predictable changes in production and marketing; (2) restricted information is available on technology; (3) production processes change over time, and economies of scale are prevalent; (4) tastes differ according to income, and thus products can be standardized at various income levels.

Figure 2.1 illustrates the product cycle hypothesis. In stage 1 (new product stage $0T_1$), development of a new product for the domestic market occurs. Product experience is gathered as suppliers experiment with different inputs, different production processes, and different design attributes. The unstandardized product with a low price elasticity of demand is produced on an experimental basis, hence producers cannot readily determine an optimum location, production, scale, or sale price. Product differentiation among suppliers plays an important role in this stage.

In stage 2 (maturing product T_1T_0') the product begins to become standardized. Exporting of the commodity occurs, and penetration into foreign markets is possible due to the advantage in new products enjoyed by the innovating country. This advantage is unlikely to last very long, although it may be prolonged by the legal monopoly afforded patents. Production and location decisions become less characterized by uncertainty.

During the course of time stage 3 (imitation stage $T_0'T_0$) arises. Product imitators enter the market, and the production processes and product attributes become increasingly standardized on an international basis.

Finally, stage 4 (standardized product) emerges in which the innovative advantages of the original product manufacturer are lost. Cost factors begin to dictate that foreign markets should be serviced

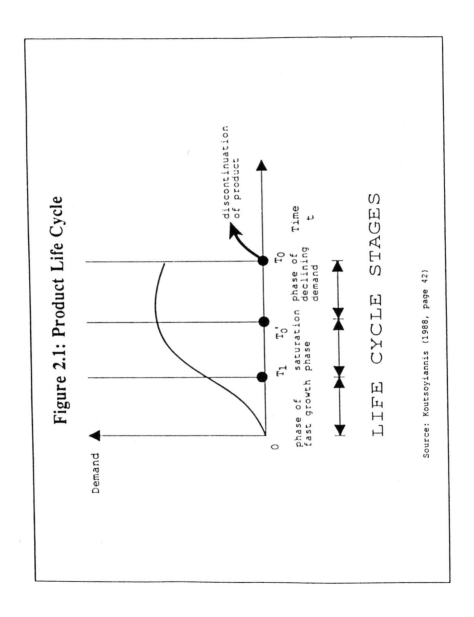

Figure 2.1: Product Life Cycle

by local production facilities. Originally production occurs in other similarly advanced countries via foreign direct investment and finally in the less developed countries where labor costs are cheapest. Discontinuation of product manufacturing may even occur.

The product life cycle may be altered in two ways (Koutsoyiannis 1982). (1) If a major innovation occurs, for example, the product may become outmoded before it reaches the maturity phase. Under such circumstances the life cycle is distorted. Effective demand is rapidly reduced, and discontinuation of the product is accelerated, as presented in Figure 2.2. If the technological breakthrough did not occur as assumed above, production of the product would be discontinued at stage T_0. Given technological change, however, product production is discontinued at stage T_0'. (2) Given slow technological change, the life cycle may be extended in two ways, as demonstrated in Figure 2.3. First, an enterprise may penetrate into markets as of yet not reached. Second, through strategies of product differentiation an enterprise can introduce minor changes which enhance the demand by creating a replacement demand or by making the product attractive to a wider range of buyers.

Vernon (1977a, 1979) has modified his model to cover the expansion of non–U.S. multinational enterprises. This modified product cycle model comes closer to the Hymer/Kindleberger tradition in basing its explanatory power on oligopoly and market structures. Now the names of the stages are the competitive devices used to construct and maintain oligopoly—innovation based on oligopoly, mature oligopoly (price competition and scale economies), and senescent oligopoly (cartels, product differentiation, and the essential breakdown of entry barriers).

The product cycle model splits the decisions of multinational strategies into three interdependent aspects: (1) investment in product development, (2) the method of servicing a market, (3) the firm's competitive stance vis-à-vis foreign firms. The product cycle model postulates that there exists a natural cycle of foreign market penetration. Exporting and investment abroad are separate stages in the decision process by which multinational enterprises expand into foreign markets. Foreign direct investment is the successor to foreign trade (exporting). A multinational enterprise undertakes foreign direct investment to protect the foreign market share obtained by exports.

Several authors have further suggested that an industry itself may follow a natural life cycle. For example, Magee (1977b) stresses that entry barriers may occur in a dynamic sense over the life of the

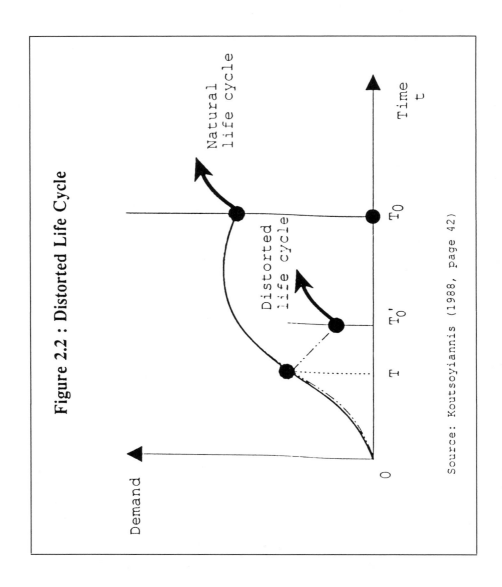

Figure 2.2 : Distorted Life Cycle

Source: Koutsoyiannis (1988, page 42)

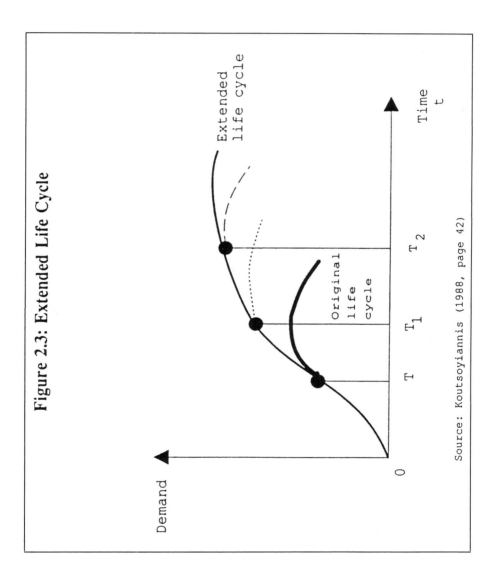

Figure 2.3: Extended Life Cycle

Source: Koutsoyiannis (1988, page 42)

industry. In the long run, the enterprise assets will be determined by its investment policy. Investing in barriers to entry may lead to (1) acquiring a temporary lead by opportunism; (2) defending this lead by branding to consolidate the pioneer's goodwill, product design to discourage reverse engineering, and tying in retailers with long-term contracts regarding service arrangements and spare parts supply; and (3) entry barriers through price policies and segmentation strategies. Research by Casson et al. (1986) has also suggested that the dynamics of global industrial competitiveness will interact with the international division of labor at various points in an industry's life cycle (as compared to a product life cycle) to produce characteristic changes in the location of production (see further Buckley and Artisien 1987). Grabowski and Mueller (1975) have also argued that enterprises experience a kind of life cycle. First, an enterprise is innovative and successful. Then a period of maturity sets in, when managers expand in accustomed ways. Grabowski and Mueller found that for the 759 U.S. enterprises they classified as "mature" or "nonmature" the returns on measured investment were significantly higher in the latter. Their interpretation is that managers in the mature enterprises make the persistent error of reinvesting too large a percentage of their internal funds.

The product cycle model's overdeterministic and programmatic nature no longer entirely captures the simultaneous decision-making strategies of present-day global competitive interactions (Buckley 1981, 76). Although there does seem to be a tendency for convergence of preferences internationally (Bartlett and Ghoshal 1988), the standardization of tastes envisioned by the product cycle model is not yet with us in high areas of demand. Enterprise strategies are commonly predicted on taste and factor differences (Buckley 1987, 51). Furthermore, being originally constructed to describe the locational activities of American multinational enterprises, it does not take into account Vernon's (1987a, 987) observation that:

> Once the US firms had established their multinational networks, the existence of those networks gradually altered the perceptions and calculations of some US-based firms. Some began to respond to conditions in foreign markets, as well as the home market, to provide the stimuli for their innovations. Some began to think in terms of world models of their products, with production facilities for component parts established in any country in the world where factor cost considerations might indicate. Trends of this sort reduced the relevance of the nationality of the parent in determining the

direction of the firm's innovations and in determining the pattern of its imports and exports.

The product cycle model has, however, established the important insight that comparative advantage does shift through time.

EVIDENCE ON THE PRODUCT CYCLE HYPOTHESIS

Vernon's product cycle model[2] has yielded a number of insights with regard to the expansion of multinational enterprise. However, as Buckley (1981, 75) and others have pointed out, although it attempts to integrate supply and demand factors, it has been outdated by events. Vernon himself became increasingly aware of this, as he states: "But certain conditions of that period are gone. For one thing, the leading MNCs have now developed global networks of subsidiaries, for another the U.S. market is no longer unique among national markets either in size or factor cost configuration." Hence, Vernon realizes that the product cycle might be less useful in explaining activities of multinational enterprise, but strong traces of the sequence are likely to remain. There is thus some degree of consensus that the product life cycle model has descriptive value.

The United States is no longer the only dominant foreign multinational enterprise investor. The framework must also include an explanation of European and Japanese foreign direct investments. Furthermore, multinational enterprises are now capable of developing, maturing, and standardizing products almost simultaneously, differentiating the product to suit a variety of needs without significant time lags.

The product cycle model has given rise to many empirical studies. The evidence is fairly persuasive that the model had strong predictive power in the first two or three decades after World War II, especially in explaining the composition of U.S. trade and in projecting the patterns of foreign direct investment by U.S. multinational enterprises (Vernon 1979, 265). Deardorff (1984) has recently surveyed this large literature. Empirical studies which support the product cycle model are presented in Hufbauer (1966), Hirsch (1967, 1975), Wells (1972), and Mullor-Sebastian (1983).

The product cycle model does exemplify the manner in which the supply-side influence of "temporary" differences in industry-specific knowledge creates trade flows based upon product and process innovation.

---

2. See further Vernon (1971, 1977a, b, 1979, 1987), Wells (1972), Moxon (1974).

The evidence presented in Figure 2.4 demonstrates the relationships between product life cycle and research and development costs as a percentage of sales. It is a fact of business life that product life cycles have been shortened in many industries. Illustrative of these effects has been the development of product life cycles in the information technology industry, which have shrunk from an average of eight years in the 1970s to barely two years in the 1980s (LAREA/ CEREM 1986a, 1; Mytelka and Delapierre 1987, 237).

For example, based on the spillover effects from the computer industry, the publishing industry is undergoing extensive changes as it moves from a paper to an electronically based industry. The time and space constraints for product development and distribution have been enormously shortened. Authors and news sources now prepare manuscripts electronically and transmit these to the publisher on floppy discs or by means of telecommunication. Word processors are used to edit manuscripts, and typesetting and graphics are now computerized. Readers can buy the product from the publisher's electronic data base network, and the promotional materials are distributed by telecommunication. The time lag between an idea for a new product and its mass distribution could be virtually eliminated (Pruijm 1990, 159).

With rising research and development costs and shortened product life cycles, competition over markets has made the successful access to foreign markets essential to the survival strategies of industrial enterprises.

Rapid acceleration of technological change and the vital role that flexible adjustment has played in the expansion of knowledge-intensive multinational enterprise have raised both the costs and risks of knowledge production itself (Mytelka 1987, 50). Delapierre and Zimmerman (1984, 12) found that in the information processing industry more than half the product variants were less than five years old. Bellon (1983, 158) observed that in the chemical and pharmaceutical industries one out of every two products was less than ten years old.

With shortened product life cycles, enterprises need to spend increasing amounts on research and development to remain at the frontier of technological change in their industry. Where technological, financial, and economic know-how and know-why replace embodied technology as the primary source of an enterprise's technological advantage, and where product life cycles barely exceed the length of time necessary to secure patent protection, the ability to capture technological proprietary rents through patenting diminishes and the importance of directly appropriating research and development re-

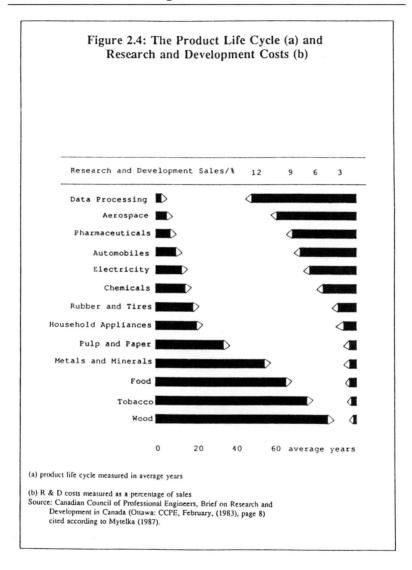

Figure 2.4: The Product Life Cycle (a) and
Research and Development Costs (b)

Research and Development Sales/%   12   9   6   3

Data Processing

Aerospace

Pharmaceuticals

Automobiles

Electricity

Chemicals

Rubber and Tires

Household Appliances

Pulp and Paper

Metals and Minerals

Food

Tobacco

Wood

0   20   40   60 average years

(a) product life cycle measured in average years

(b) R & D costs measured as a percentage of sales
Source: Canadian Council of Professional Engineers, Brief on Research and
        Development in Canada (Ottawa: CCPE, February, (1983), page 8)
        cited according to Mytelka (1987).

sults grows, promoting not only foreign direct investment but most
recently increasing acceptance of implementing preemptive network
strategies—for example, cross-licensing.

THE TECHNOLOGY GAP MODEL

The product cycle model tends to focus attention on final consumer products. Along similar lines Posner (1961) suggested that

there exists a closely related phenomenon with regard to production technology. Examining the effects of technological change on trade, he argued that a technology gap exists. Posner originally observed that U.S. exports possessed a high technological component and that many of these exports diminish or disappear when the technological lead of the United States narrows or is lost (Kindleberger 1973, 63).

Trade flows could thus not be entirely explained by homogeneous factor endowments or productivity advantages, but were often based on a technological gap which resulted as a consequence of scientific research and entrepreneurship. A country such as the United States could possess an absolute advantage due to some new invention and innovation for a limited time. As time elapses, however, technology becomes standardized. Imitators are attracted to the market and similar production functions worldwide are obtained. The quasi-monopoly situation of the original producer will be disseminated as technology becomes standardized on a global basis.

At this point, production functions being similar on a global basis, foreign locations with low costs of labor will become attractive areas of foreign direct investment flows of multinational enterprises. According to Posner, international trade will occur during a duration period (imitation lag) needed for the rest of the world to imitate the original innovation. From the viewpoint of the importing country, Posner classifies the imitation lag in three categories (Gandolfo 1987, 1:266):

> (1) Foreign reaction lag. This is the time lag between successful utilization of the innovation by entrepreneurs in the innovating country and the new good's becoming regarded as a competitive threat by some firms in the importing country.
> (2) Domestic reaction lag. This is the time lag required for all enterprises in the importing country to become aware of the competition from the new good.
> (3) Learning period. This is the time lag in which the importing country's enterprises learn to produce the new good and actually begin manufacturing and selling domestically.

Institutional characteristics of a producer's environment (e.g., a viable patent law) as well as the innovation itself will affect these behavioral responses.

Consider the following scenario illustrated by Greenaway (1986, 17). Both countries produce commodities x and y, since initial factor endowments are the same. Now allow the dynamic influences of technological change to take hold. Suppose that in industry x in country A there is process innovation which changes the production function, permitting x to be manufactured in the same specification at a lower unit cost. Or consider the more commonly found case in which unit costs remain unchanged, resulting in product innovation such that a new variety of x is produced (product differentiation). The preconditions for mutually benefitting trade now exist, depending on, as Posner terms it, the "demand" and "imitation" lag structures. The net effect of the demand lag and imitation lag determines whether or not trade occurs. Demand lags may occur due to the fact that although x in countries A and B may be acceptable consumer substitutes, consumers in country B may not immediately react to the fall in the price of x in A, or the change in product specification. On the supply side, the imitation lag is founded on the manufacturer's response in country B to the technological development in A.

EVIDENCE ON THE TECHNOLOGY GAP HYPOTHESIS

Posner's research elicited various empirical studies that supported the fact that the pace of imitation is speeding up. Hufbauer (1966) found that in the synthetic fibers industry comparative advantage is not based on raw materials. He observed that countries producing wood pulp (Canada and Sweden) and those with petroleum feed stock (in the Middle East and, e.g., Venezuela) did not engage in the production of fibers. Trade in synthetic fibers began with a technological breakthrough leading to a technological gap. Economies of scale arose and imitation occurred internationally. The original comparative advantage of the innovators shifted to those countries characterized by low wage costs. Similar studies were carried out for the petrochemical industry, office machinery, international trade in motion pictures, and semiconductors, among others, offering supporting evidence.[3]

Normally an innovation serves to decrease the amount of labor required for manufacturing relative to required capital. Countries characterized by high labor costs should thus possess an inherent propensity to be innovative. For example, the United States is characterized by high labor costs and has to date successfully managed to exceed in inventive dominance. As Caves and Jones (1977, 139) suggest, a significant proportion of U.S. exports appears to consist of "technological gap" trade.

---

3. See Kindleberger (1973, 65), and Deardorff (1984) for literature.

Indeed, Gruber, Mehta, and Vernon (1967) in an empirical study of the United States found highly supporting evidence that industries with high research and development activities (as measured by dollars spent on research and development as a percentage of sales) accounted for 72 percent of U.S. exports of manufactured goods but only 39 percent of the nation's total sales of manufactures. Further research by Hufbauer (1970) on 24 countries also confirms the relationship between innovation and high labor costs.

Given that a country can maintain a flow of innovations through time, it will enjoy a high level of income per capita. Furthermore, the durations of imitation lags vary over countries. This permits a distortion of the technological gap cycle. The innovating country will hence be capable of extending its technological advantage in other countries where the imitation lag is longer. Its greater experience in producing the good gives it an advantage over newcomers (Gandolfo 1987, 1:267).

Posner's technological gap model leaves the most fundamental question unanswered; namely, What generates the original innovation and the successive competitive patterns of imitation? His model does, however, emphasize the fact that a supply-side influence may stimulate trade, given that "temporary" differences in industry-specific knowledge exist (Greenaway 1986, 19).

INTERNALIZATION THEORY

The internalization approach is founded upon Coase's (1937) criticism of neoclassical economics.[4] As is now well known, Coase postulated that transactions within hierarchical structures of the firm are presumed to be less costly than spot market transaction costs. Consequently, firms serve to internalize markets, increasing thereby economic allocative efficiency. The level of transaction costs provides the source of economic justification for the existence of firms.

Applied to the theory of multinational enterprise, the internalization approach rests on two general axioms: (1) Enterprises choose the least cost location for each activity they perform, and (2) enterprises grow by internalizing markets up to the point where the benefits of additional internalization are smaller than the additional incremental costs (Buckley 1988, 181–82).

As mentioned earlier, explanations of multinational enterprise

---

4. Casson (1990a, 1) notes that the work of Coase follows the earlier research on the nature of the firm by Knight (1921), Robinson (1931, 1934) and Kaldor (1934). Coase has recently discussed the evolution of his ideas in Williamson and Winter (1991).

often assume the existence of some proprietary asset of a technological kind. Such firm-specific advantages permit enterprises to carry
the costs (i.e., disadvantages) of penetrating foreign markets.

Technology is commonly thought to be analogous to knowledge
or information. Due to the public-good nature of the production of
scientific knowledge (Nelson 1959; Arrow 1962; Dosi 1988), inherent
problems of appropriability in the transfer process occur. The internalization of such assets improves economic efficiency. Indeed, up
to the early 1970s the majority of most technological innovations
implemented by multinational enterprises did appear to follow this
pattern based upon systematic in-house research and development
investments (Arora and Gambardella 1990, 362).

The internalization theory was first applied to multinational enterprises by Hymer (1968).[5] His work precedes the general revival
of interest in Coase's research that began with Williamson (1971,
1975). Penrose (1959), Arrow (1969), Alchian and Demsetz (1972),
and Klein, Crawford, and Alchian (1978) have also contributed sub-
stantially with their analyses of information markets and the economics of vertical integration. Along these lines, the internalization
approach emphasizes the theory of market failure to explain multinationality.

Following McManus (1972), Buckley and Casson (1991) incorporated the various strands of the internalization literature, asserting
that multinational enterprises will be created wherever markets are
internalized across international boundaries. Their original objective
was to apply the concept of internalization of markets to develop a
model of the growth of the enterprise. As Buckley (1988, 182) notes,
later writers who have taken technological capabilities and management skills to be fixed unduly "straightjacketed the analysis."

McManus (1972) pointed out that the essence of the phenomenon of international production is not the transfer of capital, but
rather the international extension of managerial control over foreign
subsidiaries. Ownership-based control permits management to allo-
cate resources more effectively than would be possible through the
market. The following factors are found to be significant for enterprises deciding on market sourcing policies in international markets:

(1) the coordination of resources over time, when research
and development is involved;

---

5. Casson (1990a, 1): "What has only just been realized is that the theory was
first applied to international business by Hymer (1968), who temporarily abandoned

(2) the need for discriminatory pricing to maximize profit
on quasi-monopolistic information;
(3) the existence of bilateral monopoly;
(4) buyer uncertainty over the value of knowledge to be
traded;
(5) perishability of products and uncertainty over security
of supply;
(6) investment in durable transaction-specific goods
requiring planning;
(7) ex ante monopoly of a unique resource requiring
discriminatory pricing.[6]

The process of multinational internalization will continue until
the benefits and costs of further internalization are equated at the
margin. Buckley and Casson (1991) first examine the orthodox theory
of location, which ignores the factors relevant to internalization. One
may, however, interpret the location economic approach also as an
aspect of internalization; for example, in a spatial context the firm
minimizes transport costs of transaction per se. Dean and Carroll
(1977) have presented a general framework of plant location under
uncertainty. Various decision environments can be "mapped" in such
a way that the enterprise can obtain a "lay of the land" before em-
barking on some specific location analysis.

In a second stage, Buckley and Casson (1991) analyze the extent
to which internalization interacts with and modifies location strategy.
They find that trade flows in knowledge or commodities often face
imperfect markets. This implies high transaction costs which inhibit
free trade across borders. Here the insights of Coase (1937) are applicable, since presumably international markets are characterized by
greater imperfections and higher transaction costs than domestic
markets.

One of the important results of the research of Buckley and
Casson is that the higher the general level of similarity between
nations, the lower the cost of contracting internationally as compared
to foreign direct investment. Their second finding is that nation-spe-
cific costs (political, legal, and fiscal policies of governments) may
raise the costs of using external markets relative to internalization.
Finally, they find that at the firm level an enterprise's expertise both

---

his market structure emphasis (Hymer 1960) to articulate internalization theory before
returning to the market structure theme in his Marxist phase (Hymer 1971)."
    6. Discussions on internalization theory and the multinational enterprise are
found in Dunning (1977), Giddy (1978), Hood and Young (1979), Casson (1979), and
Clegg (1988).

in transacting with outside agents and in administering resources internally is often based upon experience. The embodied value of such transaction-specific investments is such that the price the investment receives internally is often higher than its external market value. Along these lines, the possession of an internal market gives the multinational enterprise superior ability to produce and distribute goods and services that are intensive in the use of such intermediate inputs (most importantly, the intermediate input information). It is the ability to effectively utilize an intermediate input on an international level that distinguishes the multinational enterprise from other domestic corporations.

The internalization approach contributes to explaining the route by which an enterprise chooses to exploit the firm-specific advantages it has over its foreign competitors. Caves (1971a, b) observed that a specific factor model is needed since foreign direct investment involves a bundle of capital, technology, and marketing skills. Thus, each sector has its own specific type of capital (+ technology + marketing skills).[7] Hirsch (1976) first formalized the optimization problem of an enterprise's options of servicing a foreign market. His model identifies the conditions under which an enterprise has an economic incentive to exploit its ownership advantages through exports or foreign direct investment.[8]

Hood and Young (1979, 56) have rightfully raised the question: How does this internalization approach differ from the theories of technological advantage presented earlier? As they state, the difference is that it is not the possession of some unique asset per se which gives a firm its advantage. Rather it is the process of internalizing that asset as opposed to selling it to a foreign producer which gives the multinational enterprise its competitive edge.

According to Buckley and Casson (1991, 68) firm-specific assets of multinational enterprises are

> the rewards for past investment in (1) research and development facilities which create an advantage in technological fields, (2) the creation of an integrated team of skills, the rent from which is greater than the sum of the rewards to individuals, (3) the *creation of an information transmission*

7. See further the specific factors model developed by Jones, Neary, and Ruane (1983).

8. McManus (1972), Brown (1976), Magee (1977a), Hood and Young (1979), Caves (1982), Casson (1990a), Lall (1980), Buckley and Davies (1979), Giddy and Rugman (1979), and Grosse (1985) have elaborated on this theme.

network which allows the benefits of (1) and (2) to be trans-
mitted at low cost within the organisation, but also protects
such information, including knowledge of market conditions,
from outsiders [emphasis added].

EVIDENCE ON THE INTERNALIZATION HYPOTHESIS

The internalization hypothesis is now generally considered common sense in much of the literature on multinational enterprises. There has been little or practically no critical assessment of the applicability of the internalization approach as applied to the globalization of enterprise markets.

The internalization hypothesis in its general form cannot be directly tested. However, as suggested by Buckley (1988), this does not imply it is useless. Specific versions may be formulated that can indeed be confronted with observed evidence.[9] In so doing, Buckley suggests that "a major bridge" may be built with transaction cost economics and the distinct markets and hierarchies approach associated with Williamson and Teece. Since much of the arguments are based upon transaction costs in internal and external markets, studies need to be undertaken that attempt to measure transaction costs under alternative transactional configurations.

Perhaps somewhat surprisingly, some of the original major advocates of the internalization approach to multinationality (e.g., Hennart 1982; Casson 1990a) have become critical of the common oversimplified misinterpretations of the internalization approach. In a similar vein Williamson (1991, 271) states: "Hierarchies are more than a continuation of market mechanisms. Hierarchy is not merely a contractual act, but also a contractual instrument, a continuation of market relations *by other means*. The challenge to comparative contractual analysis is to discern and explicate the *different* means." Dunning (1988b, 343) has pointed out that internalization theory may also be applicable to networks of inter-enterprise collaborations. As he notes, the form of governance in strategic alliances (abstracting from distributional questions) is group oriented. Networks of strategic alliances may be regarded as *group internalization*.

Hennart (1986, 793) raises the following critical point:

---

9. Studies undertaken on the mode of transferring technology between countries but within firms (Davidson and McFeteridge 1984) revealed that such variables as existing overseas commitment, research intensity, and degree of product diversification were positively and significantly correlated with the extent of an enterprise's internalization (Dunning 1988a, 8).

Does internalization consist in the substitution of internal for external prices? Is the distinguishing characteristic of firms the use of internal prices? Although the concept of "internal markets" accounts for some features observed in firms, my view is that it fails to capture their most specific characteristic. The productive activity of the overwhelming majority of employees is not directed by prices, but by directives, either formalized through company rules, directly voiced by superiors, or internalized through indoctrination. Most employees are not rewarded on the basis of their output, measured at market prices, but according to their obedience to rules, orders or traditions. At the division level, internal prices also play a limited role. Firms which are functionally organized do not make use of internal prices. Even in multidivisional firms the use of internal shadow prices is seriously limited by interdependencies and measurement problems.

Furthermore, the description of internalization as setting up an internal market does not seem to adequately describe business behavior. A firm that integrates vertically forward or backward does not use "internal markets" to coordinate upstream and downstream activities. Setting up such a market would mean, in this context, using transfer prices to guide, measure, and reward the performance of the managers of its upstream and downstream divisions. A firm that integrates vertically does not make use of this coordination mechanism, for to do so would re-create the bargaining situation it has sought to avoid by taking over its supplier or customer. . . .

Although firms do sometimes rely on internal prices as a method of organization, the use of such prices is not their distinguishing mark. *The firm does not displace the market because it is better at doing what the market does, but because, as we will see, it uses a completely different method of organization. To describe internalization as the replacement of an imperfect external market by a more efficient internal market seems therefore to obscure what is distinctive about internalization* [emphasis added].

As Casson (1990a, 1, 27) has commented, "The major problem of the [internalization] theory [is] that it is too often trivialised and over-sold." Furthermore, "internalization theory does not generate a uniquely international theory of the firm. Internalization is only one of a number of principles needed to explain international business behavior—location factors, the philosophy of scientific research and the social principles of engineering trust are all key elements in the package too."

THE TRANSACTION COST VIEW

The internalization approach emphasizes the advantages and costs associated with internalizing market imperfections in intermediate markets, especially the markets for knowledge. As Teece (1986, 23) has remarked, "At one level the internalization school and the transaction cost approach are one and the same. Both see the firm as a response to market failure. Profit-seeking firms internalize operations when by so doing the costs of organizing and transacting business will thereby be lowered."

In order to go beyond this general conclusion of internalization, Teece, among others,[10] emphasizes the "nature of the transactions which are to be internalized." They stress that "the unit of analysis should be the transaction (Williamson 1975, 1979, 1981), and explicit attention must be given to ex ante versus ex post conditions of competition in the markets which the multinational enterprise internalizes. In short, the internalization paradigm developed in the literature to date needs to have transaction cost economics embedded within it if a deep understanding of the multinational enterprise is to evolve" (Teece 1986, 23).

The analysis of transaction cost economies as applied to multinational enterprises extends the internalization framework and attempts to systematically analyze where and when transactions should be internalized internationally. The comparative institutional approach of Williamson, which attempts to explain why production and exchange are organized administratively by fiat within firms as well as contractually between them, has been applied by Teece to multinational enterprises. He directs attention thereby to the distinctive governance properties of multinational enterprise and the consequences of restricting the employment of this particular organizational form. Profit-seeking enterprises choose their boundaries in order to minimize the sum of production and transaction costs (Teece 1981).

Galbraith and Kay (1986) suggest that the rationale for multinational enterprises must be sought in terms of potential economies of information. Figures 2.5 and 2.6, developed by Williamson (1979,

---

10. E.g., Toyne (1989), Rugman (1981), Hennart (1982, 1988), Jones and Hill (1988).

253), summarize the essential dimensions of information or know-how transactions for which, according to the transaction cost approach, governance structures need to be designed. Although highly simplistic, the figures demonstrate effectively the match of governance structures with transactions, which economizes on transaction costs and facilitates an efficient know-how transfer.

Teece (1980, 1982), Kay (1983a), and Hennart (1989a) have extended the transaction cost approach to diversification, merger, equity and nonequity cooperative agreements and takeover by rejecting the assumptions of separability and independence of product markets. The transaction cost approach has taken an important step in the right direction by incorporating economies of market and technology interdependencies into the analysis of multinationality.

Along the lines of Figures 2.5 and 2.6, the goal of the transaction cost model is to identify which institutional alternative or governance structure is most effective in economizing on transaction costs. The range or scope of governance structures among institutions typically includes the spectrum from markets to hierarchies which, due to their nature and incidence of their respective frictions, often hinder transactors from reaching cooperative outcomes.

According to Williamson (1985a, 41–42), "implementing transaction-cost economics mainly involves a comparative institutional assessment of discrete institutional alternatives." In transaction cost economics, two behavioral characteristics are postulated: (1) decisions and actions are characterized by bounded rationality, and (2) opportunistic behavior (Williamson 1986, 20; Galbraith and Kay 1986; Teece 1986; and Masten 1988).

The intermediate case of firm-specific/partially product-specific information provides a strong rationale for multinational enterprise (Teece 1986). Foreign location is necessary to exploit product-specific economies, while the multinational option internalizes and guards the nonproduct-specific informational content of foreign direct investment.

EVIDENCE ON THE TRANSACTION COST HYPOTHESIS

Modern economic theories of vertical integration of firms are all basically transaction cost explanations. As pointed out by Langlois (1989, 86), "If there were no costs but production costs, we would expect the least possible vertical integration; every stage would be its own firm, and each thus could take best advantage of the particular production economies open to it. Production would be fully decentral-

Figure 2.5 : Illustrative Knowhow Transactions

CHARACTERISTICS OF KNOW-HOW

NON PROPRIETARY → PROPRIETARY

FREQUENCY OF CONTEMPLATED TRANSACTIONS	nonspecialized application	specialized application	nonspecialized application	specialized application
occasional	transfer of standard engineering service for particular product or process	transfer of custom engineering service for particular product or process	transfer of "spin off" technology with nonspecialized application	transfer of "spin off" technology with specialized application
recurrent	transfer of know-how for well known process (e.g. thermal cracking of petroleum)	application of well known process (e.g. packaging technology modified for new product)	transfer of process know-how in standard formulation to firms in other markets (e.g. petroleum platforming technology)	transfer of know-how for specialized application in another industry (e.g. aircraft technology applied to aerospace development)

Source: Williamson (1979, page 253), cited according to Teece (1980, page 231)

Figure 2.6:
Some Elements of Organizational Design

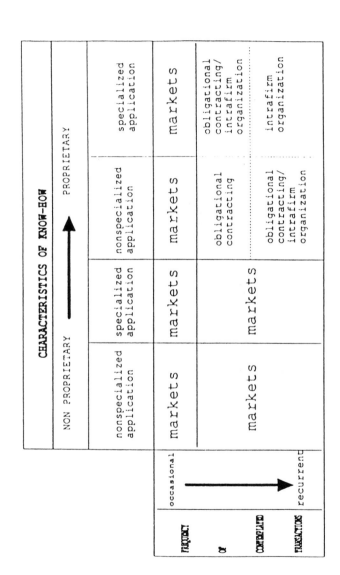

Source: Williamson (1979, page 253), cited
according to Teece (1980, page 231)

ized, and all coordination would be a matter of price-mediated spot transactions."[11]

Without doubt transaction costs play an important role in networking strategies. Just the same, mixed evidence is available as to the awareness of the role that such costs perform. For example, in their survey study of seventy collaborative agreements for the year 1980, Mariti and Smiley (1983) defined transaction costs as all costs of negotiating contracts, including management's time, legal fees, and all other identifiable costs. When interviewed, senior executives in all cases replied that avoiding transaction costs was not an issue in deciding to undertake collaborations. Senior executives perceived that the benefits and costs other than simple transaction costs from cooperative agreements overwhelmed the costs of making the transaction. Mariti and Smiley note, of course, that their definition of transaction costs is very narrow.

Coase's (1937, 390) now famous insight was to recognize that there "is a cost of using the price mechanism." Transaction costs, as well as production costs, determine the extent of the internal organization of enterprises.

The questions arise: But what are these transaction costs? And where do they come from? At a general level, a transaction cost originates from any hindrance to price-mediated spot-market exchange that makes internal organization profitable. Transaction costs are hence the counterpart to the opportunity costs of market exchange.

Transaction costs, being intangibles, are very difficult to measure empirically. Economists have studied details of the costs of market exchange such as asymmetric information (Arrow 1975), technological indivisibilities in team production (Alchian and Demsetz 1972), and differential risk perception (Blair and Kaserman 1978). However, such explanations commonly suffer from a lack of generality (Langlois 1989). A predominant dilemma of all such approaches is the measurement of transaction costs.

Casson (1985), Buckley and Casson (1985), and Teece (1983) have, however, been able to demonstrate that the incidence of transaction costs in vertically integrated process industries, knowledge-intensive industries, quality assurance–dependent products, and communication-intensive industries are especially important.

---

11. See further Jarillo (1988, 33). According to Williamson (1991, 13), economics has been too intent with issues of allocative efficiency, in which marginal analysis was emphasized to the neglect of organizational efficiency.

Borrus, Tyson, and Zysman (1987) offer evidence that the know-how and know-why transactional aspects, with regard to the understanding of how a technology was developed as well as to the potential ways it may be applied, extend beyond the product itself into the network or community of people who initially developed and applied it. Investigating the semiconductor industry, they found that potential users of a new technology often require knowledge of products in order to secure their own effective research and innovative activities. As the chips industry moved through large-scale integration, the nature of the products it produced changed. Increasing complexity of the integrated circuit technology required integration forward into computer systems' production. This was necessary to capture the increased value to offset rapidly rising research and development investment costs associated with placing so much complex circuitry on chips. Also, "captive" production—either through acquisition or in-house start-ups—evolved rapidly as the strategic nature of the integrated circuit for future product development and market growth was recognized.

Along these lines, Polanyi (1967) earlier recognized the importance of "tacit knowledge"—that is, the competence embodied in individuals or groups of individuals to understand and react to situations. The necessary advanced competence required for complex business decisions cannot easily, if at all, be communicated to others (Eliasson 1987, 333). Thus it cannot be traded in bits and pieces in markets. Monteverde and Teece (1982), Masten (1984), and Anderson and Schnittlein (1984) offer similar empirical evidence. Given transaction costs, enterprises will wish to integrate activities that could have been subcontracted. With regard to the relevance of the transaction cost approach to network theory, Jarillo (1988, 33) has noted that "if an entrepreneur is able to lower those transaction costs (relative to its competitors), the resulting firm will be less integrated and more efficient (ceteris paribus): the firm can concentrate exclusively on its comparative advantages. There is, of course, an assumption here, not discussed by Williamson: transaction costs can be affected by the conscious actions of the entrepreneur. We shall see that this is the case, and how this is the foundation for the concept of 'strategic network'."

THE COMPETITIVE ADVANTAGE VIEW

Today national competitiveness has become an outstanding issue in every nation, and most attempts to explain national competitiveness have taken an aggregate perspective. As the world becomes increasingly integrated, competitiveness will become more important. The literature on multinational enterprises has focused mainly on the problem of becoming a multinational rather than on strategies for established multinationals. From the more microeconomic perspective of the firm, Michael Porter among others has done research on the questions: "What does international competition mean for competitive strategy? In particular, what are the distinctive questions for competitive strategy that are raised by international as opposed to domestic competition?" (Porter 1986b, 9).

The goal of competitive strategy is to obtain, utilize, and sustain competitive advantages to the optimal level (Grosse and Kujawa, 1988). For Porter (1990a, 73), "A nation's competitiveness depends on the capacity of its industries to innovate and upgrade. Companies gain advantage against the world's best competitors because of pressure and challenge. They benefit from having strong domestic rivals, aggressive home-based suppliers, and demanding local customers." Table 2.5 lists briefly the competitive advantages of multinational enterprises commonly based upon some proprietary asset as the foundation for their competitive strength. A good discussion of these advantages is found in Grosse and Kujawa, so we will not repeat it here.

Based upon this list of competitive advantages a basic framework of competitive strategy is developed which views enterprises as organizations that carry out a set of economic activities as sketched in Figure 2.7.

Multinational enterprises are value-maximizing organizations that calculate the optimal combinations of inputs at each stage of the production process. In Figure 2.7 the relevant dimensions of the production process are illustrated. Important in seeking competitive advantages is that managers realize that enterprises must evaluate the costs and benefits expected from that advantage in terms not only of the enterprise's own activities but also the strategic behavioral actions of their competitors, both at home and abroad. Since it is basically impossible that an enterprise can excel in all key competitive advantage areas, management should thus evaluate the relative importance of each advantage in the industry (and country) and then implement those offering the largest benefits. Such benefits commonly go hand in hand with activities that establish the greatest barriers to entry and exit from industry (Grosse and Kujawa 1988, 38).

According to Porter (1980, 1985, 1990a), enterprises face five

Table 2.5: Competitive Advantages of Multinational Enterprise

Advantage	Description
General Competitive Advantages	
Proprietary technology	Product process, or management technology held by a firm that others can obtain only through R & D or contracting with the possessor
Goodwill based on brand or trade name	Reputation for quality, service, etc., developed through experience
Scale economies in production	Large-scale production facilities that lower unit costs of production
Scale economies in purchasing	Lower costs of inputs through purchasing large quantities
Scale economies in financing	Access to funds at a lower cost for larger firms
Scale economies in distribution	Shipments of large quantities of products/inputs to necessary locations, lowering unit shipping costs
Scale economies in advertising	Sales in several markets, allowing somewhat standardized advertising across markets
Government protection	Free or preferential access to a market limited by government fiat
Human resource management	Skill at fostering teamwork among employees and optimizing productivity
Multinational Competitive Advantages	
Multinational marketing capability	Knowledge of and access to markets in several countries
Multinational sourcing capability	Reliable access to raw materials, intermediate goods, etc., in several countries that reduces single-source costs
Multinational diversification	Operations in several countries so that country risk and business risk are reduced
Managerial experience in several countries	Skill for managing multicountry operations gained through experiance in different countries (learning curve gains)

Source: Grosse and Kujawa (1988, page 31).

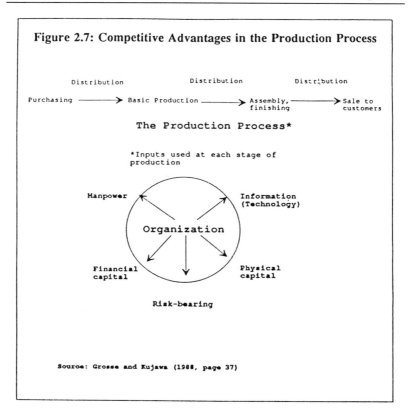

Figure 2.7: Competitive Advantages in the Production Process

Source: Grosse and Kujawa (1988, page 37)

competitive forces that require them to respond strategically to changes in the competitive environment (see Figure 2.8).

For Porter (1980, 34) competitive strategy involves "taking offensive or defensive actions to create a defendable position in an industry, to cope successfully with the five competing forces [i.e., threat of entry, intensity of rivalry among existing firms, pressures from substitute products, bargaining power of buyers, and bargaining power of suppliers] and thereby yield a superior return on investment for the firm." Along these lines an industry will be characterized by high profits whenever enterprises within the industry can deal effectively with potential new entrants and substitutes, neutralize the bargaining power of suppliers and buyers, and establish a moderate to low rivalry among themselves.

Generic Strategies

Porter (1986b, 13) emphasizes that, "It is only at the level of discrete activities, rather than the firm as a whole, that competitive

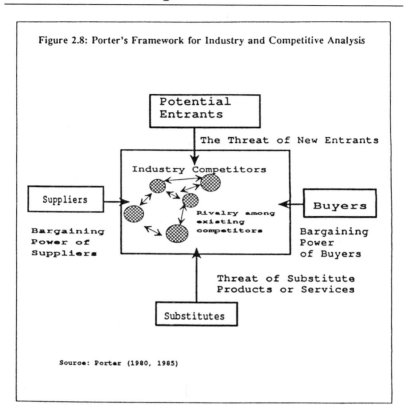

Figure 2.8: Porter's Framework for Industry and Competitive Analysis

Potential Entrants

The Threat of New Entrants

Industry Competitors

Suppliers

Rivalry among existing competitors

Buyers

Bargaining Power of Suppliers

Bargaining Power of Buyers

Threat of Substitute Products or Services

Substitutes

Source: Porter (1980, 1985)

advantage can truly be understood." He suggests three generic strategies for outperforming other enterprises: overall cost leadership, differentiation, and focus. Strategy is aimed at securing long-term sustainable advantage.

Cost Leadership

The competitive cost leadership position of an enterprise may arise from three main sources: economies due to learning effects, economies of scale, and economies of scope. According to Porter (1980, 35), "Cost leadership requires aggressive construction of efficient-scale facilities, vigorous pursuit of cost reduction from experience, tight cost and overhead control, avoidance of marginal customer accounts, and cost minimization in areas like R & D, service, sales force, advertising, and so on."

Learning by doing as a result of repetition suggests that as more is done, less time must be devoted to each individual activity. Learning is in this sense very similar to economies of scale. Shachar and Zuscovitch (1990) in their study on learning patterns within the technological network of the European space program have recently documented such cumulative learning processes.

Economies of scale arise from a number of possibilities as a function of production volume. Commonly mentioned are the economies from massed resources, economies of increased volumes, economies of specialization, and indivisibilities. For example, original costs of research and development may be spread over a larger output at the outset of manufacturing such that costs per unit decrease whenever the output is increased.

Economies of scope affect the strategic position of an enterprise in markets. Scope economies can be obtained by moving into a new market with an existing good or by introducing new products into existing markets. Willig (1979, 346) has pointed out that "economies of scope arise from inputs that are shared or utilized jointly without complete congestion." Baumol (1977, 807) defines economies of scope more technically: "The initial concept is strict subadditivity of the cost function, meaning that the cost of the sum of any output vector is less than the sum of the cost of producing them separately." Galbraith and Kay point out that economies of scope are basically quite similar to Ansoff's (1965) concept of synergy often used in business literature. Both concepts deal with potential links between respective product markets and synergy effects. According to Galbraith and Kay (1986, 5), "There is no effective formal distinction between the earlier concept as employed by Ansoff and economies of scope."

Differentiation

The two polar cases most often discussed as forms of price determination are models of perfect competition and pure monopoly. The perfectly competitive model assumes that there are numerous firms which produce the same homogeneous product. Producers are price takers, having no influence over price. In the pure monopoly model, in the simplest case, assuming that the firm is the seller of a single good, the firm is a price maker. Real world situations are, however, often characterized by market structures that appear to fall in between these two extremes. Although many firms do have some control over price and do not face a perfectly elastic demand curve, they are not really oligopolists or pure monopolists; rather, the market structure is one of monopolistic competition.

Basically, one is interested in analyzing the effects of market structure upon the fundamental principle of exchange underlying economic reasoning: If economic agents possess different goods or services, and the valuations which they place on them differ respectively, then a necessary condition for exchange (transaction) exists. The rate of exchange (or price) corresponding to transactions will be determined by the relative strength of the agents' valuations. Differences in market structures create differences in marginal valuations and thus affect the corresponding transactional outcome, since differences in marginal valuations are a precondition for exchange (trade).

The main feature of the monopolistically competitive market is product differentiation. Products in this market structure, although very similar, are not identical in comparison to those in a perfectly competitive market structure. Many markets exhibit monopolistic competition—cigarettes, toothpaste, cereals, soap, automobiles, and so on. Indeed most markets appear to be characterized by product differentiation. A number of similar but different products are commonly available for each product group (classification).

One may distinguish between product differentiation that is real in an objective physical sense and that which is artificial in a consumer perceived sense. Real product differentiation involves different combinations of physical characteristics, such as actual chemical differences between two brands of paints. Artificial product differentiation depends upon such factors as different packaging materials, brand names, advertising expenditures, the basis of location, and services rendered with the product sold. The main characteristic of the monopolistic market structure is that each individual producer has an absolute monopoly in the production and sale of a differentiated product, even though many close substitutes for that product are available.

Whatever the ultimate source of product differentiation is, the fact remains that consumers believe that a considerable range of differences exist between individual varieties in any product group. Furthermore, consumers are willing to pay higher prices for some products than for others, this willingness to pay being prescribed by the consumers' perceived quality differentials.

Focus

Porter's third strategy is to focus, i.e., to find a market niche. Enterprises may focus on some particular buyer group, segment of a product line, or a geographical market. "Overall size is largely irrelevant to competitive advantage. Diversification to build size for the sake of size is exactly the wrong strategy for most European companies to be following today—the American example is a poor one to follow. Instead, they should be narrowing their range of businesses and investing to build focused international market position in core businesses, in readiness for the competitive challenges ahead" (Porter 1990b, 21).

The Value Chain

The old microeconomic concept of a value chain is reintroduced by Porter in his book *Competitive Advantage* (1985). It is used to describe the various steps a good or service goes through in the transformation process of production from raw materials to consumer end product. The profitability of an enterprise depends upon an enterprise creating value (i.e., the amount consumers are willing to pay for a product or service) such that value exceeds the cost of performing the value activities. "To gain competitive advantage over its rivals, a company must either perform these activities at a lower cost or perform them in a way that leads to differentiation and a premium price (more value)" (Porter and Milar 1985, 150).

The value chain is exhibited in Figure 2.9. Porter classifies value activities in nine generic categories. A value chain perspective of the enterprise studies the primary and support activities of production. Activities of physical production of goods and services, their marketing and delivery to buyers, their support and servicing after sale are regarded as primary activities. Five primary services are identified by Porter. Inbound logistics deal with receiving and handling inputs. Operations deal with converting the inputs to the product or service. Outbound logistics are activities that collect, store, and distribute to the consumer. Marketing and sales provide the means and incentives for buyers to buy the product. Service includes activities to enhance or maintain the value of the product. Support activities such as firm infrastructure, human resource management, technology development, and procurement provide the inputs and infrastructure which permit primary activities to take place.[12]

EVIDENCE ON THE COMPETITIVE ADVANTAGE VIEW

In his most recent book Porter (1991) has documented empirically his research covering ten nations and over one hundred industries. His main findings suggest that (1) there is no such thing as a "competitive nation";[13] (2) nations are only competitive in certain industries and industry segments; (3) competitive industries in a na-

---

12. For a more detailed version of the value chain see Hax and Majluf (1984).
13. See further Porter (1990a, 84–85).

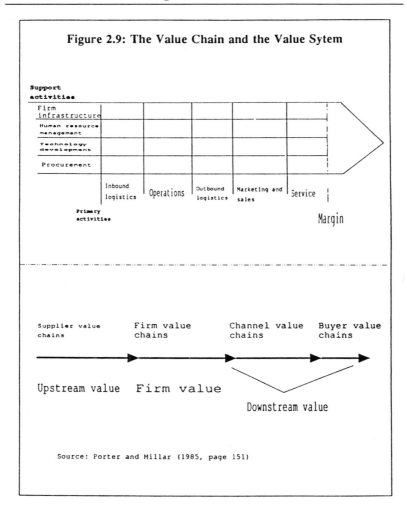

Figure 2.9: The Value Chain and the Value Sytem

Source: Porter and Millar (1985, page 151)

tion are clustered; (4) patterns of international competition are changing.

Despite the appeal of the competitive advantage view, various authors have criticized its conceptualization as being oversimplified.[14] The value-added chain concept has found many admirers in articles

---

14. E.g., Hall (1980), White (1986), Hill (1988), Buckley, Pass, and Prescott (1988), Pruijm (1990).

on business strategy.[15] According to Kogut (1984, 151), for example, the challenge is "to differentiate between the various kinds of economies, to specify the link and which factor captures the firm's advantage, and to determine where the value-added chain would be broken across borders."

THE ECLECTIC APPROACH

The eclectic approach to multinational enterprises arose out of the dissatisfaction with current partial explanations of international production and the lack of a formal model relating it to trade or other modes of resource transfer. The eclectic approach was originally associated with the writings of Dunning (1973, 1977, 1979a, b, 1981a). Early contributions were also made by Hirsch (1976) and Lundgren (1975).[16]

As the name suggests, the eclectic approach draws upon and integrates three strands of economic theory to explain why and under which modus enterprises service foreign markets. According to Dunning (1988a, 1), "The intention was to offer a holistic framework by which it was possible to identify and evaluate the significance of factors influencing both the initial act of foreign production by enterprises and the growth of such production."

No single theory alone can explain all the vital aspects of multinational enterprise. An eclectic approach implies that location theory, industrial organization theory, property rights theory, etc., all have something to add to any explanation of why enterprises transact with other nations. The principal hypothesis of the eclectic approach[17] is that an enterprise will engage in foreign direct investment if three conditions are fulfilled (Dunning 1979a, 275):

(1) Enterprises possess net ownership advantages vis-à-vis firms of other nationalities in servicing particular markets. These ownership advantages commonly take the form of the possession of intangible assets (e.g., "headquarters services") which, at least for a period of time, are exclusive or specific to the enterprise possessing them.

(2) Given that condition (1) is satisfied, it must be more beneficial to the enterprise possessing these advantages to utilize them internally rather than to sell or lease such services to foreign firms.

(3) Assuming that conditions (1) and (2) are satisfied, it must be

---

15. As pointed out by Pruijm (1990, 204–205), Starreveld (1962) and Starreveld et al. (1985) have even developed a value cycle to describe the flow of values within the trading firm. More recently, see Forbis and Mehta (1981), Kogut (1984), Johnston and Lawrence (1988).

16. See Clegg (1988, 22).

17. A full account of the eclectic approach may be found in Dunning, (1988a, b).

profitable for an enterprise to employ these advantages in conjunction with at least some factor inputs (e.g., cheap labor and natural resources) outside its home country.

If the above three conditions are not fulfilled, foreign markets will be served entirely by exports, and domestic markets by domestic production. As was the case with internalization theory, emphasis is placed here upon the cost of transactions in external markets, complemented by an analysis of location costs. The eclectic approach to international production is summarized below in Figure 2.10.

The eclectic approach makes the internalization theory operational by including locational factors, thus permitting an assimilation of the theory of multinational enterprise into international economics (Clegg 1988). The degree to which a nation engages in international production and the industrial composition of that production depends, first, on the structure of its economic activities and, second, on the ability of its firms to generate ownership specific advantages which are best exploited by these same enterprises in a foreign rather than (or in addition to) a domestic location (Dunning 1979a, 277).

Multinational enterprises, according to the eclectic approach, therefore commonly represent an appropriate institutional vehicle for transacting internationally. Foreign direct investment will occur whenever enterprises possess net competitive advantages over enterprises of other nationalities which can best be exploited by foreign rather than domestic production. An internalization strategy is often more profitable than selling or leasing activities to other firms.

The eclectic view stresses, however, that net competitive advantages are not evenly spread over industries, countries, and enterprises. Consequently, any full explanation of the pattern of international production of multinational enterprise must consider the relevant industry and firm-specific characteristics making for ownership, locational, and internalization advantages.

The terminology "competitive advantage" is interpreted in the eclectic paradigm—as compared to its usage as set out by Porter (1985) and Kogut (1985a)—as ownership-specific advantage, while the comparative advantage of countries appears synonymous to location advantage. Dunning (1988a, 27) notes, that "while the business strategy approach gives more emphasis to the positioning of firms in the sectors in which they compete, the eclectic paradigm places more stress on the organizational form of transactional relationships."

EVIDENCE ON THE ECLECTIC APPROACH

A wide variety of empirical evidence exists to support different aspects of the eclectic paradigm. However, Dunning (1988a, 1) ac-

Figure 2.10: The Eclectic Theory of International Production

1. **Ownership Specific Advantages**

(a) **Advantages which need not arise due to multinationality.** Those due
     mainly to size and established position, product or process diversification, ability to take
     advantage of division of labor and specialization; monopoly power, better resource capacity
     and usage. Proprietary technology, trade marks (protected by patent et. al. legislation).
     Production management, organization, marketing systems; research and development
     capacity; "bank" of human capital and experience. Exclusive or favored access to inputs,
     e.g. labor, natural resources, finance, information. Ability to obtain inputs on favoured
     terms (due e.g. to size or monopsonistic influence). Exclusive or favoured access to
     product markets. Government protection (e.g. control on market entry)

(b) **Advantages which those branch plants of established enterprise may
     enjoy over de novo firms.** Access to capacity (administrative, manangerial,
     research and development, marketing, etc.) of parent company at favored prices.
     Economies of joint supply (not only in production, but in purchasing, marketing, finance
     etc. arrangements).

(c) **Advantages which specifically arise because of multinationality.**
     Multinationality enhances above advantages by offering wider opportunities. More favored
     access to and or better knowledge about information, inputs, markets. Ability to take
     advantage of international differences in factor endowments, markets. Ability to diversify
     risks e.g. in different currency areas.

2. **Internalization Incentive Advantages.** (e.g. to protect or exploit
    against market failure). Avoidance of transaction and negotiation costs. To avoid costs of
    enforcing property rights. Buyer uncertainty (about nature and value of inputs (e.g.
    technology) being sold). Where market does not permit price discrimination. Need of seller
    to protect quality of products. To capture economies of interdependent activities (see 1(b)
    above). To compensate for absence of futures markets. To avoid or exploit Government
    intervention (e.g. quotas, tariffs, price controls, tax differences etc.). To control supplies
    and conditions of sale of input (including technology). To control market outlets (including
    those which might be used by competitors). To be able to engage in practices e.g. cross-
    subsidization, predatory pricing etc. as a competitive (or anti-competitive) strategy.

3. **Location Specific Variables** (These may favor home or host countries).
    Spatial distribution of inputs and markets. Input prices, quality and productivity e.g.
    materials, components, semi finished goods. Transport and communication costs. Go-
    vernment intervention. Control on imports (including tariff barriers), tax rates, incentives,
    climate for investment, political stability etc. Infrastructure (commercial, legal, transporta-
    tion). Psychic distance (language, cultural, business, customs etc. differences). Economies
    of research and development production and marketing (e.g. extent to which scale econo-
    mies make for centralization of production).

Source: Dunning (1979a, page 276)

cepts that "because of its generality, the eclectic paradigm has only limited power to explain or predict particular kinds of international production; and even less, the behaviour of individual enterprises. But this deficiency, if it is a deficiency, which some critics have alleged, could no less be directed at attempts to formulate a general but operationally testable paradigm of international trade." Dunning (1988a) reviewed the various criticisms of the eclectic paradigm and found that the theory remains "a robust general framework for explaining and analyzing not only the economic rationale of economic production but many organizational and impact issues in relation to MNE activity as well."

SUMMARY

This chapter has reviewed theories of multinationality. Each of the reviewed paradigms may to some valid extent claim proficiency in explaining aspects of multinational enterprises and their strategies. Standing as they do alone, there still remains much effort needed to establish a general consensus. However, along the long and winding road in the search for a paradigm, progress is being made. For example, an important development has been the incorporation of internalization theory into imperfect competition models of trade (Krugman 1979a, b; Jones and Dei 1983; Helpman 1984; Helpman and Krugman 1985; Markusen 1984; and Ethier 1986). Dynamic environmental changes are necessarily focusing our attention toward studying the creation of global networks.

As Dunning has suggested, the shifting of the balance of advantages of hierarchies and external markets for international transactions, together with the emergence of new contractual arrangements and interlocking networks of cross-border alliances, is a present-day feature that industrial organization economists and strategists are only just beginning to understand. He points out that here too an eclectic approach needs to be developed to obtain a full understanding of common multinationality. Dunning (1988a, 25) anticipates "a gradual interweaving of the approaches of the economist, business analyst and organizational theorist" as theorizing and empirical work on multinational enterprises becomes both more technically sophisticated and more policy oriented.

It is commonly stated that international markets are characterized by tremendous uncertainty. What has often been overlooked in theorizing on multinational enterprises "is that the creation of a global network provides the benefit of profiting from the uncertainty of the world market" (Kogut 1985, 27). In Kogut's (1984, 165) terminology,

"The hallmark feature of the multinational corporation is its evolutionary structure that transforms the variance between different national markets into profit opportunities and bargaining strength. In this perspective, the distribution of rewards and losses between firms may indeed be less affected by marginal shifts in strategies than by differential abilities in managing the environmental variance of world competition."

CHAPTER 3

Economic Rationale of Networks

> The real problem is to integrate choice and structure, not to depreciate or conflate the distinction.
> —Charles Lipson

In the newly evolving context of the partner and rivals model of multinationality based upon emerging global network structures, this chapter provides insights into the economic rationale for international collaborations between multinational enterprises. Transaction cost economics concentrates on the discrete choice in time of an appropriate institutional form of organization. The network approach applied in the following pages goes a step further by emphasizing the continuous time dimension and dynamics of the relational transaction process.

Multinational enterprises are embedded in a complex transactional environment in which firm-specific asset complementarities exist between enterprises. The network approach basically reverses some of the internalization arguments of transaction cost analysis. Along the lines of transaction cost analysis, the accumulation of quasi-rents is explained by internalization strategies. Under the observed new forms of internationalization, the accumulation of quasi-rents is achieved by externalization strategies through global networks of strategic alliances.

If one goes beyond the traditional boundaries of common price theory of the firm where necessary, valuable insights may be obtained, offering a theoretical foundation for the rapidly increasing observations regarding the incidence of multinational networking. The emphasis is placed on networks, because "networks are the original [organizational] form from which all other forms develop" (Ireland 1990, 113).

The complementarities between firm-specific assets create constantly evolving contractual and noncontractual arrangements, i.e. interfaces, among multinational enterprises, as observed in the new forms of internationalization and accumulation of respective quasi-rents. The boundaries of the enterprise depend on its capabilities (Penrose 1959; Langlois 1989).

Richardson's (1972, 833) "rediscovered" observation that industries are characterized by a "dense network of cooperation and affiliation by which firms are interrelated" through subcontracting,

101

supplier relationships in manufacturing and marketing, and the pooling or transfer of technology offers highly relevant examples of coordination across enterprise boundaries. Richardson posed the question, "What kinds of coordination have to be secured through conscious direction within firms and what can be left to the working of the invisible hand?" which appeared to be the key question in the theory of industrial organization. He argued that the habit of working with models which assume a fixed list of goods may have the unfortunate result of causing us to think of coordination merely in terms of the balancing of quantities of inputs and outputs, and thus leave out the need for qualitative coordination.

Richardson's accomplishment was that he recognized the fact that the organization of industry has to adapt itself to the fact that activities may be complementary. As he pointed out, a variety of potential gains may be provided by grouping activities without respect to their character. In so doing, risks can be spread, the general managerial capacity of the enterprise may be kept fully employed, and the allocation of finances can be planned from the center. Such a network strategy does not contradict the principle that it usually will pay for enterprises to expand into activities for which they possess an inherent comparative advantage.

Interdependency exists as a result of the enterprises in these network relationships. Along these lines, in order to diagnose sources of comparative advantage, a disaggregated view of the enterprise is needed focusing on its value chain at the enterprise level and at the environmental network level.

An enterprise competing internationally must decide how to spread the activities in the value chain among countries. Coordination among interdependent enterprises requires the establishment of exchange relationships at an economic cost. A recent important cost reduction tendency can be observed concerning the choice between transactional modes. On the basis of employing networks to get the job done faster, time has become one of the main sources of enterprise comparative advantage (Stalk 1988).

The process of bonding as a result of long-term transactional relationships is also very important to the establishment of network relationships (Johanson and Mattson 1987). Bonds may be of a technical, planning, knowledge, socioeconomical, or legal nature. The manifestation of these bonds occurs through product and process adjustments, logistical coordination, knowledge about the counterpart, personal confidence and liking, special credit agreements, and long-term contracts.

Economists must study a continuum passing from international transactions arranged in commodity markets with minimal cooperation, through intermediate areas characterized by linkages of traditional connection and goodwill, and finally to those complex and interlocking clusters, groups, and alliances which represent cooperation fully and formally developed in a global network.

Strategic elements of various forms of industrial cooperation are becoming increasingly relevant to enterprise decision-making structures on a global basis. The multinational enterprise may be interpreted as a differentiated form of a national corporation that has evolved organizationally in such a manner that it possesses an enhanced flexibility to transfer resources across national borders through a globally maximizing network.[1]

Entering a new foreign market requires that an enterprise establish new relationships. Correspondingly, an enterprise may be dropped from a network if it is displaced by a new entrant with stronger bonds. The network approach of industrial markets implies that an enterprise's activities are constantly being established, maintained, developed, and broken to give short-term satisfaction ensuring long-term enterprise survival. For example, in being part of the network an enterprise has access to external resources controlled by other firms. The position of the enterprise in the network affects resource accessibility. Consequently, an enterprise's short- and long-run success will be network dependent. Thus, the operational aspects of multinationality are stressed. Two key functional elements (Gottinger 1982) underlie the design of any organization: its structure and the set of behavioral rules that make an institution work and perform.

From the perspective of individual enterprises today three main regimes or categories can be observed within which complementary worldwide activities (transactions) are quantitatively and qualitatively coordinated:

(1) trade on international spot markets (external
    transacting),
(2) foreign direct investment (internalizing transactions),
    and
(3) cooperative networks of external collaboration
    (interpenetration of market and hierarchy).

The basic economic logic of these three transactional perspec-

---

1. See Kogut (1983), Johanson and Mattson (1987), DeMeza and Van Der Ploeg (1987), Stalk (1988), Johnston and Lawrence (1988) for this line of thought.

tives allows the tracing of transactional activities of internationally active firms within the range of the traditional trade paradigm to the currently evolving networking paradigm.

Along the lines of Arrow (1969), it may be argued that market exchanges of information are more costly than intra-firm exchanges. However, as Mariti and Smiley (1983, 439) have suggested and as recent developments seem to corroborate, intermediate forms of interfirm agreements may also have certain advantages which permit enterprises to take advantage of economies of scale in one or more of their production processes while remaining separate entities.

The important aspect here is that active cooperation in interenterprise industrial networks must not necessarily diminish the private appropriation of quasi-rents. Rather, it is much more the case that externalizing various transactions internationally through interenterprise collaboration liberates funds for further development activities that are more likely to enhance an enterprise's competitive position (Mytelka 1987). This is largely due to the growing distinction between evolving "base" and "key" technologies.

A base technology ("blueprint technology") is common to all or most industry participants and to most products of a business, whereas the key technologies may be regarded as applications of engineering techniques—that is, process and product differentiation developments which, building upon the base technology of networks, still permit competitive private appropriation of market advantages. As emphasized, however, by Ohmae (1989b, 145), "Nothing stays proprietary for long. . . . The inevitable result is the rapid diffusion of technology."

Arrow (1975) has demonstrated that vertical integration can generate better information, increasing the profit level when input supply uncertainty exists and when an investment type decision is of an ex ante nature. However, he shows further that the upstream industry can appropriate the benefits of better information by giving the information to the downstream industry. Thus, while vertical integration is sufficient, it is not always necessary.

Networks exist because of the need to coordinate closely complementary but dissimilar activities. Since these activities are dissimilar, the coordination cannot be left entirely to the internal control of multinational enterprises. It also cannot be left to spot market transactions because it does not involve balancing the aggregate supply of something with the aggregate demand for it but, instead, matching both quantitatively and qualitatively individual enterprise strategic planning of transacting partners.

A formal theory of multinational networks is still nonexistent.[2] Consequently, the remaining sections of this chapter present fragments of the emerging network theory, and an attempt has been made to keep the mathematics to a minimum emphasizing the analytical insights of networks. After a review of traditional contract curve analysis from microeconomics, four basic network strategies are presented. Applying these four strategies, the economic optimization problem of strategic alliances is briefly presented according to a model developed by Arora and Gambardella (1990). In a somewhat broader context, a partners and rivals model recently suggested by Tucker (1991) is then evaluated. To obtain a more complete understanding of the economic rationale of networks new production concepts and changing industry structures are briefly analyzed. In conclusion, the question is raised "When is a network arrangement efficient?" Borrowing analysis from Jarillo (1988), a simple yet thorough answer is given.

TRADITIONAL MICROECONOMIC ANALYSIS OF NETWORKS

In this section the principle of arbitrage is applied in a simple manner to highlight, along the lines of traditional microeconomic contract curve analysis, the beneficial economic aspects of multinational enterprise network structures. The line of argument presented is borrowed from Malinvaud (1976, 155–57) and Varian (1987a).

The process of institutional differentiation and institutional arbitrage is founded upon the coordinating properties of institutions and their respective relations to the relative availability of resources they possess. In this vein, the recent increased usage of strategic alliances may be viewed as a transformation process of industrial structures by multinational enterprise resulting from institutional arbitrage. Network arbitrage links markets and hierarchies.

The importance of arbitrage conditions has been extensively studied in the field of financial economics (e.g., Varian 1987a). Modigliani and Miller (1958) first demonstrated that if a firm could change its market value by purely financial operations such as adjusting its debt-equity ratio, then individual shareholders and bondholders could engage in analogous portfolio transactions yielding pure arbitrage profits. An efficient market, however, would eliminate arbitrage profits. The Modigliani–Miller theorem thus states that the value of

---

2. As pointed out by Williamson (1991, 13), economists have neglected study of organizational efficiency in part because the mathematics for dealing with "clusters of attributes" is only now beginning to be developed (e.g., Topkis 1978; Milgrom and Roberts 1990).

a firm is independent of its financial structure, due to the absence of arbitrage. The value of the firm should thus depend only upon the sum of the value of its stocks and bonds and not on whether the firm is weighted more heavily to debt or equity.

The Modigliani–Miller theorem is, however, restricted in its practical application, one important restriction being that it applies only to combinations of existing assets. Institutional arbitrage is the operation by which enterprise coalitions move from one allocation state to another that is better for the members of the network. The possibility of asset creation and cumulative learning through networking will economically shift the evolving payoff matrix, creating new production and consumption possibilities across states of nature.

Enterprises $(i = 1,2,...,m)$ are a priori in possession of quantities ω_{ih} of different information (some form of a firm-specific asset, e.g., headquarter services) with $h = 1,2,...,1)$. Given transactional exchanges, they consume quantities x_{ih} such that each vector $\mathbf{x}_i$ belongs to the corresponding set X_i.[3] The vector $\mathbf{x}_i$ is the more advantageous the higher value it gives for the expected profit function $E(\pi(\mathbf{x}_i))$, which is assumed to be continuous.

Allowing for situations characterized by imperfect competition a priori, we now wish to discover which states (networks) are capable of being established.

Let there be two individual enterprises, i and α, who respectively own the quantities x_{ih} and $x_{\alpha h}$ of various knowledge. These are either the quantities ω_{ih} and $\omega_{\alpha h}$ they originally possessed or quantities they have acquired after some exchanges. Now let us assume that both enterprises will benefit from a cooperative transaction between them; let z_h denote the quantity of h that i would give to α in this transaction, or $-z_h$ the quantity of the same knowledge given by α to i. Since the transaction is postulated to be mutually advantageous,

$$E_i (\Pi_i (x_i - z)) > E_i (\Pi_i (x_i))$$

and

$$E_\alpha (\Pi_\alpha (x_\alpha + z)) > E_\alpha (\Pi_\alpha (z_\alpha)).$$

The enterprises i and α may be unaware of this possibility of ex-

---

3. The similarity to standard consumer theory is apparent: the value of a commodity bundle is expressed as the sum of the expenditures on the various goods. The important difference is, however, that the goods (intermediate factor inputs) that are being chosen (firm-specific assets) are not the ultimate end of consumption. They are only the means to an end. See e.g., Varian (1987a, 58).

change. Consequently, any third party that intervenes to enable them to carry out the operation has the possibility of profiting from it.[4] Since Π_i is continuous, there is a nonzero vector $\mathbf{w}$ with no negative component, such that

$$\Pi_i(x_i - z - w) > \Pi_i(x_i).$$

So the enterprises will benefit from a transaction where the quantities of h in their possession vary by $-(z_h + w_h)$ for i, by z_h for α and by w_h for the middleman if a third party (e.g., consultant agency) is involved. Such a transaction is called an arbitrage ("buy cheap and sell dear strategy"). The illustration above dealt solely with arbitrage involving two enterprises; this is bilateral arbitrage. Analogously, a mutual arbitrage regime could be constructed involving several enterprises.

A "stable allocation" will be that network state in which no further arbitrage, bilateral or multilateral, is possible; all transactions are concluded and there is no further incentive for exchange (cooperation). It should be mentioned that there is no reason for such a network state to coincide with a competitive equilibrium.

A stable allocation E^0 as defined here is a distribution optimum. Otherwise there is another feasible network state E^1 preferred by one enterprise and judged at least equally good by all the others. To say that E^1 is feasible is equivalent to saying that passage from E^0 to E^1 constitutes an exchange. The possibility of arbitrage (perhaps even involving all enterprises) therefore exists. This is contrary to the fact that E^0 is a stable allocation.

The notion of arbitrage can be used to describe the rudimentary process of institutional design. In the initial situation the varying quantities ω_{ih} may not be a stable allocation; certain exchanges and arbitrages between enterprises will occur. The quantities owned by various enterprises are therefore changed as often as needed for the realization of a stable allocation. Assuming $E(\Pi_i(x_i))$ is nondecreasing over exchanges (for simplicity) and given that no advantageous possibility remains ignored indefinitely, the process in question is convergent (Hahn and Negishi 1962). There are, however, multiple paths to a stable allocation. This is illustrated in Figure 3.1, examining the

---

4. One is reminded of the rapid expansion of consulting services that often initially bring network partners together. The middleman in the arbitrage is able to profit by it. The following assumes either that he is himself one of the agents or that his deducted proceeds w_h are small enough to be ignored.

case of two types of (enterprise-specific) knowledge and two enterprises within a common Edgeworth box diagram. PR and PS are the "iso-network information curves" passing through the point of complementary knowledge factor endowments P. RS is the traditional contract curve locus of Pareto optimum. A path implying three network exchanges is demonstrated (P to E^1, E^1 to E^2, E^2 to E^0).

Each exchange improves the value-added of the two enterprises. By combining the existing assets into "strategic internationalization" portfolios, enterprises can achieve different patterns of wealth across the states of nature. The potential patterns of wealth that evolve through networks are dependent upon the entire set of available assets. Since proprietary information is known to be characterized by a high level of appropriation risk, diversification also has a natural value in a market with risky assets (Varian 1987a, 57–61). Consequently, the market value of an enterprise will typically depend on other assets that are available to combine with it. But there are many possible network paths, and the final state can be represented by any point on the "network" contract curve RS.

As illustrated by Figure 3.1, "alliance exchanges should be viewed as a process that began with a central or primary transaction that ultimately expanded into a diverse collection of exchange relations and benefits added considerably to the adaptive and innovative capacities for all the firms" (Larson 1991, 183). Through the leveraging of external ties, entrepreneurial performance is enhanced.

Coase (1937) originally treated transactions as the basic unit of exchange and associated costs as the fundamental determinant of organizational form. The important fact is that Coase explains the boundary between firm and market in terms of the relative cost, at the margin, of the kinds of coordination they respectively provide (Richardson 1972, 896). The manner of explanation applied in this book is not inconsistent with Coasian ideas, but it gives content to the notion of this relative cost by specifying network factors such as different modes of cooperation that affect the enterprise boundaries.

From an institutional choice perspective it is important how the particular details of a transaction affect the differential efficiency of alternative organizational forms; that is, when one institutional arrangement can, for economic reasons, be substituted for another.[5] The existence of various contractual arrangements according to the

---

5. See e.g., Cheung (1969), Alchian and Demsetz (1972), Klein, Crawford, and Alchian (1978), Williamson (1979, 1987), Hauser (1981a, b, 1986), Masten (1984), Hart (1987).

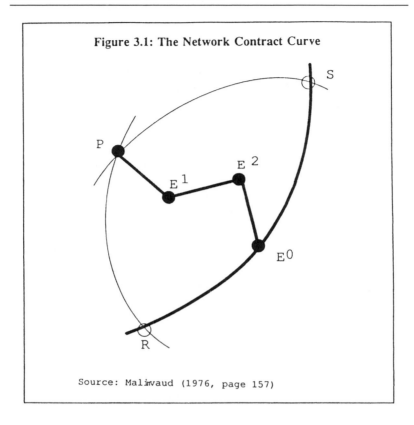

Figure 3.1: The Network Contract Curve

Source: Malinvaud (1976, page 157)

transaction cost model discussed above in chapter 2 is due to natural risk, defined as the contribution by nature or the state of the world to the variance (or standard deviation) of the product value (Hirschleifer 1965; Cheung 1969, 24).

In a world of nonzero variance for the expected outcome of a transaction (the total income for the contracting parties), different contractual arrangements permit different distributions of income variances among the contracting parties. If risk-averse behavior is postulated,[6] contracting parties will wish to avoid risk, if the cost of

6. Although risk aspects are undoubtedly relevant in choosing between alternative institutional forms of mediating transactions, in a wide variety of circumstances relationship-specific investments play a more fundamental role in explaining the existence of long-term contracts. A basic reason for long-term contracts (implicit or explicit) is the existence of investments which are to some extent party-specific; that is, once made, they have a higher value inside the relationship than outside (Masten 1982).

doing so is less than the gain (Caves 1982, 82–83). Risk may be averted either by obtaining more information (which in an international context, due to the higher levels of transactional complexity, may not be attainable even at an infinitely high cost), by selecting investment options that are less risky, or by using contractual arrangements in which risk may be dispersed to various extents among the participants of a network value system. The existence of a continuum of contractual alternatives for transactions is found in the different transaction costs associated with a specific transaction. The choice of contract is made so as to maximize the gain from risk dispersion subject to the constraint of transaction costs (Cheung 1969).

The absolute costs of coordinating transactions are not as important as the comparative costs of alternative modes of exchange (Hauser 1981a, 184). A relevant theory of international business collaborations requires that the boundaries of the enterprise be derived by analyzing the nature of exchange processes at the microeconomic level of the individual transaction (Toyne 1989). Such an analysis assesses, on the one hand, the efficiency properties of internal organization against the efficiency properties of the market and contractual agreements (Teece 1981; Cheung 1969; Hart 1987). On the other hand, "the fact that the process of economic exchange may be relation-driven, not always efficiency-driven, is not ignored" (Toyne 1989, 13).

Kogut (1989b, 151) in examining the life histories of 92 joint ventures also emphasizes the fact that the "transaction itself cannot be a unit of analysis in the absence of a broader understanding of the relationship among the parties. In particular, there is evidence that other horizontal ties, including technology transfer, promote cooperation." Kogut's study suggests that the governance of a transaction must include the wider network of ties among the partners, if not also other affected parties. Going even further, he argues that the economic relationship as opposed to the transaction, is the proper unit of analysis.[7]

A strong argument can be made that all transactions entail some form of a contract. Transactions conducted in the marketplace are simply characterized by outright or partial transfers of property rights among the contracting parties. Any trade—as a quid pro quo—must be mediated by some form of contract, explicit or implicit. Multinational enterprises, however, are characterized not by the dis-

---

7. See further the discussions in Jarillo (1988, 33–34), Ouchi (1980), and Imai and Itami (1984).

crete choice between alternative transactional modes, but rather by the scope or span of mediating international transactions efficiently in order to profit from their actions in a risky global environment.

FOUR BASIC NETWORK STRATEGIES

There has been a fundamental change in thinking about global competition during the past decade. Previous analysis concentrated on the decision to invest overseas. Current analysis is increasingly shifting to questions concerning the strategic value of operating assets in multiple countries. As Kogut (1989a) suggests, an important element in this shift is the distinction between increased economies due to serving a larger market and the acquisition of advantages built upon the multinational network.

Four basic types of external linkages (i.e., strategic alliances) are commonly exploited in networks (Arora and Gambardella 1990):

  (1) research and/or joint development agreements with
       other firms;
  (2) research agreements with universities;
  (3) equity investments in the capital stock of other firms
       (minority participations);
  (4) acquisitions and mergers.

Each such external linkage targets some perceived set of firm-specific assets complementary to the assets of the mother enterprise necessary for new production or marketing developments. In analyzing such network linkages the problems of appropriability of firm-specific assets play a major role in deciding which strategy will be chosen (Masten 1982; Gilroy 1989). However, increasingly one observes that such appropriability problems may not be the whole story. In many industrial sectors multinational enterprises apparently are no longer capable of internalizing all the resources necessary to produce and commercialize new products and technologies. More importantly, the strategic positioning of an enterprise within a global network is vital to long-run survival.

Often the research or joint development agreements with other enterprises are product-specific. Such strategies focus their efforts on the development and commercialization of "downstream" activities of the innovation cycle.

Universities are establishing new research and development alliances and partnerships. Equity arrangements with industry enterprises are emerging to advance development and commercialization of faculty research (Feller 1990). University research teams take on the character of quasi-firms eager and willing to cooperate in research and development programs aimed at commercial application (Etzkowitz 1983; Feller 1990). From the perspective of the enterprise, research agreements with universities aim at more fundamental research objectives. The basic strategy of financing research activities is designed to appropriate basic scientific knowledge in some relevant field. Generally, such research finance agreements contain a first option on the license of any new discovery made by the researchers. Over and above this underlying objective, such agreements often provide a highly efficient means of recruiting qualified researchers or access to such research service potential while leaving the researchers in environments they find most congenial.[8]

Minority equity participation in the capital stock of enterprises provides a means of monitoring the internal research activities of the enterprise. Furthermore, this strategy attempts to establish a "preferential" link with the new equity partner, offering the possibility of preempting rivals in the commercialization of any important discovery made. This strategy also may be helpful in averting problems of moral hazard and serve as tokens of good faith.

Acquisitions and mergers provide large multinational enterprises that have substantial in-house technology with additional core research potential. This strategy is sometimes applied as a way of catching-up if the multinational enterprise is a late entrant in the business, and may be considered the "ultimate intercorporate alliance" within the hierarchy of alliances (see Figure 1.3). The acquisition of the foreign enterprise in large reflects the network-specific position in which the investing enterprise finds itself (Forsgren 1989, 37). Of course simply having financial control over an acquisition does not account for the human resource network aspects regarding worker and management commitment. Neglect of human network relationships at the floor level of the firm often resulted in the highly publicized "buy-'em-and-bust-'em-up" escapades of the 1980s.[9]

THE OPTIMIZATION PROBLEM OF STRATEGIC ALLIANCES

The traditional extensions of the "theory of the firm" to the open economy have largely assumed profit maximization, which is Pareto-optimal under certainty. The neoclassical approach breaks down to

---

8. See further the discussions in Arora and Gambardella (1990), Van Dierdonck, Debackere, and Engelen (1990), and Feller (1990).

9. See, e.g., the discussion in Ohmae (1989b, 153–54). Forsgren (1989) also discusses acquisition as a network stretegy in greater detail as exemplified by Swedish multinational enterprises.

some extent under uncertainty. Profit maximization no longer ranks alternative decisions, profits being now a random variable, not completely controllable. Value maximization is then the next applicable option for decision making.

Taking this into consideration, this section very briefly illustrates the model developed by Arora and Gambardella (1990), which examines the value maximization problem of multinational enterprises taking into consideration the necessity of the four basic forms of strategic alliances discussed above.[10]

Assume that $V(\mathbf{x};\theta)$, the payoff function of the enterprise, is a function of the strategies $\mathbf{x} = [x_1,x_2,x_3,x_4]^T$, and a vector θ of firm characteristics, i.e. $\theta = [\theta_1,\theta_2,....,\theta_m]$.[11] $V(\mathbf{x};\theta)$ is postulated to be concave in $\mathbf{x}$. Two strategies are said to be complementary if an increase in one raises the marginal payoffs of the other. Given $V(\mathbf{x})$, any two strategies x_i, x_j, for $i \neq j$, are complementary if and only if $V_{ij} \geq 0$, where V_{ij} is the second order cross-derivative between x_i and x_j, i.e. $V_{ij} = \partial^2 V/\partial x_i \partial x_j$. For example, an increase in in-house competence from an acquisition raises the marginal value of links with universities (which is the same as saying that they are complements). As such, one would expect to observe that enterprises which make more acquisitions also tend to have a higher number of interactions with universities. Two strategies that are complements should be positively correlated.

Each enterprise must solve the following strategic alliance optimization problem:

$$\underset{\mathbf{x}}{Max}\ V\ (\mathbf{x};\ \theta) - (\mathbf{w} + \epsilon)^T \cdot \mathbf{x}$$

V is a scalar. $\mathbf{w}$ is a vector $[w_1,w_2,w_3,w_4]^T$ of (constant) marginal costs of undertaking each of the strategies in $\mathbf{x}$, *common to all enterprises,* and ϵ is a vector $[\epsilon_1,\epsilon_2,\epsilon_3,\epsilon_4]$ of stochastic perturbations across enterprises of the "true" unit costs of the different linkages. The elements of ϵ are "unobserved" and firm-specific. The "true" unit cost $(\mathbf{w} + \epsilon)$ of pursuing the strategies $\mathbf{x}$ is equal to a common factor $\mathbf{w}$ and a firm-specific element ϵ. Arora and Gambardella (1990) suggest that one

---

10. For a more detailed discussion of the model the interested reader is referred to Arora and Gambardella (1990), who tested the hypothesis for the strategies of the large firms in biotechnology. Their theoretical and empirical results support the argument that the four external network linkages discussed above are complementary with one another in the sense that the covariance between any two strategies, conditional upon a set of firm characteristics, is positive (i.e. value increasing).

11. The superscript T denotes transpose vectors or matrices. Bold lower case or Greek letters represent vectors, and upper case variables are used for matrices.

interprets these "costs" as the direct expenditure incurred and the transaction costs.

The first order conditions of the strategic alliance optimization problem are given as

$$V_x^* = \mathbf{w} + \epsilon$$

where the left-hand side V_x^* is the vector $[V_1, V_2, V_3, V_4]^T$ evaluated at the optimum $(\mathbf{x}^*; \theta)$ and $(\mathbf{w} + \epsilon)$ designates the corresponding costs $(V_i \equiv \partial V/\partial x_i, i = 1,2,3,4)$.

TUCKER'S PARTNERS AND RIVALS MODEL

Often the high costs of research and product development and the rapid pace of product obsolescence have forced enterprises to cooperate in research and development while they still compete in production, marketing, and servicing of their product variants (Gray 1983).

The fierce and rapid expansion of global competition has made two factors vital for enterprise survival: (1) flexible and quick reaction to changing market conditions; (2) positioning of enterprises ("strategic partnering") in such a manner that they themselves compete to influence the functioning of future markets (Michalet et al. 1983; Madeuf and Ominami 1983; Mytelka 1987). This dual concern of multinational enterprise has promoted the rate of technological change, obliging enterprises to engage in new growth and internationalization strategies of strategic alliances that reduce costs and enhance the flexibility of knowledge production.

A rich amount of information concerning the growth of international collaborations and strategic alliances is to be found in a recent article by Jonathan Tucker (1991). In order to answer the question, "What are the factors that influence the ability of enterprises that are current or potential competitors to collaborate and work effectively?" he has developed a comprehensive partners and rivals model. Tucker's view explains the terms, organizational structures, and outcomes of collaborations based upon the relative capabilities of the transacting enterprises. Although Tucker's model was originally conceived to deal with mixed motive situations in world politics, it possesses enough generality to cover interfirm multinational network situations in which the participants follow collective interests at one level and competing interests at another. The model can also be adapted to a two-level partners and rivals paradigm to describe the broader political context of public policy in strategic industries such as defense or aerospace. Networks of interstate government—industry relations and strategic alliances may be examined.

Using concepts from bargaining theory and the theory of clubs[12] a rational actor model may be constructed which views networks of multinational enterprises as "clubs" in which two or more enterprises pool their technical, financial, human, and organizational resources to pursue economic opportunities (such as appropriating proprietary information, profits, and markets) that each enterprise would be incapable of gaining on its own. Tucker's model incorporates the important fact that partnerships, strategic alliances, or collaborations unavoidably necessitate transfers of technology, which simultaneously intensifies the competitive potential of rivals. As Tucker states, "A fundamental characteristic of international collaboration in advanced technology is that players have a mixture of common and conflicting interests: a mutual desire to combine their resources synergistically to increase the size of the 'pie,' yet divergent interests when deciding how the joint benefits from collaboration (such as gains in technological know-how) are divided between them" (Tucker 1991, 86).

Although contemporary strategic alliances frequently generate first-stage benefits for all committed, the multistage network environment may prove to be an economic disaster in the long run if it facilitates one enterprise to secure a greater relative advantage in competence, making it a formidable rival. The important insight of Tucker's model is that each network player is consequently not solely concerned with its expected payoff from cooperation but also with the difference between its remuneration and that of the partner.

The structure of networks imposes constraints on the behavior of network peers, which must conform to the network's prevailing norms or risk losing their network position. Networkers accordingly are inclined to be "defensive positionalists" that endeavor to sustain or improve their relative capabilities vis-à-vis those of potential rivals.

The more each network peer is concerned about protecting its relative position, however, the more difficult it will be to achieve an evolution of mutual cooperative benefits. Given extreme competitiveness, a "game of pure difference" (Taylor 1976) emerges, in which agents maximize the difference between their payoff and that of the partner. Such behavior results in a zero-sum game in which one part-

---

12. Axelrod (1984) and Oye (1986) are the relevant introductions to general cooperation theory. The theory of clubs was discussed originally in Buchanan (1965), more recently in Hartley (1983). For a somewhat different approach to rivalry see Brenner (1990).

ner benefits from another's losses. Due to the incentive structure, cooperation does not evolve.

Collaboration and Payoffs

In the partners and rivals model, each network peer pursues two types of payoff from collaboration: a short-term welfare payoff and a longer-term positional payoff.[13] Three aggregate enterprise capabilities are postulated: financial capital, technological know-how, and market share. Tucker's model assumes realistically that one network peer is stronger than the other in aggregate capabilities.

Welfare Payoffs

Welfare payoffs represent short-term benefits to network participants based upon profits and licensing fees, cost and risksharing, economies of scale and scope, and larger markets for the product in question. Given large disparities in capabilities between enterprises, the stronger enterprise's potential welfare benefits from collaboration are low since the weaker partner possesses fewer complementary financial, technological, or market assets.

Collaboration on a coequal basis would compel the stronger player to transfer technology to the weaker partner without receiving much in return, the outcome being that the stronger enterprise will only collaborate with a much weaker partner through subcontracting agreements, which involve limited transfers of technology (see Figure 1.3) in the hierarchy of alliances. The stronger enterprise's expected welfare payoff from collaboration tends to increase in direct proportion to the relative capabilities of the weaker enterprise.

Positional Payoffs

The positional payoff from collaboration for the stronger partner consists of a net gain or loss in its relative capabilities and hence in its network position. Given that partners improve their technological capabilities but their relative positions stay the same, the positional payoff for both is zero. If, however, one partner secures a larger net benefit from the collaboration than the other, it collects a positive positional payoff whereas its partner acquires a negative positional payoff.

There exists a natural tendency for technological know-how to flow from the stronger to the weaker partner, thus the weaker partner can commonly expect a larger positional payoff from collaboration. International collaboration generates increasing returns to scale for

---

13. Along similar lines Krugman (1988) has developed an applicable model of international multistage competition.

partners with low levels of resources yet renders decreasing returns to scale for partners with high levels of resources (Ruggie 1972). This to a large extent may explain the observed differences in the literature with regard to the propensities to network among nations (e.g., Contractor and Lorange 1988a; Harrigan and Newman 1990).

Jarillo (1988) has also argued along similar lines that networks are an organization mode that can be implemented by managers or entrepreneurs to position their enterprises in a stronger competitive stance. The network approach as developed by Swedish researchers (Johanson and Mattson 1987, 36) also stresses the cumulative nature of network relationships "in the sense that relationships are constantly being established, sustained, developed, and broken in order to give satisfactory, short-term economic returns and to create positions in the network that will assure the long-term survival and development of the firm." They have correctly argued that individual enterprises in the network model are dependent on resources controlled by other enterprises. The enterprise obtains access to these external resources through its network position. In this view, an enterprise's position in the network takes time and effort to develop; as such, it is basically a partially controlled, intangible, market asset that generates revenue.

Smaller enterprises also benefit positionally through cooperative alliances with a more prestigious enterprise due to reputation effects. Such benefits are not to be underestimated. The smaller enterprise gains in "legitimacy," since in the business world view the stronger partner will usually only collaborate with reputable enterprises who possess enough potential capacity. A "market alliance signal" is advertised to future potential partners which increases future business prospects for the smaller partner (Larson 1991). Reputation capital (enterprise goodwill) is created which enhances the competitive position of the smaller partner. The possibility that a smaller enterprise will deviate from the original interest of an alliance with a larger, well-known partner also is limited due to the negative reputational consequences that emerge affecting the smaller enterprise's stream of future profits if its performance is poor.

The Disparity Principle

As mentioned above, collaboration enables the weaker partner to enhance its relative position at the stronger partner's expense.[14] The weaker partner is hence motivated to collaborate by the sum of

---

14. See, e.g., the discussions in Abegglen (1982), Reich and Mankin (1986), and Omestad (1989) regarding the U.S.–Japanese relationship. See Ishihara (1991) for the Japanese perspective.

its (positive) welfare payoff and (positive) positional payoff, while the stronger partner is motivated to collaborate by the sum of its (positive) welfare payoff and (negative) positional payoff. Under these circumstances, the limiting factor is the stronger partner, who readily collaborates only when its expected welfare benefits exceed its positional costs.

The Welfare Payoff Curve

Tucker then studies the situation in which the stronger partner's capability is constant and the weaker partner's is variable. For simplicity, it is assumed that the stronger partner's welfare payoff from collaboration increases linearly with the increasing capability of the weaker partner. The payoff scale is indeterminate to a constant, thus the welfare payoff is kx, where k is a constant and x is the ratio of the weaker partner's capability to that of the stronger player. x may vary between 0 and 1.

The Positional Payoff Curve

The positional cost of collaboration starts out very low when the disparity in partner capabilities is large, but increases quickly as the gap diminishes. The marginal value of each positional payoff from collaboration for the strong partner is negative and varies as a function of the gap in capabilities between the two partners. As long as the disparity gap is large, the stronger partner views increments of loss in its relative position as a drop in the bucket compared with the total disparity in capabilities. The stronger partner is willing to collaborate under these circumstances since the short-term welfare benefits from a strategic alliance such as a joint venture (e.g., access to new markets, cost savings, and economies of scale) exceed the risks of transfers of technology to the weaker partner. The disparity in capabilities stays within a "security zone" in which the position of the stronger partner is not challenged.

Due to the increasing rate of change in the value of positional losses, the stronger partner's positional payoff curve declines exponentially as a function of the shrinking disparity in capabilities. Though the specific form of the positional payoff curve will vary from partner to partner, it may be illustratively regarded by the exponential function $-\alpha e^x$, where x is the ratio of player capabilities and α is a "sensitivity coefficient" that affects the slope of the curve by reflecting the relative importance that the stronger partner assigns to positional costs over welfare benefits. According to Tucker, six "contextual parameters" influence the stronger partner's choice of collaborative strategy, since the sensitivity coefficient decreases or increases based upon salience, complementarity, appropriability, concentration, vulnerability, and the discount rate.

The exponential form of the positional payoff curve suggests that the stronger partner only becomes conscious of the positional costs of collaboration as the curve begins to fall off rapidly. After it reaches a certain threshold, the weaker partner may be perceived as a potential competitor. The stronger partner will begin to defend its position against further decay. Incentives to cooperate will be reduced greatly.

The Net Payoff Curve

Over time the weaker partner of a strategic alliance will shift its position. As it becomes stronger, the weaker partner now has more to offer in terms of financial assets, technological know-how, and market access; the result corresponds to the formula kx that the stronger partner's payoff from collaboration increases linearly. Simultaneously, the weaker partner threatens the stronger partner's positional payoff from collaboration, reducing it exponentially according to the formula $-\alpha e^x$.

Combining the welfare and positional payoff curves, Tucker has derived the following counterintuitive result: Equals do not make the best partners. According to the disparity principle, optimal conditions for collaboration arise when the capabilities differential is marginal enough that the weaker partner has suitable assets to engage in mutually beneficial exchanges yet at the same time large enough that the stronger player feels safe in its superior position and therefore will be willing to transfer technology since the positional costs of collaboration are low and outweighed by the welfare benefits.

This may be illustrated by Figure 3.2. As Tucker (1991, 91) demonstrates,

> The stronger player's net payoff from collaboration is the sum of its (positive) payoff and its (negative) positional payoff, or $y = kx - \alpha e^x$. This function has a single peak: it is low when the disparity in player capabilities is large (i.e., when the ratio of the aggregate of the weak player to that of the stronger player is between 0 and 0.3), rises to a maximum when the disparity in capabilities is moderate (a ratio of 0.3 to 0.6), starts to decline when the disparity is small (a ratio of 0.6 to 0.9), and drops off steeply as the capabilities of the two players approach parity (a ratio of 0.9 to 1.0).

The single peak of the net payoff curve suggests that the incentives for collaboration among partners are greatest when the ratio of

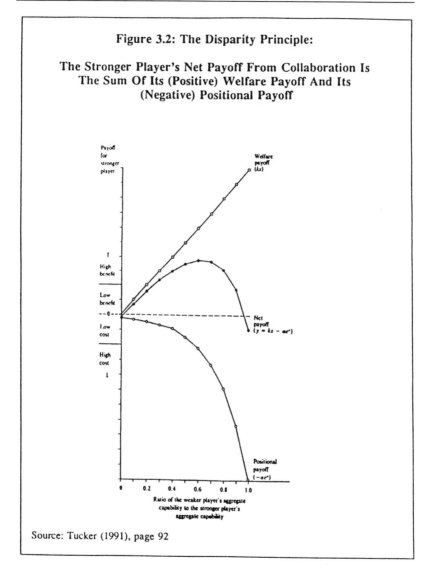

Figure 3.2: The Disparity Principle:

The Stronger Player's Net Payoff From Collaboration Is
The Sum Of Its (Positive) Welfare Payoff And Its
(Negative) Positional Payoff

Source: Tucker (1991), page 92

the players' capabilities is intermediate and are lowest when the ratio
is close to 0 or 1.0. Given a large disparity between partners, there
is no basis for the mutually beneficial exchange of assets.

The Compensation Principle

In situations in which the stronger partner's expected positional
costs from collaboration surpass its expected welfare benefits, it will

agree to some form of partnership with the weaker partner only on the proviso that the arrangement accommodate the stronger partner with a larger share of the joint welfare benefits. The readjustment is essentially a compensatory "side-payment" as applied in game theory (Luce and Raiffa 1957, 168–69).

Side-payments commonly consist of the following: project leadership; a disproportionate share of the contract either in terms of development and production operations or in terms of work on the high value-added components; a disproportionate division of the financial and technological benefits; or a mixture of these. As noted by Tucker (1991, 100), "Although the stronger player may appear to be exploiting the weaker one by demanding a disproportionate share of the benefits from collaboration, its demand for a side-payment can be considered a just compensation for its expected positional losses."

Tucker's Four Modes of Collaboration

Tucker's model distinguishes between four modes of collaboration that can be associated with the amount of disparity in technological capabilities between partners of strategic alliances (see Table 3.1). Each of these four modes—leadership, symbiosis, transition, and parity—is related to a preferred organizational structure and to a particular strategy followed by the stronger partner with regard to the size and type of side-payment it entails.

Given large capability disparities, the leadership mode implies that licensing or subcontracting serve as the preferred organizational alliance form. The weaker partner collaborates on a voluntary basis as the licensee or subcontractor, paying a small side-payment in recognition of the stronger partner's superior technological capabilities and the potential of appropriating new knowledge.

In the symbiosis mode of collaboration optimal conditions for mutual benefit from strategic alliances emerge. The weaker partner is in a position to exchange assets, yet the stronger partner perceives no positional threat. Therefore, side-payments are not required as compensation to net welfare positional loss. Customarily, a "pilot" scheme will be initiated in which the stronger partner will be the prime contractor and the weaker partner is a junior partner.

Under the transition mode the weaker partner is increasingly in the position of challenging the leadership position of the stronger partner. The stronger partner's positional payoff curve begins to drop exponentially and demands for a large side-payment emerge. The organizational structure of strategic alliances is a "hybrid" between the pilot and integration schemes.

Finally, in the parity mode of collaboration partners possess simi-

Table 3.1: Tucker's Four Modes of Collaboration

Disparity capabilities	Mode of collaboration	Strategy of stronger player	Preferred organizational structure
Large	Leadership	Demands project leadership and a small side-payment (such as a licensing fee)	Licensing or subcontracting agreement
Moderate	Symbiosis	Demands project leadership but no other side-payments	"Pilot" structure, with stronger player as prime contractor and weaker player as junior partner
Small	Transition	Demands a large side-payment (such as project leadership and a work share greater than that specified by juste retour)	"Hybrid" structure combining elements and of "pilot" and "integration" structures
Negligible	Parity	Insists on strict reciprocity in technology transfer to prevent partner from gaining a net positional advantage	"Integration" structure, with joint-venture management company established and run by both players

Source: Tucker (1991), page 101.

lar capabilities and are rivals for the same markets. Collaboration commonly degenerates into a zero-sum game in which any gain for one partner is perceived as a loss for the other.

The Principle of Strict Reciprocity

The principle of strict reciprocity alleviates the problem that collaboration can commonly degenerate into a zero-sum game. The principle of strict reciprocity requires that all of the technologically valuable work be divided on an equal basis. Under circumstances of parity the strict reciprocity principle permits both enterprises to profit from a net gain in welfare benefits from collaboration (including absolute gains in technological know-how), whereas their relative positions remain unchanged. In the parity mode of collaboration partners usually institutionalize a joint management unit in which responsibility and control are allocated equally along the lines of Figure 1.4.

According to Powell (1987, 81), observed collaborations among enterprises simply represent modern-day version of a centuries-old means of allocating goods and services, a method Polanyi (1967) termed "generalized reciprocity." In the reciprocity model of resource allocation, transactions occur neither through discrete exchanges nor by administrative fiat, but through networks of individuals engaged in reciprocal, preferential, mutually supportive actions. Reputation, trust, tacit collusion, and a relative absence of calculative quid pro quo behavior guide this system of exchange. Buckley and Casson (1988) and Casson (1990b) have also developed a theory of cooperation much along these lines. They view cooperation as an output. Partnerships, collaborations, and strategic alliances that enhance mutual trust between the parties reduce the transaction costs of subsequent undertakings in which they are involved.

Throughout the literature on cooperative agreements other scholars have also noted that the principle of reciprocity reinforces the stability of collaborations. Schelling (1960), Telser (1980), Williamson (1983), Axelrod (1984), Buckley and Casson (1988), and Kogut (1989b) have all advanced the insight that cooperation is often founded upon the ability of partners to reciprocate penalties and reward altruistic behavior.

Telser (1980), for example, has suggested that the probability of cooperative behavior can be increased through bundling one agreement with other contractual relationships of value to the transacting parties. Noncooperative behavior of network peers is punishable by reciprocating in the context of other agreements. Thus, collaborations are more likely to survive and be stable if they are part of a larger network of agreements among the participating parties. Preliminary supporting evidence of this sort of enterprise behavior is to be found in Hagedoorn and Schakenraad (1990) and Kogut (1989b).

Framing the phenomenon of know-how trading among rivals within the context of a prisoner's dilemma, Von Hippel (1989) has also studied what he terms "collective invention" and reciprocity. His data appear to show that individuals and enterprises commonly revealed information of apparent competitive value to both existent and potential rivals based upon reciprocity. Informal know-how trading possesses a lower transaction cost than more formal agreements to license or sell information.

NEW PRODUCTION CONCEPTS AND CHANGING INDUSTRY STRUCTURE

Tucker's model is capable of explaining many of the dynamic economic behavioral aspects of networking; however, it does not explain the entire basis of recent competitive success of enterprises practicing extensive networking.

According to Ohmae (1989b, 146):

> In the past, for example, you tried to build sustainable competitive advantage by establishing dominance in all of your business systems's critical areas. You created barriers to entry where you could, locked away market shares wherever possible, and used every bit of proprietary expertise, every collection of nonreplicable assets to shore up the wall separating you from competitors. The name of the game in most industries was simply beating the competition. If you discovered an ounce of advantage, you strengthened it with a pound of proprietary skill or knowledge. Then you used it to support the defensive wall you were building against competitors.

Powell (1987, 79) has observed that "among the principal disadvantages of large-scale organization are a bias toward internal procurement and expansion, problems of structural inertia, risk aversion, and decreased employee satisfaction and commitment."

Forces of globalization are chipping away the foundations of the above logic (Ohmae 1989b). Especially, information technology is transforming the economic relationships among scale, automation, and flexibility. Due to the declining costs of information technology, large-scale manufacturing is no longer essential to achieve automation. Hence, entry barriers in various industrial segments are falling (Pruijm 1990, 209). In the past, large vertically integrated multinational enterprises, such as General Motors, were well suited to apply strict and well-stipulated mass production operational methods to deal with a relatively stable international environment. Nowadays multinational enterprises face rapid fluctuations in demand and unanticipated changes, subjecting enterprises to the liabilities of large scale. Enterprises such as, for example, IBM could not have marketed their products with such success in the short time they did if they attempted to keep their product development 100 percent proprietary. Lotus Development Corporation provided the applications software, and Microsoft wrote the operating system on an Intel microprocessor. According to Ohmae (1989b, 145), "The heart of IBM's accomplishment with the PC lay precisely in its decision—and its ability—to approach the development effort as a *process of managing multiple external vendors*" (emphasis added).

Automation no longer necessarily leads to inflexibility. The simultaneous matching of automation and flexibility is altering the pattern of rivalry among global competitors. Possession of a superior technology is still an integral part of any economic strategy of multinational enterprise, but it is no longer sufficient to guarantee success. "Meeting customer needs is the key—no matter what the source of the technology" (Ohmae 1989b, 146).

To obtain a more comprehensive understanding of evolving global markets it is necessary to briefly survey a series of new production concepts: process over operation efficiency, just-in-time for material resource planning, single-minute exchange of dies for economic order quantities, automation for automotion, and technology and organizational learning (Best 1990).

Process over Operation Efficiency

Traditional methods of mass production emphasize operations engineering—the reduction of time required per machine or labor hour. In the past, the development of low cost, centralized power, and efficient but costly production machinery tipped the competitive advantage toward large enterprises that could achieve economies of scale (Johnston and Lawrence 1988).

Operational efficiency focuses upon the amount of time needed for the transformation process of factor inputs, machine operations, and final commodity output. Process efficiency encompasses both productive and unproductive time. Unproductive time includes the time which materials spend in inventory or other nonoperational activities such as handling, moving, inspecting, reworking, recording, batching, chasing, counting, and repacking. More recently, operational throughput efficiency is the indicator of success for mass producers, evaluated in terms of productivity per labor or machine input per hour. Process throughput efficiency is the ratio of the time a commodity is being transformed to the time it is in the production system (Best 1990).

The success of an enterprise's process efficiency may be measured by the work-in-process (WIP) ratio: the ratio of work in progress to annual sales.[15] Abegglen and Stalk (1985, 113–14) estimate that every doubling of the WIP turn improves labor productivity by 38 percent. They found that during the late 1970s Western automobile manufacturers had WIP turns at most of around 10 to 25. Toyota's WIP turn was larger than 300 per year.

At the center of traditional operational efficiency analysis management was mainly concerned with methods of increasing worker and machine productivity. The amount of time, however, that labor actually transforms material is a small percentage of the total production time. In comparison, process efficiency requires that management be consciously aware of activity sequences which involve a comparatively greater time allotment (covering the entire time flow of manufactured goods and services from the entry to the exit point of the plant).

Much of the success of Japanese manufacturers is to some extent due to the fact that they effectively turned their strategic behavior into one of time-based strategies. That is to say, they broke down the traditional planning loop of manufacturing mainly based upon operation efficiency and emphasized process efficiency. In addition, they implemented faster new product introductions, and improved their operation efficiency, utilizing swift sales and distribution networks (Stalk 1988). Economies of time are a vital strategic component of global markets and a source of competitive advantage.

Success in international markets where rapid delivery plays a significant competitive role requires that multinational enterprises abolish nonoperational cost- and time-adding activities that inhibit process throughput efficiency. Increasingly, competitive success depends upon optimizing economies of time on a global basis. Current advances in operational process engineering are overcoming the traditional cost versus scale tradeoff.

Just-in-Time for Material Resource Planning

Just-in-time manufacturing is founded upon the idea that inventories can be virtually eliminated in the production process. Ac-

15. The WIP turn is comparable to the stock turn ratio applied as a success indicator by the first mass retailers (Chandler 1977, 223; Best 1990, 148).

cording to Nayak and Ketteringham (1986, 212), the concept was originally created by Kiichiro Toyoda, the founder of Toyota Motor Works. His idea was, paradoxically perhaps, that the assembly line should be designed after the American supermarket. The economic advantage of a supermarket is that the production orders for replacement supplies are managed by purchases off the shelf, the last stage of the production system. "Thus instead of the planned coordination by a material resource planning staff to assure that each stage in the production process was supplied with the requisite materials at the right time, coordination could be spontaneous" (Best 1990, 149).

Time-based manufacturing strategies differ from those of conventional manufacturing along three key dimensions: (1) length of production runs, (2) organization of process components, and (3) complexity of scheduling procedures.

In the past, multinational enterprises have followed a strategy of maximizing production runs. The more recent enterprise strategy of time-based manufacturing, on the contrary, is to minimize (shorten) production runs as much as possible through strategic alliances. The economic logic of such a reverse strategy is founded in the dynamics of an enterprise's search for competitive success. By reducing the length of production run time, the complete range of enterprise product variety is more frequently produced with a faster response to customers' demand. This effect evolves out of the manner in which information is processed throughout the value chain.

The notion of economies of time goes back to Adam Smith. One of the three sources of productivity gain he analyzed in describing the division of labor was "the saving of time which is commonly lost in passing from one species of work to another" (Smith 1970, 112). Unfortunately, Smith's economies of time became defined in economics in terms of specialization and not throughput. The timeless dimension of optimal allocation theory "makes it blind" to the fact that the criterion of competitive success is contingent not only upon allocative efficiency but increasingly upon throughput (process) efficiency (Best 1990, 73).

Time flows affect information processing and communication linkages within enterprises. Information is distortedly passed on within the system, further distorting enterprise market perceptions. The result is inefficiencies and bad planning, which are potentially devastating for competition in international markets. Secondly, time-based manufacturing is organized by product. Recently multinational enterprises have often granted world product mandates to selected affiliates abroad. Ideally, under the terms of a world product mandate, the local subsidiary is responsible for all aspects of product research and development, including design and conceptualization and international marketing (Pearce 1988; Mytelka 1987; Rutenberg 1982; Poynter and Rugman 1982). This allows a minimal requirement for the handling and movement of parts. Consequently, the manufacturing functions for a component or a product are as close together as possible. The successive flow of parts in the production run proceeds quickly and efficiently thus eliminating costly inventory investments.

Earlier multinational enterprise manufacturing was characterized by complex scheduling procedures. Central scheduling of material resource planning on an international basis is difficult, requiring enormous amounts of information flows which also need to be effectively processed. Time-based scheduling, however, is of a local nature. Production control decisions are made at the factory floor level, eliminating the time-consuming loop back to some central management. The product-oriented layout of the entire enterprise network together with local input scheduling policies (inter- and intrafirm cooperation at local levels) make the total production run more smoothly. These differences between conventional and time-based manufacturing enterprises embedded in international or regional networks add up.[16] Enterprise capacity increases to produce a range of products economically with short changeover times (Best 1990, 150).

Single-Minute Exchange of Dies for Economic Order Quantities

The traditionally long production runs implemented by multinational enterprises tend to be operationally efficient but process inefficient. This is due to the common observation that while any product is being assembled, the materials for all of the other products are being manufactured for inventory. As mentioned above, process efficiency implies short runs which reduce the inventory duration period of materials (Best 1990). Network supplier enterprises characterized by process efficiency level out production runs.

Short-run production changes from product to product in manufacturing are often inhibited by the time necessary to modify the configuration and settings of machinery. Machine changeovers could be efficiently minimized by long production runs; however, the trade-off requires the generation of increasing nonproduction costs. Figure 3.3 illustrates the economics of mass production from the cost viewpoint. Changeover times have been traditionally regarded as exogeneous constraints with batch sizes being dictated by economic order

---

16. For an illustrative discussion of Toyota see Stalk 1988, 48.

quantities, that is, that output quantity which equated the rising cost of inventories with the unit decreasing changeover costs.[17]

In a network system changeover times are not fixed. Given mutually beneficial alliances, changeover times may correspond to small batches that may be run with minimal interference with the principle of flow in which production is organized to exploit economies of time optimizing the speed and volume of throughput.[18] As Best (1990) formulates it, "What had been an invariable constraint to the mass producers became a challenge to the entrepreneurial firm."

The General Motors–Toyota joint venture in Fremont, California, is a recent illustration of how by applying the concept of single-minute exchange of dies a reduction of changeover times was obtained.[19] A typical die change was reduced from 12 hours to 15 minutes, enabling an assembly line operator to switch from four- to six-cylinder engines in minutes.

The single-minute exchange of dies principle reflects the logic of networking in its most absolute form. After distinguishing between internal and external setup activities, the fundamental goal is to convert what had been internal to external activities in order to obtain changeover time reductions. Applying the principle permits usage of more general machines capable of producing a greater variety of products in less time, inventory reductions, space saving, higher capital turnover rates, and "level scheduling" with suppliers (Best 1990).

It is not simply a matter of pushing inventories upstream to suppliers. The main point in just-in-time and single-minute exchange of dies methods is that the division of labor in a network permits transactors to optimize dynamically on short runs and changeover times. The consequence is that enterprises can even out production over time, raise their span of product variety, and reduce costs of inventory.

Automation for Automotion

Ohno (1984, 90) distinguishes automation from automotion. For example, he argues that whereas the Ford assembly line was "self-moving," the Toyota line is "self-working." Toyota employs machines which were designed to detect production part deviations and auto-

---

17. As Best (1990, 151) notes, "A tension exists in every multiple product firm between optimal production runs and consumer orders. Put differently, consumer purchases do not come in batches that match optimal production runs. Instead, consumers, as a group, are simultaneously purchasing the whole range of a company's products. This is the problem that just-in-time addresses."

18. See further the discussion in Best 1990, 51–52.

19. *Business Week* Nov. 4, 1985: 43; Abegglen and Stalk (1985).

Figure 3.3: Setup Times and Economic Order Quantity

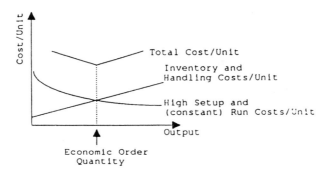

Case I: High Setup and Constant
Non-Setup Costs

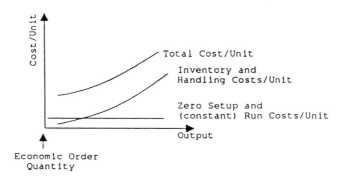

Case 2: Zero Setup and Constant
Non-Setup Costs

Source:Best(1990),page 151.

matically stop. Automatic machinery with the built-in capacity to stop revolutionized the organization of production (Best 1990, 153–56). Machine operators could now be employed using the concept of multimachining. Toyota set up machines in U shapes in their factories so that a single worker could supervise a group of machines simultaneously. Through multimachining a distinct increase in labor productivity was obtained based upon organizational innovation.

This simple organizational innovation had an important additional positive effect. It made conscious problem solvers out of workers. "The worker, instead of being perceived as merely a factor of production, became an active force in the continuous upgrading of the production system" (Best 1990, 154).

Ohno (1984, 93), using a baseball analogy, has described the just-in-time production system and automation link:

> How can I best express the connection between the two pillars of the Toyota production system, "right on time" and "automation"? Using metaphors from baseball, I would say that "right on time" represents teamwork; it displays the essence of cooperation. "Automation" enhances each player's skills. When "right on time" has been implemented, every player in the field will show good timing in catching balls, and base runners will be put out through cooperative teamwork. Each section can systematically develop good team play. Again to use baseball terms, supervisors and directors are like hitting, fielding, and running coaches. A good baseball team uses system plays, perfecting their teamwork so they can respond to any situation. A plant where "right on time" has been thoroughly understood is like a baseball team with good teamwork.

Technology and Organizational Learning

A flexible manufacturing system alters the mode of effective competition. It is no longer simply a question of achieving large scale economies in operating a factory. The competitive edge must nowadays be established at the earlier stage in which the layout of the production facilities and human resources themselves are planned. It is important to recognize that only people who are also involved in daily operations can accumulate the experiential knowledge necessary to make a new technology perform to its full potential.

New production concepts are redefining the tasks of management. In the words of Jaikumar (1986, 76): "The new role of management in manufacturing is to create and nurture the project teams whose intellectual capabilities produce competitive advantage. What gets managed is intellectual capital, not equipment."

WHEN IS NETWORK ARRANGEMENT ECONOMICALLY EFFICIENT?

Jarillo (1988) has recently posed the above question and offered a simple but very effective answer.[20] From the economical perspective, final total costs for a given activity decide whether or not the activity will be performed internally or subcontracted. Total costs of external transactions *(EC)* consists of the price charged by the supplier in the case of subcontracting *(EP)* and the transaction cost *(TC)* that arises. Thus, $EC = EP + TC$.

Integration of an activity occurs when $EP + TC > IC$, where *IC* designates the internal cost of the activity.

The important insight of Jarillo's model is that the entrepreneur can in fact lower *TC* for activities supplied to (or by) his or her enterprise. If *TC* can be lowered up to a point where $EP + TC < IC$, enterprises will prefer not to integrate the activity and, precisely by doing so, will be more efficient than their competitors. "This is the essence of the effectiveness of the network arrangement" (Jarillo 1988, 35).

Enterprises organized within efficient networks therefore enjoy lower costs and increased economies of scale, scope, and time as compared to their rivals who due to their transaction cost environment are forced to integrate. As pointed out by Jarillo (1988, 35), "This will be the case if and only if $EP < IC$ (a technological consideration) and *TC* can in fact be lowered enough so that [part of] the savings can be realized by subcontracting."

Economic efficiency of a network requires that *EP* be lower than *IC* for some activities necessary for the production of the good delivered by the network. Networks of strategic alliances permit enterprises to specialize in Porter's core activities of the value chain reaping the benefits of specialization, focus, and size. Economies of scale emerge from organizational change, not from technology (Leijonhufvud 1986; Langlois 1989). Complementary to this, the enterprises that perform the externalized activities gain, based upon the same logic.

As MacMillan and Farmer (1976, 283) pointed out earlier, "The market test is still applicable." Networking introduces a cost discipline that may be absent in an integrated enterprise, with its captive internal markets (Jarillo 1988, 35). Furthermore, enterprises de-

---

20. Williamson (1991) has also recently discussed efficiency aspects of "hybrid" transactional arrangements.

crease costs for those activities it internalizes through economies of scale and specialization.

Williamson (1991) also notes that a network may be interpreted as a nonhierarchical contracting relation in which reputation effects are quickly and correctly communicated. Network collaboration, or in Williamson's terminology "hybrid contracting," increases in relation to hierarchy and markets in regimes where interfirm reputation effects are more highly perfected. Further, given greater levels of uncertainty, Williamson (1991, 291) finds that "although the efficacy of all forms of governance may deteriorate in the face of more frequent disturbances, the hybrid model is arguably the most susceptible." If the above conditions of Jarillo's model are fulfilled, network structures provide an effective governance mechanism for entrepreneurial enterprises. However, given instances in which the frequency of disturbances reaches high levels, the hybrid mode may become economically inefficient, resulting in a return to markets and hierarchies as governance structures.

The concluding point is, that when an enterprise decides upon its internal or external procurement strategy, the *real complete internal cost* must be calculated and evaluated. The fact that multinational network strategies are increasingly emerging suggests that the costs of internalization strategies may often be higher than first glance examination suggests, since in-house production may also mean a substantial efficiency loss for the overall enterprise (Jarillo 1988, 36).

SUMMARY

The production of research-intensive components of skills and final assembly operations may be locationally separated but integrated through trade within hierarchical networks or within regional or global markets. The existence of an economically integrated market promotes the tendency toward a joint determination of production decisions in different countries by multinational enterprises operating within the region (Cantwell 1987). Static scale economies associated with rising production levels have had a significant effect, but dynamic scale economies accomplished through production automation and better coordination of successive production stages through new managerial, organizational, and contractual techniques have permitted a higher total value-added. Regarding the new forms of internationalization, flexible contractual arrangements with component or service suppliers have facilitated production planning, production efficiency, product development (through the upstream and downstream diffusion of technology), and quality control.

The success of the Japanese motor vehicle industry especially illustrates the analytical and empirical network effects presented in this chapter, permitting institutional arbitrage by multinational enterprises (see, e.g., OECD 1983, 1987b; Cantwell 1987, 143; Johnston and Lawrence 1988). Toyota, for example, produces approximately 20 percent of the value of its automobiles, while General Motors and Ford produce 70 percent and 50 percent respectively. The successful market comeback of Chrysler was partly due to its newly instituted value-added partnerships with its suppliers, distributors and union (Iacocca and Novak 1984). Chrysler now produces roughly 30 percent of the value of the automobiles it sells. The publishing industry has also strongly developed value-added partnerships. The key technologies in publishing are now brokerage and marketing. Changes over time in technological, legal, and market characteristics were seen to be highly relevant in assessing the shift in the relative costs of enterprise, market and network organization, and the rise in new forms of internationalization as multinational enterprises compete to transform their industrial structures.

Once an enterprise has become multinational, the basic goal is no longer simple internalization; rather, it is to find the formal structure and conditions which provide multinational enterprise with the right organizational and competitive positional fit. Transactions among affiliated and nonaffiliated parties evolve out of a complex process motivated by strategic, behavioral, and economic considerations. Intermediate input procurement is structured rather differently in different industries. Within industries, intermediate input procurement may also be organized differently at each stage of manufacturing.

The potential gains of strategic alliances through network linkages are relatively high in certain industries. When the internalization costs of procurement are high as well, enterprises have been often able to improvise contractual and noncontractual arrangements which permit them to obtain the benefits of internalization without all the costs through the use of strategic alliances.

Factor and product market imperfections, as stressed throughout much of the literature on multinational enterprises, are commonly mentioned as the Coasian economic incentive for the internalization strategies of multinational enterprises. Market imperfections, however, may come about quite naturally, as Caves (1971a), Casson (1990b), and others have stressed. Firms seek specifically to establish unique competitive positions through their procurement strategies—that is, their network linkages on an international basis. This aspect has been stressed by the value chain business strategies of Porter (1986b).[21] Competition among enterprises in international markets is a continuously changing process which is a great deal more complex than the now common internalization theory at first glance suggests.

Current models of foreign direct investment strategies do not take into account the value-added advantages of a global network. They stress instead motivational and structural advantages—for example, proprietary knowledge, static domestic industrial structure, and product differentiation. These are all important aspects of multinational enterprise. However, the initial motivations for establishing subsidiaries in foreign locations are conceptually quite different from subsequent investment decisions as exhibited through strategic network linkages and alliances. Networking represents largely sequential flows of information stemming from the advantages of flexibility inherent in a multinational enterprise network system.

A global network perspective of the multinational enterprise implies a collection of valuable transactional options which permit the discretionary choice of changing real economic activities or financial flows from one country to next. We have stressed the importance of a strategic multinational network as an important contribution to the overall value of the enterprise and its economic opportunities.

Rapid technological change along with the shifting patterns of international trade and global competition have intensified multinational enterprises' search for new competitive alternatives to explicit overall foreign direct investment. These developments were foreseen by researchers such as Dunning (1979b) and Casson (1979). They were well aware, at an early stage, of the potential development of the now rapidly growing cross-hauling of international investment and joint ventures or quasi-contractual resource flows among enterprises.

Dunning suggested that if governments attempt to "unpackage" the activities of multinational enterprises, or if technology becomes more standardized, then contractual ventures will take the place of foreign production and the "traditional" multinational enterprise may become less important. The acceleration of technical progress (along with shortened product life cycles) and the improvement of both inter- and intrafirm communication networks have counterbalanced

---

21. Porter (1990a, 93) has recently taken a somewhat more skeptical view of the importance of strategic alliances. He suggests that using alliances as a strategy may only ensure an enterprise's mediocrity, not its international leadership. According to Porter, alliances are best used as a selective tool, employed on a temporary basis or involving noncore activities.

these effects. This is basically due to the fact that the distribution of innovations continues to be uneven across nations, and if the world moves closer toward economic interdependence rather than away from it, international networking will remain a dominant force affecting the organizational structures of multinational enterprise.

The literature on multinational enterprise offers sufficient guidance for explaining the initial foreign direct investment decision. It focuses mainly on the problem of becoming a multinational rather than on competitive strategies for established subsidiaries. Although this is a still rather neglected area of research, equally important are the operational aspects of established affiliate production centers and potential inter- and intraenterprise collaborations through networks.

Successful enterprises achieve strategic organizational and positional fit with their market environment and support their strategies with appropriately designed structures and management processes (Miles and Snow 1984, 1986; Kotha and Orne 1989). Less successful enterprises commonly exhibit poor fit externally and/or internally.

The search for new competitive approaches in multinational enterprise is producing new organizational forms culminating in international dynamic integrated networks. These new structures are both a cause and a result of today's global market environments in which enterprises compete to combine strategy, structure, and management processes most effectively. Relative disparities of enterprise capabilities and their respective gains are transforming the nature of multinational enterprise collaborations. In earlier times contractual forms of internationalization were to a large degree ad hoc. More recently, as the input factor time has begun to play a more significant role due to life cycle and technology gap aspects, enterprises are increasingly seeking to hedge against the risk of defection by establishing more stable partnerships ("strategic alliances") within long-term global networks diversified over a vast series of projects (Tucker 1991, 119).

In the uncertain environment of international markets, production flexibility is achieved by the ability to change a process from one mode of operation to another. One of the most significant benefits of such flexibility is to provide the manufacturing process with an ability to modify itself in the face of uncertainty (Kulatilaka and Marks 1988). The rapid rise in the volume of intrafirm trade and in network linkages reflects these developments. Intrafirm trade and network linkages manifest strategic attempts to diversify over broad ranges of industries, allowing for specialization along product lines or according to processes within industries, rather than the traditional interindustry specialization. The upshot of this is a relative ease in adjusting to structural change in international markets, adding to the expected profit value of the firm.

Strategic alliances, however, may often result in a loss of profits for partners, as recently illustrated by the failure of the Olivetti and AT&T joint venture. Originally these enterprises were considered to be a good match with high levels of synergy effects due to complementary research and development strategies as well as their complementary geographical locations.

After realizing the potential importance of strategic alliances and networks, future research should concentrate its efforts on analyzing the managerial and economic problems of effective implementation of strategic alliances. The international consulting agency Deloitte Haskins and Sells in a recent study of 880 corporate partnerships found that only 45 percent of the participating parties regarded their alliances as successful. Forty percent of the strategic alliances had a life span of no more than four years, and only 14 percent of the alliances managed to last longer than ten years (see Rubner 1990, 66). Michael Porter has also estimated that the track record for acquisitions is apparently equally poor. More than half of the acquisitions in related fields of business and approximately 60 percent of the acquisitions in nonrelated fields of business have proven to be failures, according to Porter.

It is potentially incorrect, however, to interpret the well-documented instability of strategic alliances as being representative of their low strategic value. Based upon the evolutionary process of technological development and structural changes in international markets, strategic alliances are predestined to be inherently unstable. In judging the success or nonsuccess of strategic partnerships it is necessary also to take into account the positional payoff—that is, any additional competitiveness derived for the involved parties that arose out of the venture. Since it is only natural that the complementary firm-specific advantages of the involved parties change over time, so will the organizational and competitive positional fit of strategic alliances change enterprise boundaries over time, depending upon the learning curve effects that occur in playing the iterated game in the merry-go-round of strategic alliances. Preliminary evidence as well as economic theorizing suggest that intensified levels of inter- and intrafirm cooperation will no longer be the exception but the rule. Rivalry among multinational enterprises will, however, remain very intense "since strategic alliances have something of the flavour of tennis doubles partnerships where each player is free to pursue a single career" (O'Brien and Tullis 1989, 13).

CHAPTER 4

Successful Management of Innovative Networks

> As far as the professional experts in these methods are concerned, one claims, "We often spend so much time analyzing the stem, stamen, pistal, and petal that we do not see the flower." The floral metaphor is appropriate. Networking is like trying to cultivate wild flowers. You don't plant and hover over them. You permit or create an environment where they can come out and grow. —Robert K. Mueller

In light of the rapidly rising incidence of worldwide network structures of strategic alliances as a distinctive competitive strategy of multinational enterprise, this chapter examines the critical success factors such as human resource management required in the entrepreneurial process of networking. Although technological aspects of networking have been emphasized throughout this book, strategic alliances and network structures depend even more fundamentally upon the attitudes and practices of the participating managers (Johnston and Lawrence 1988; Doz and Prahalad 1988).

Today's multinational enterprise executives face the exciting challenge of cultivating an avid assessment proficiency of the international global business environment while simultaneously being confronted with shortened competitive time restraints. The role of global scanning in business planning is nowadays put at the top of the list in strategic planning (e.g., Davidson 1991); however, effective implementation in day-to-day activities is often still a Pandora's Box, the problem being that no guaranteed recipes may be given for success.

As demonstrated by Porter's (1986a, 1991) recent works, a single global strategy does not exist. Rather a strategy is constrained by the value chain (i.e., vertical integration imperatives), configuration (location costs of interrelated activities internalized within the enterprise) and coordination issues. This leads to a typology of global strategies (Buckley 1988, 189).

Despite this fact, effective global scanning through networks is vital for success if executives are to perceive and follow through on profitable international opportunities. International business executives face the horrendous task of reviewing and assessing endless

138

sources of information.[1] At the same time, executives must keep abreast of the identification of potential strategic alliances and network business relationships.

If executives, general management, and employees in general are to exploit the emerging global networks of competition and cooperation, they must obtain a fundamental understanding—a "mind mapping"—of the dynamics and complexities of networking and strategic alliances. The following discussion briefly highlights fundamental managerial aspects of networking and strategic alliances. An understanding of network processes begins with recognition of the problem of identifying prospective partners and the role of task and organizational complexity. Management issues of international partnerships are then examined as a two-stage process, in which the sequential aspects of network management are elaborated. The importance of monitoring network processes is then discussed. Finally, the managerial implications for organizational design and the associated human resource management issues of global strategic alliances ranging from licensing and joint venture to consortia, keiretsus, and chaebols are examined.

FUNDAMENTAL ASPECTS OF NETWORKS

Networking is an evolutionary or cumulative process, hence it is not possible to establish a simple standard overall checklist typology of relevant factors of success. Certain levels of generality are, however, common to all network structures. This does permit to some extent practical aid in establishing efficient network structures and avoiding costly failures. Figure 4.1 elaborates briefly on fundamental aspects of enterprise networking.

IDENTIFYING PROSPECTIVE PARTNERS

The first step in network management is to identify prospective partners and knowledgeably initiate and construct partnerships with complementary enterprises.

Enterprises contemplating a strategic alliance should scrutinize potential partner attributes with regard to a listing of relevant criteria (Baranson 1990). Such a listing will naturally vary according to the specific alliance decision at hand. External key resources such as high product quality (reputation), rapid delivery, cost, service, and a

---

1. For an interesting discussion of problem-solving issues in international business entrepreneurship see Casson (1990b, ch. 3).

Figure 4.1: Fundamental Aspects of Networks

● The development of network structures, involving mutual trust capital, often takes considerable time. Management time horizons should preferably be based upon long-term prospects.

● Management must be aware that networking is a distinct form of international competition. Networking peers are simultaneously competitors and collaborators.

● Networks involve bilateral monopoly exchanges of complementary information. Transacting parties attempt to learn as much as possible from one another, while at the same time attempting to limit the exchange of information being transmitted. Today's collaborators are often tomorrow's most vicious rivals.

● Successful network strategies require early implementation of flexible rules and performance requirements to monitor the distribution of potential benefits among the transacting parties. Network partners must learn to be flexible within a set of rules.

● The mere possession of some firm-specific advantage or "core asset" does not guarantee network success. Managers should especially be aware of the vast amount of sociocultural differences among international transactors, both at the level of business partners as well as the equally important differences at governmental levels.

● "Indicative" economic planning of rival governments commonly plays a significant role in the establishment of multinational enterprise networks. Policy makers intermingle in the networking game.

● Management must avoid alliance traps. All strategic alliances are inherently risky. Partnerships and networks must be evaluated accordingly. "Alliances don't work for you - you work through them (Business International (1990, page 102))."

● If you do not possess in-house capabilities, the question must be asked "Should we produce it ourselves or look for a partner?"

● The phenomenon of networking and strategic alliances is not a new vogue, it is, however, a new multinational enterprise strategy.

potential partner's ability to grow and adapt during the alliance's life cycle commonly play an important role in any collaboration.

An examination of the "commitment record" of a potential partner should be undertaken. What is a potential partner's history and reputation pertaining to earlier alliances? Such information may be routinely collected at little cost by simply talking with an enterprise's current or earlier partners (Larson 1991, 186).

After prospective partners have been identified and evaluated, the architectural design of the cooperative network must be considered. Management should conceive tentative design options that serve as a foundation for the negotiation process among participants emphasizing simplicity as well as feasibility. The logic—that is, the purpose and objectives—of the partnership should be clarified and the economic rationale as a whole understood (Lorange 1988).

Design issues must be put on the management agenda. The establishment of realistic structure and complementary managerial processes and systems can make the collaboration work. "Without such a consistent approach to structure/systems/processes, it will be difficult for the cooperative venture to succeed" (Lorange 1988, 383).

THE ROLE OF TASK AND ORGANIZATIONAL COMPLEXITY

The next assignment in network management is to learn to manage complexity. Reducing organizational complexities of networks facilitates network performance. Tight fit is the governing force which fosters superiority.

The concept of networks was first introduced outside the fields of economics and business strategy (Jarillo 1988; Ghoshal and Bartlett 1990). Scholars in organizational theory[2] began to study interorganizational relationships in nonprofit organizations.

Contemporary researchers are only now beginning to emphasize the role of organization theory in the reconceptualization of multinational enterprises. Ghoshal and Bartlett (1990) recently delineated an interorganizational network approach to multinational enterprise based upon the foundations of organization theory.

At the management strategy level of analysis Miles and Snow (1984, 1986) and Killing (1988) have emphasized the role of organiza-

---

2. E.g., Evan (1966), Aldrich and Whetten (1981), Levine and White (1961), Hall et al. (1972), Benson (1975), Van de Ven (1976), Van de Ven and Ferry (1980), Pfeffer and Salancik (1974), Bacharach and Aiken (1976), Van de Ven and Walker (1984). Such studies have commonly focused their analysis on interorganizational groupings not connected by ownership ties (Ghoshal and Bartlett 1990).

tional complexity in the design of enterprise alliances. Since alliances are increasingly emerging in advanced technological areas of product and process development, managers often lack the required skills and commitment levels to effectively deal with the task and organizational complexity in the design of alliances.

Management should consider, according to Killing (1988, 54), the following basic points:

> 1) Alliances that undertake complex tasks do not always need to be organizationally complex. Task complexity does impact on organizational complexity, but so do a number of other factors.
> 2) Firms wishing to create an alliance to undertake a complex task should first enter a simpler alliance with their chosen partner, in order that a degree of mutual trust may be established, prior to the formation of the more complex alliance.
> 3) Relatively weak firms should be wary of entering alliances with strong firms, if those alliances are intended to take on complex tasks.

Alliance Complexity

Surveying managers involved in fifteen alliances (roughly half of which were in the automobile industry), Killing's 1988 study suggests that the key to successful alliance building is to develop an alliance that is simple enough to be manageable. Complexity, it was found, entices failure. Figure 4.2 highlights two relevant aspects of all alliances: the complexity of the task to be undertaken and the complexity of its organizational design.

Task Complexity

Figure 4.3 summarizes the three factors that significantly influence alliance complexity: the scope of an alliance's activities, the environmental uncertainty, and the adequacy of the skills within the alliance.

The scope of an alliance's activities naturally will depend on its objectives, the number of business functions, duration of the alliance, number of products, and the number of markets to be served. A rather wide range of possible arrangements are conceivable regarding the scope of partnership agreements, as will be discussed in more detail below.

Environmental uncertainty due to overall demand, customer preferences, competitors' actions, government actions, and supplier competence are areas in which it is difficult to make any form of

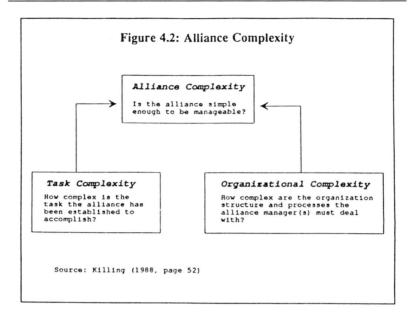

Figure 4.2: Alliance Complexity

Alliance Complexity

Is the alliance simple
enough to be manageable?

Task Complexity

How complex is the
task the alliance has
been established to
accomplish?

Organizational Complexity

How complex are the organization
structure and processes the
alliance manager(s) must deal
with?

Source: Killing (1988, page 52)

sound management forecasts. Consequently, management should follow these areas closely.

Potential partners must be evaluated as to the resources, competence, and familiarity they possess. The distribution of enterprise capabilities may be quite widespread. Effective alliance building requires recognizing potential complementary partners that meet the necessities of good organizational fit.

Organizational Complexity

Figure 4.4 illustrates that the more frequent and less routine in nature the interactions between alliance partners are, the greater will be the organizational complexity involved. Problems may arise between partner interactions since (1) partners must originally become familiar with one another, (2) corporate cultures may differ, and (3) partners will commonly have different objective functions. The more partners that are aligned in the alliance network, the greater will be the degree of organizational complexity. Cooperative arrangements between equals enforce organizational complexity. Decision making may become tedious. Generally, however, the more partner skills coincide, the more likely shared decision-making alliances may arise (Killing 1983).

As pointed out at various times by authors such as Peter Drucker

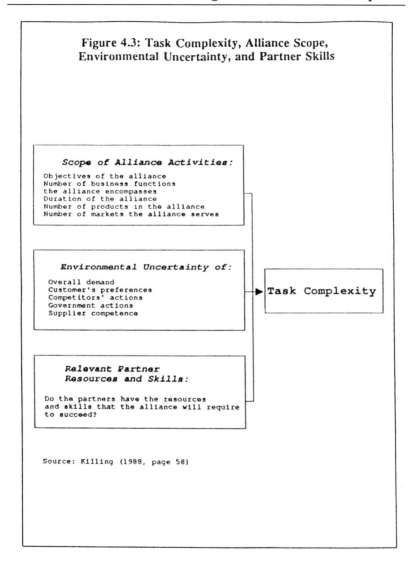

Figure 4.3: Task Complexity, Alliance Scope,
Environmental Uncertainty, and Partner Skills

Scope of Alliance Activities:

Objectives of the alliance
Number of business functions
the alliance encompasses
Duration of the alliance
Number of products in the alliance
Number of markets the alliance serves

Environmental Uncertainty of:

Overall demand
Customer's preferences
Competitors' actions
Government actions
Supplier competence

Task Complexity

**Relevant Partner
Resources and Skills:**

Do the partners have the resources
and skills that the alliance will require
to succeed?

Source: Killing (1988, page 58)

(1954), Thomas Peters and Robert Waterman (1983), enterprises
with enduring records of high performance "tended to have a clear
business focus, a bias for action, and lean structures and staffs that
facilitated the pursuit of strategy" (Miles and Snow 1984, 14).

The managerial and organizational characteristics of globally
successful enterprises are hence the result of tight linkage fits with

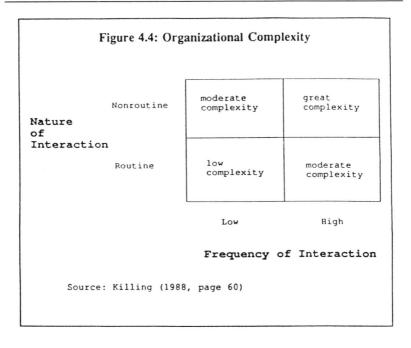

Figure 4.4: Organizational Complexity

		Low	High
Nature of Interaction	Nonroutine	moderate complexity	great complexity
	Routine	low complexity	moderate complexity

Frequency of Interaction

Source: Killing (1988, page 60)

environment and among strategy, structure, and process. "The trick is the matching of information collection costs to the impact on strategy" (Buckley 1988, 184).

As Miles and Snow (1988, 15) have summarized, the governing dynamic of tight fit tends to operate in four stages:

> First, the discovery of the basic structure and management processes necessary to support a chosen strategy create a *gestalt* that becomes so obvious and compelling that complex organizational and managerial demands appear to be simple.

> Second, *simplicity* leads to widespread understanding which reinforces and sustains fit. Organization structure and key management processes such as reward and control systems "teach" managers and employees the appropriate attitudes and behaviors for maintaining focus on strategic requirements.

> Third, simplicity *reduces the need for elaborate coordinating mechanisms,* thereby creating slack resources that can be reallocated elsewhere in the system.

Fourth, as outstanding performance is achieved and sustained, its *association* with the process by which it is attained is reinforced, and this serves to further simplify the basic fit among strategy, structure, and process.

The evolving global network structures represent an enterprise's search for organizational forms that are both internally and externally compatible. As put forth by Miles and Snow (1988, 27), "Minimal fit is necessary for survival, tight fit is associated with corporate excellence, and early fit provides a competitive advantage that can lead to the Organization Hall of Fame. Tomorrow's Hall of Fame companies are working on new organization forms today."

FORMING THE PARTNERSHIP: A TWO STAGE PROCESS

Entrepreneurship through networking is the creative cultivation of internal and external relationships and a corporate environment in which long-run mutual trust between partners matures and grows through cooperation. Trust creation depends inherently upon the quality of management processes.

The process of networking is, according to Mueller (1986), "a search for a new social geometry." He regards the search for networking geometry as an indirect "around end" approach to organizational effectiveness based upon human interactions. Doz and Prahalad (1988) go even further and suggest that the strategic management of existing resources is becoming more important than how new resources are deployed over product lines and global markets. The quality of the organization and management processes is a vital source of competitive advantage. As the resource configurations of enterprises become increasingly similar throughout world markets, the quality of management and the manner in which it leverages resources globally is the key to enterprise success. A network "is only as good as the administrative infrastructure that facilitates its dynamic and selective use against active global competitors" (Doz and Prahalad 1988, 367).

The initial exchange between two transactors is the beginning point of any future linkages. Market exchanges based upon arms-length price-driven transactions are characterized by their short-term nature and often are carried out under adverse circumstances. Given the right constellation, binary transactor associations between enterprises and individuals emerge which, if cultivated, may evolve into full-grown alliances that need to be adequately managed.

In order to grasp the general overall structure of networking, it is useful to break down the management process into two main stages, as Larson (1991) has recently demonstrated. Figure 4.5 illustrates Larson's analysis that after some initial trial period, a sequence of transactions emerges which, if properly managed, may culminate in a partnership, i.e., network dyad.

Stage One: The Trial Period

After prospective partners have been identified, a trial period should ensue in which supplementary transactions and exchanges of information permit further partner evaluation. Before becoming committed to a full-fledged strategic alliance, partners should attempt to gradually reduce the risks of being noncompatible with each other through preliminary arrangements.

During that trial period of alliance building, the main task of management is to screen partner performance efforts and conduct, while at the same time visibly establishing their own commitment and credibility. The establishment of good partner rapport and fair contribution reinforces an enterprise's reputation, which can be strategically significant in oligopolistic industries (Moxon, Roehl, and Truitt 1988).

Ground rules for routine interactions between partners emerge incrementally, institutionalizing a given set of patterns of interaction and exchange. Daily interactions on a trial-and-error basis enable management to learn "the systems and procedures" of collaborating (Larson 1991).

At an early stage of the management process, both enterprises should develop the "transparency of executive process" (Doz and Prahalad 1988). Management transparency builds trust and legitimates dissent inhibiting a degenerate process. During the trial period formal contracts are not the driving motivational force behind alliances. Contracts serve as a "safety net." They often prove, however, to be inefficient given the fact that recourse to the law can be highly expensive and time consuming. In international alliances contracts often illustrate part of the commonly found culture gap between partners. In the United States and Europe, for example, a contract is viewed as a binding legal document defining the rights and responsibilities of the involved parties. Koreans, Japanese, and Chinese, on the other hand, view contracts as "organic" documents that are due to evolve as conditions change. Ignorance of such cultural differences can forcefully disrupt a peaceful coexistence of any relationship (Tung 1991). As unanimously pointed out in the literature (e.g., Mueller 1986; Buckley and Carson 1988; Larson 1991), more im-

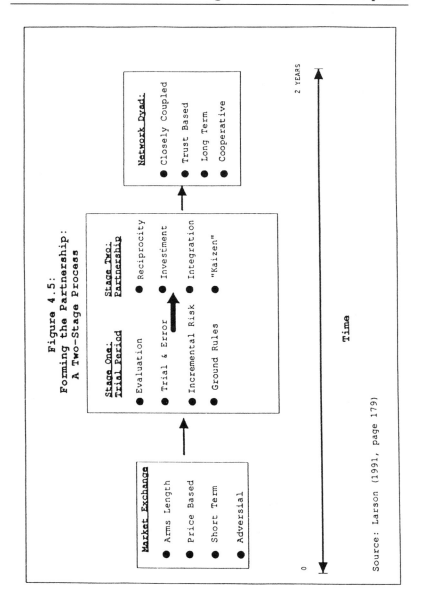

Figure 4.5:
Forming the Partnership:
A Two-Stage Process

Market Exchange

● Arms Length
● Price Based
● Short Term
● Adversial

Stage One:
Trial Period

● Evaluation
● Trial & Error
● Incremental Risk
● Ground Rules

Stage Two:
Partnership

● Reciprocity
● Investment
● Integration
● "Kaizen"

Network Dyad:

● Closely Coupled
● Trust Based
● Long Term
● Cooperative

2 YEARS

0

Time

Source: Larson (1991, page 179)

portant than reading the small print of the contract is the production
of trust. Comprehensive cooperation commands trust-building processes, founded on the original motives for collaboration, the principle
of reciprocity and how often partners interact (Buckley and Casson
1988; Casson 1990b).

Where the partitional brink is between the trial period and stage
two, the partnership is somewhat difficult to assert. Conceptually, the
trial period ends the time in which an implicit contract has been
developed based on trust "and the reciprocity in actions that trust
encourages. Trust [has] emerged as a central component of the exchange" (Larson 1991, 177).

Stage Two: The Partnership

Partnerships may be distinguished by what Larson (1991) has
termed a "trust threshold," that is, a common understanding of fair-
ness and the assumption of trust. Restraint from cheating on a reciprocal basis becomes the essence of cooperation (Buckley and Casson
1988). "Short-term losses are set against long-term gains; and each
side begins to play for future as well as present stakes" (Larson 1991,
177). Alliance partners begin to make long-term investments in one
another on a reciprocal basis rather than short-term trial-and-error
investments.

Stage two is distinguished from the first stage by the extent of
integration that has occurred. Enterprises become integrated through
frequent contact across organizational and functional boundaries.
The principle of reciprocity intensifies management commitment to
successive improvement of the relationship, thereby lowering the
transaction costs of future interactions (Buckley and Casson 1988).

Larson (1991) views the dynamics of partnership exchanges
based upon reciprocity as being founded upon what he calls kaizen
orientation,[3] *kaizen* being a Japanese term which reflects constant
improvement in any given situation. Continual improvement is a result of experimentation, risk taking, innovation, and a focus on quick
response and problem solving. Comprehensive information sharing
through dense communication networks and intensified patterns of
reciprocated investments of time, people, and equipment distinguish
stage two. Interorganizational and interpersonal learning occurs.

Casson (1990b) has also demonstrated how differences in the
degree of trust between economic agents may explain some of the
differences between the United States and Japan that existing theo-

---

3. See further Imai (1986).

ries do not sufficiently explain. As he notes (p. 105), "Other things being equal, high levels of trust promote economic performance. Japan, it is claimed, benefits from a relatively high degree of trust between economic agents. This high level of trust is engineered and sustained by economic institutions which have adapted ancient traditions for modern purposes."

The sequential expanded exchange processes of strategic alliances finally culminate in the network dyad. Benefits materialize for all parties involved based upon the greater speed, volume, and quality of information exchanged. These information flows augment an enterprise's innovative capabilities, improve product quality, reduce costs, and reposition the enterprise's market competitiveness.

MONITORING THE NETWORK PROCESS

Management must periodically review the competitive strength of the network as a whole. The value-added chain constructed may need to be revised to maintain competitive positioning.

An essential function of management in the network process is to periodically monitor network performance along the iterative steps, taken in the shaping of the network. The international business environment changes at a rapid pace. Since networking is an iterative process, the management of such processes also requires management review procedures.

Ideally there are no dominate-subordinate relationships in a network. To a certain extent assessment procedures may, however, require the implementation of hierarchical structures. Hierarchies and network structures both have essential functions. "They can exist coetaneously if the inherent conflicts in communications, and command and control processes are understood and resolved" (Mueller 1986, 49). The management challenge is to balance hierarchies and networks without overstressing either at the expense of the other.

Lorange (1988) has proposed that a senior-status management committee consisting of key executives from each of the focal organizations should be established to work out the basic objectives for the network. Such a committee should possess the necessary political influence to enforce relevant decisionmaking. Although objective setting originally is embedded in stage one of the network process, environmental changes may require a modification of original objectives throughout the process. Simple extrapolative thinking, being unimaginative, should preferably be avoided in the continual process of objective setting.

The division of responsibilities in a network are commonly less well defined than in hierarchies. In order to avoid unnecessary dissonance among alliance partners and enable early evaluation and correction procedures, it is vital that management be capable of identifying who is responsible for doing precisely what. Project teams may be created who report directly to the senior management planning committee on their progress. As mentioned above in chapter 3 under the aspect of possible side-payments within the partners and rivals approach to collaboration, the "symbolism" of which partner should maintain the lead role in what aspects of a collaborative agreement is also consequential (see further Lorange 1988).

The process of networking requires the mobilization of enterprise resources. Strategic alliances often place high demands on an enterprise's resources, especially on human resources. If a shortage of executive resources exists from the start, the risks of failure increase enormously. As pointed out by Lorange (1988), it is therefore necessary in the preliminary budgeting phase of alliance building for management to analyze the resource requirements of potential collaborations beforehand as well as during the networking process. Underallocation of critical resources, such as executive personnel, to a given project greatly reduces the chances of success. Unfortunately, as recent evidence suggests, partners in international alliances often first establish the alliances and then turn later to the recruiting and staffing considerations (Cascio and Serapio 1991).

Along the lines of thought regarding the product and technology gap hypotheses described in chapter 2 above, alliance management should monitor the growth potential of their products. The executive planning committee should meet at regular intervals to monitor any possible changes in critical environmental aspects of the partnership (Lorange 1988). Enterprise management must resist the temptation of analyzing the benefits and costs of alliances in a fragmented and isolated manner. Tracking network performance requires not only assessment of one's own network, but also a competitive assessment analysis of one's competitors (Kogut 1984; Lorange 1988).

TYPES OF COOPERATIVE ARRANGEMENTS

Global strategic alliances and their managerial implications for organization design and the associated human resources management requirements have been recently elaborated upon by Lei and Slocum (1991). This section borrows heavily from their research.

As Table 4.1 summarizes, international transactions of multinational enterprises may be ranked according to their increasing interorganizational dependence which is generally, but not necessarily, correlated with strategic impact (Pfeffer and Nowak 1976; Contractor and Lorange 1988a, 9). As noted by Contractor and Lorange (1988a), little comparative empirical work exists on the various types of cooperative agreements and the extent of interorganizational dependence they create.

Licensing Arrangements in Manufacturing

In the hierarchy of alliances (see Figure 1.3) licensing arrangements are the least complex. No equity position is involved among the transacting parties. Licensing commonly means selling off an enterprise's technology. Consequently, licensing often creates new competitors. A strategical tradeoff exists, however, that may still make licensing a feasible strategy since licensing can be used to preempt potential future competition by establishing industrywide standards early in a product's life cycle. This offers an enterprise considerable market breadth as well as faster entry into growing markets.

The computer industry illustrates the efforts of firms racing to license their technologies to potential users in an attempt to set industrywide standards. MIPS Computer Systems, for example, have licensed their newest microprocessor designs to Siemens of Germany in an attempt to preempt the Sun Microsystems—Philips' designs from penetrating the market too rapidly. MIPS has also simultaneously established cross-licensing agreements with Digital Equipment Corporation, Texas Instruments, Cypress Semiconductor, and Bipolar Integrated Technology of the United States and with Fujitsu, NEC, and Kubota of Japan to manufacture its chips and market new computers that are based upon its design (Lei and Slocum 1991, 45–6).

The pharmaceutical and chemical industries are further examples in which networks of cross-licensing agreements function to maintain sources of industrywide discipline and innovations. For example, the international market for pharmaceutical products is artificially highly segmented. The real reason why pharmaceutical profits are so high is that multinational enterprises have partitioned the international market through cross-licensing with prohibition clauses on exports. Such practices enable pharmaceutical enterprises to practice serious price discrimination. A patent is basically a territorial monopoly. This right is imparted to the licensee (De Jong 1981, 230; Contractor 1985).

When technological innovations occur discontinuously, licensing helps enterprises avoid bearing the costs of plant and product obsoles-

Table 4.1: Global Strategic Alliances

Strategy	Organization design	Benefits	Costs	Critical Success Factors	Strategic Human Resources Management
Licensing-Manufacturing Industries	Technologies	● Early standardization of design ● Ability to capitalize on innovations ● Access to new technologies ● Ability to control pace of industry evolution	● New competitors created ● Possible eventual exit from industry ● Possible dependence on licensee	● Selection of licensee that is unlikely to become competitor ● Enforcement of patents and licensing arrangements	● Technical Knowledge ● Training of local managers on-site
Licensing-Servicing and Franchises	Geography	● Fast market entry ● Low capital cost	● Quality control ● Trademark protection	● Partners compatible in philosophies/ values ● Tight performance standards	● Socialization of franchisees and licensees with core values
Joint Ventures-Specialization Across Partners	Function	● Learning a parter's skills ● Economics of scale ● Quasi-vertical integration ● Faster learning	● Excessive dependence on partner for skills ● Deterrent to internal investment	● Tight and specific performance criteria ● Entering a venture as "student" rather than "teacher" to learn skills from partner ● Recognizing that collaboration is another form of competition to learn new skills	● Management development and training ● Negotiation skills ● Managerial rotation
Joint Ventures-Shared Value-Adding	Product or line of business	● Strengths of both partners pooled ● Faster learning along value chain ● Fast upgrading of technological skills	● High switching costs ● Inability to limit partner's access to information	● Decentralization and autonomy from corporate parents ● Long "courtship" period ● Harmonization of management styles	● Team-building ● Acculturation ● Flexible skills for implicit communication
Consortia, Keiretsus, and Chaebols	Firm and industry	● Shared risks and costs ● Building a critical mass in process technologies ● Fast resource flows and skill transfers	● Skills and technologies that have no market worth ● Bureaucracy ● Hierarchy	● Government encouragement ● Shared values among managers ● Personal relationships to ensure coordination and priorities ● Close monitoring of member-company performance	● "Clan" cultures ● Fraternal relationships ● Extensive mentoring to provide a common vision and mission across member companies

Source: Lei and Slocum (1991, page 48)

cence. Just the same, the costs of licensing may be disproportionately high relative to their benefits for manufacturing enterprises. In the terminology of chapter 3 above, the long-term positional payoffs of a licensing agreement may become negative, thereby eliminating any short-term welfare benefits.

Strategic alliances through cross-licensing also possess a technological synergy rationale. For example, Contractor (1985) has found that in the pharmaceutical and biotechnology fields, through the pooling of patents, a superior product is expected. Based upon the different aspects of the state-of-the-art know-how of the partners the creation of "eclectic atmospheres" supports creativity and innovations not likely to be achieved in any one parent organization's "monoculture" context.

In attempting to minimize the risks of licensing in manufacturing industries, management should avoid entering into a licensing agreement with enterprises that are liable to become real competitors in the future. Licensing arrangements inherently benefit the licensee, consequently high costs of management control and monitoring are usually unavoidable.

Licensing Arrangements in Service- and Franchise-Based Enterprises

Licensing arrangements are commonplace in service- and franchise-based enterprises. They provide a low-cost method of rapid market penetration and often entail a standardized marketing approach to creating and monitoring a global image. The spectrum of licensing arrangements in service- and franchise-based industries ranges from fast-food restaurants (McDonald's, Kentucky Fried Chicken), hotels (Hilton Hotels, Holiday Inns), to professional services such as accounting (see Table 4.2). The use of licensing and franchising as a viable strategic alliance often is due to local legal regulations that inhibit explicit foreign direct investment. McDonald's franchise chains in Russia are a recent example.

The international activities of the largest accounting firms in 1986 are shown in Table 4.2. These multinational service enterprises have developed extensive networks of affiliates in developed and developing countries. Typically, accountant enterprises have joined forces with existing local entities, "creating a network of national affiliates that are owned and managed locally but are linked to an international organization that retains coordinating and standardizing responsibilities" (Mallampally 1990, 98). Frequently, local regulatory requirements demand that branch offices be set up in partnership with locally licensed accountants.

Table 4.2:
The International Activities of the Largest Accounting Firms, 1986

Firm name and home country	Number of foreign affiliates			Number of staff		Fee (millions of dollars)	
	Total	Developed countries	Developing countries	Total	Percentage foreign	Total	Percentage foreign
Arther Anderson (United States)	141	82	59	36,117	44	1,924	30
Coopers & Lybrand (United States)	397	249	148	38,500	65	1,695	50
Peat-Marwick (United States)	297	168	129	32,183	55	1,672	35
Ernst & Whinney (United States)	332	211	121	28,800	56	1,492	39
Klynveld Main Goerdaler (Netherlands)	498	396	102	30,894	n.a.	1,137	89
Binder, Dijker, Otte (Netherlands)	294	258	36	13,027	n.a.	531	n.a.
Dearden Farrow (United Kingdom)	193	137	56	5,717	84	211	86
Spicer and Oppenheimer (United Kingdom)	227	166	61	7,775	72	263	75

n.a. Not available
Note: The firms included are the top firms for each of the three countries included in a list perpared by UNCTC of the twenty largest firms worldwide. The data for different firms may vary in terms of coverage of member, representative, correspondent, and affiliate firms. For details see UNCTC (1989).

Source: UNCTC (1989), pages 194-95.

Training and development costs, personnel, and a unique brand of accounting methods are shared within the accountant networks. Noyelle and Dutka (1987, 39) have estimated that in 1983 the world's nine largest accounting enterprises probably controlled more than one-third of the world's accounting business.

The benefits of licensing agreements in service-based industries, according to Lei and Slocum (1991), outweigh the costs. Enterprises whose products or services have reached the maturity stage of the life cycle (such as the fast-food and beverage industries) gain the most since foreign market potential may be exploited at low cost. The latent costs of licensing and franchising consist of potential misuse of trademarks and deficient product/service quality control.

In service industries, licensing and franchising need to be coordinated geographically. Legal trademark protection is vital to success, as are performance and quality controls at an early stage of the partnership. This requires the establishment of overall standards and procedures for evaluation. Licensees/franchisees should be carefully selected based upon their compatibility with regard to sharing the same values, working styles, and corporate philosophy. After an agreement has been reached, local management must be socialized to the licensing/franchising enterprise's values, methods, and mission. "Socialization is the only real long-term mechanism for guiding independent action" (Lei and Slocum 1991, 50).

Joint Ventures: Specialization and Shared-Value Ventures

Joint ventures entail establishing a new entity in which the originating partners jointly participate in formulating strategy and decision-making processes. Four general objectives for entering into a joint venture may be listed: (1) to share and lower the costs of high-risk, technology-intensive development projects; (2) to promote economies of scale and scope in value-adding activities; (3) to seek access to a partner's technology, accumulated learning, proprietary processes, or protected market position; (4) to shape a basis for future competition in the industry involved. Joint ventures may be either specialized ventures or shared value-adding ventures (Lei and Slocum 1991).

Specialization ventures are usually organized around functions—manufacturing, marketing, distribution, etc. Each partner contributes a particular core ability in a distinctive value-adding activity (e.g., one designs the product while the other produces it). In shared-value ventures, partners equally assume the execution of value-adding activities (e.g., through joint designer teams and joint production facilities).

The benefits of specialization ventures are to be found in aspects of risk pooling, acquisition of new proprietary skills and processes, and entry into new distribution channels. Specialization ventures allow partners to achieve a level of quasi-vertical integration without having to carry the otherwise enormous fixed cost investments. Shared value-adding ventures provide partners with necessary strengths and skills to acquire economies of scale, faster learning, and a quick upgrading of technology.

The most eminent cost of all joint venture arrangements is a loss of competitive positional advantage as the partner becomes more competent. Coordination costs may emerge, compromising trust. If corporate cultures do not "fit," inflexibility arises which inhibits interorganizational learning. Value-adding activity exchanges may even come to a stop given atmospheres of mistrust. In specialization ventures a dominant partner frequently forces a position of permanent weakness upon the weaker partner. Management should attempt to avoid alliance partner core asset dependency. Self-learning processes should be emphasized rather than the teaching of partners, at least to the extent of some formal level of reciprocity of exchange. Shared value-adding partnerships permit partners to enjoy economies of scale and rapid learning. If they are successfully managed, the involved parties continuously upgrade their technologies and improve their market positions.

Corning Inc. of the United States is an example of an enterprise that has successfully implemented a progressive network strategy based upon shared value-adding partnerships (Hammonds 1991). Corning has collaborated with Siemens (Germany) in optical cable, with Asahi Glass (Japan) in large-screen television and television bulbs, and Mitsubishi Petrochemicals (Japan) in ceramic devices to control noxious power plant emissions (Baranson 1990, 57).

Focusing on quality, Corning sent its employees to quality-training courses with the final goal being complete customer satisfaction. Presently Corning is involved in nineteen strategic alliances in which it shares technology and marketing skills, thereby permitting a competitive leverage of expenditures. Joint ventures and other alliances accounted for 37 percent of Corning's net income in 1990. These external strategic alliances have enabled Corning to develop and market new products faster, providing size and power without the bulk.

Internal alliances with labor were also established at Corning. The glass worker's union and Corning management undertake joint decision making. Factory design and job scheduling are planned and managed by worker teams. In order to avoid staffing problems, a network of managerial counselors aids blacks and women on questions concerning occupational planning. Asians and Hispanics are the next group to be targeted by Corning. Corning has also promoted community facilities, such as hotels, museums, and libraries, in order to upgrade the locational attractiveness for employees and management.

The success of any joint venture is founded upon numerous factors. It is therefore necessary that performance criteria be established early on in the venture. Even more important, management must be continuously cognizant of the fact that joint ventures represent a distinct form of competition. Therefore, one of management's most important tasks is to create an environment in which the ability to learn from another partner's strength while preserving one's own core advantage capabilities is given top priority. Management must contrive mechanisms for successful organizational learning, retention of personnel, and transfer of management skills. This requires constant monitoring and adjustment during the network process. A decentralized and committed managerial staff flexible in terms of different international management cultures enhances the implementation of the principle of reciprocity. Give-and-take relationships evolve that formal contracts cannot achieve.

All joint ventures require extensive training and team-building managerial methods. Unfortunately, the important insight that international collaborations represent an "alliance of people" is commonly overlooked or ignored (Cascio and Serapio 1991). Significant economies of maintaining team continuity exist which promote corporate identity that outlasts any one member or even generations of members (Casson 1990b, 72). Human resource management is becoming even more important given the fact that high-technology skills are increasingly people-embodied rather than machined-based (Lei and Slocum 1991). Managers must be well versed in negotiation and conflict-resolution skills, such as third-party consultation and integrative negotiations.

Furthermore, managers must become acculturated to working with a foreign partner. New employees must be prepared to deal with the social context of international alliances. Differences in sociocultural methods of doing business strongly influence transaction costs and ultimately enterprise performance. Any business strategy of continuous innovation will depend largely upon whether or not a scientific outlook is perceived to be culturally legitimate. In the long run, access to a foreign culture is one of the most important assets a multinational enterprise can possess (Casson 1990b). Negotiations may come to a halt in alliance building if sociocultural differences are not paid due respect (Tung 1991). For example, the role of implicit communication—the practice of conveying information through gestures, facial expressions, and other nonverbal messages—should be well recognized as an important aspect of many foreign management cultures. This may not be as trivial as first impressions suggest. As Bartolomé (1989, 142) put it, "Using information properly is largely a matter of not *misusing* it."

Any gains from joint venture specialization may be countervailed by costs of communication. Communication processes often fail due to simple misunderstandings. Misinterpretation of messages may be minimized by complementing formal communication structures with informal communication structures. Such personal-ized communication is, however, relatively expensive. A large portion of management time will be consumed in the process of communicating. All the same, such efforts are becoming increasingly essential in areas where human-embodied technologies exist. Personal interaction on a face-to-face basis enforces degrees of confidence and the accumulation of trust capital (Casson 1990b, 62).

Joint ventures often serve as windows through which competitors learn about technologies and core competencies of partners outside of the original agreement. It is rather difficult to demonstrate goodwill and at the same time inhibit a too extensive flow of information. One possible method of inhibiting a potentially dangerous information overflow across enterprise borders is to rotate different managers through the venture, thereby preventing a foreign partner from accumulating too much information from any one person (Lei and Slocum 1991, 56). Organizational boundaries may also be established to diminish threats of substitution or encroachment where competitive dimensions are most vital to long-run survival. Doz (1988, 182) and his associates have over the years gathered evidence supporting the insight that "it is critical to ensure that organizational boundaries to the flow of information and the transfer of skills between the partners reflect the scope of the partnerships, allow for value creation and circumscribe areas where concern for protecting core skills—or for extracting them from the partner—would compromise value creation."

If managed correctly, joint ventures may also be viewed as windows of opportunity. Dynamic global competitive advantage may be accumulated by operating with global partners, providing a strategic advantage over enterprises with less experience (Thorelli 1986; Lyles 1988).

In shared value-adding ventures, short- and long-term dependencies arise as management teams accommodate daily operating procedures. Flexibility of team structure is an essential success factor for adapting to rapidly changing global markets. Ideally, a harmonization of management cultures is obtained such that international alliance management teams create their own distinctive corporate culture.

Consortia, Keiretsus, and Chaebols

"The key to successful networking is to ask questions and listen to others" (Sonnenberg 1990, 58).

The final network management strategy in the hierarchy of

global alliances is the creation of consortia, keiretsus, and chaebols. In response to Asiatic keiretsus and chaebols and international competition in general as discussed above in chapter 1, European technology initiatives or consortia such as the airbus industry, ESPRIT (European Strategic Program for Research and Development in Information Technologies), RACE (Research and Development in Advanced Communication Technologies for Europe), JESSI (Junior Engineers' and Scientists' Summer Institute), BRITE (Basic Research in Industrial Technologies for Europe), and EUREKA (European Research Coordination Agency) are currently attempting to harmonize European efforts to surmount the fragmented and segmented nature of important high-technology markets in Europe (Hauser 1988).

In the United States such developments are still less intense. This may basically be due to American management's current view of the usefulness of such arrangements. The ongoing controversy Ohmae versus Porter is illustrative of the polar viewpoints on these issues (see "Porter vs. Ohmae," *The Economist*, Aug. 4, 1990:55). If one leaves the intellectual battleground of management strategists, however, it cannot be left unobserved that American enterprises are also increasingly implementing network ties at both a domestic and international level.

For example, IBM and Motorola, among others are pooling their resources in an attempt to free themselves from being held hostage to Japanese chip producers (Lei and Slocum 1991). Most recently, Digital Equipment Corporation and Compaq have formed an alliance. IBM is also currently attempting to alleviate its core asset dependency on Microsoft operating systems software. In the business press one finds articles on the formation of a new alliance between the two old rivals IBM and Apple Computer, Inc. Apple is to license its basic software to IBM and receive IBM's RS/6000 chip technology in return. Both technologies are complementary, and cooperation could enhance the competitive position of both while at the same time transforming the future structure of the computer industry worldwide.

The unique function of such consortia, keiretsus, and chaebols lies in the creation of networks of strategic alliances which enhance the productivity of the international research and development system (Fusfeld 1988, 41). At the firm and industrial level risks and costs are shared in networks designed to maximize the value of potential cooperative benefits while still sanctioning industry specialization.

Resource flows and skill transfers are more flexible in a functioning network. Network partners diversify risks and costs, thereby enabling obtainment of minimum efficient scale production and a long-term focus regarding the accumulation of a critical mass in process and production technologies. The costs of applying a consortia strategy, according to Porter (1990a, 92), entail "coordinating two separate operations, reconciling goals with an independent entity, creating a competitor, and giving up profits." He argues that these costs ultimately make alliance building a short-term transitional device that commonly ensures a company's mediocrity, not its international leadership. Such a perspective may indeed prove to be correct given that management does not understand the rules and principles of network structures. It must also, however, not be overlooked that excessive enterprise individualism may also be a source of weakness, limiting the enterprise in its capacity to be successful in international markets (see Casson 1990b, 76). Divestment of assets through strategic alliances on the basis of reciprocity may well bring benefits that outweigh the costs on a long-term basis.

"Indicative" economic planning is a common critical success characteristic of government-initiated networks. The apparent success of a powerful central government pursuing an industrial policy which encourages the establishment of industrial groupings is well documented for Japan, Korea, Taiwan, Hong Kong, and Singapore. The role of governments in networking raises a variety of important questions and management issues that will be taken up in greater detail in chapter 6. Let it suffice here simply to state that a single institutional configuration regarding the role of government should be regarded with great care (Best 1990).

Essential to success in global strategic alliances and networks are the close personal relationships between managers that cooperate over periods of business transactions. Shared managerial values induce implicit mutual understandings that augment efficient investments in tomorrow's industries. Close monitoring of member company performance and the fear of losing face within the group encourage constant effort and productivity even when few formal monitoring mechanisms exist (Lei and Slocum 1991).

The most important human resource management task of networking is the provision of constant training, development, and socialization of managers in the organization's values, mission, and philosophies. As pointed out by Lei and Slocum (1991) among others, American management is inclined to promote individualism rather than a more corporate wide purpose. Individualism inhibits the establishment of trust and commitment needed to build long-term network relationships.

SUMMARY

Returning to the floral metaphor presented at the beginning of this chapter, Ohmae (1990, 12) offers an adequate response: "Not every kind of plant grows well in the same patch of soil. And patches of soil can vary considerably in the kinds of growth they support." As can be seen from the discussion of management issues covered in this chapter, successful management of innovative networks requires a conscious implementation of the following principles:

(1) The first step in network management is to identify prospective partners and knowledgeably initiate and construct partnerships with complementary enterprises.

(2) The next assignment in network management is to learn to manage complexity. Reducing organizational complexities of networks facilitates network performance. Tight fit is the force that fosters superiority.

(3) Entrepreneurship through networking is the creative cultivation of internal and external relationships and a corporate environment in which long-run mutual trust between partners matures and grows through cooperation. Trust creation depends inherently upon the quality of management processes.

(4) Management must periodically review the competitive strength of the network as a whole. The value-added chain constructed may need to be revised to maintain competitive advantage.

(5) Continuously asking questions and listening is fundamental to achieve effective network structures.

(6) Management must be cognizant of the fact that international collaborations represent alliances of people; consequently human resource management issues are highly important.

American and European managers are often still reluctant to explore the global industrial landscape defined by today's emerging interlinked economy. Entrepreneurial management, however, dictates a more open-minded viewpoint. As recently emphasized by Ohmae (1990, 18), "They must make the trip for themselves. And they must have the vision to understand what it is they have seen."

CHAPTER 5

Networking in Developing Countries

> The experience of the 1980's underlie the impor-
> tance which various forms of foreign investment and
> enterprise linkages can have for export success of
> developing countries. The steep growth of manufac-
> tured exports from developed countries in recent
> years has gone hand in hand with a rapid intensifi-
> cation of co-operation between firms from developed
> and developing countries. —UNCTAD

There has been justified dissatisfaction with attempted development strategies in which the "trickle-down" or "trickle-up" effects
have not reached desired levels. It is now obvious that development
from "above" models, as well as development from "below"—or employment, growth, and basic needs—models alone offers no satisfactory solution for development.

These "simple" solutions need to be integrated into a network
development strategy. Over a decade ago, Lall (1980) argued suc-
cinctly that the development literature underemphasizes the importance of network linkages.[1] Linkages are essential to the functioning
of any normal industrial market (Richardson 1972; Casson 1990b).
The creation of strategic alliances stimulates the development of
linked activities and industrial diversification in less-developed countries. Effectively implemented, they speed up the realization of the
natural division of labor (Lall 1980).

In the past, less-developed countries (LDCs) have exported those
commodities for which developed countries (DCs) possess a relatively
low income elasticity of demand. This had the effect of worsening
the LDCs terms of trade. Prebisch strongly argued that the income
elasticity of the center for peripheral countries' exports was an important factor contributing to the evolution of the net barter terms
of trade. One policy implication comes quickly to mind: Individual
LDCs should attempt to concentrate higher levels of their commodity
exports in those branches in which relatively high income elasticities
in DCs exist, thus achieving better terms of trade. Unfortunately, the
necessary material and personnel capacities needed for such large-
scale adjustments are commonly not available in LDCs, at least not

---

1. For a short review of the literature on linkages see Caves (1982, 270–72).

in the short run. In the long run, however, as Raffer (1987) has suggested, differentiation of products according to their importance in the center may be a means of improving net barter terms of trade and development.

Traditionally, commodity exchanges between highly developed countries are dominated by an *intra*-industrial division of labor, whereas commodity exchanges with their less developed partners are commonly characterized by an *inter*-industrial division of labor. Although the traditional complementary division of labor betwen DCs and LDCs still largely remains, a trend toward a more substitutive division of labor in the form of intraindustrial trade flows and intra-industrial investment flows is emerging (Schumacher 1983; Wells 1983; Lall 1984).

Recent evidence (e.g., Havrylyshyn and Civan 1983; Singer, Hatti, and Tandon 1988) suggests that for a growing number of rap-idly industrializing countries the intensity of trade overlap in similar products between the same industrial sector is quite high. In addition to this observation it has also been noted that a clear and strong positive relationship between the level of intraindustry trade and the stage of development as measured by national income exists (Loertscher and Wolter 1980; Erzan and Laird 1984). Furthermore, membership in a successful trade-integration scheme seems to be an important factor in intraindustrial trade levels (Greenaway 1983; UNCTAD 1990b).

The ongoing discussion on the consequences of the rising integra-tion of the developing countries in international trade and investment flows is of increasing importance to world network structures. These developments may be interpreted in light of a common technological base for the nations involved (Broll and Gilroy 1988), or it may sim-ply be that different production stages are integrated through the use of regional resources and market complementarities, thus offering a significant infrastructural element for subsequent trade and techno-logical flows among developing countries (Monkiewicz 1985).

Such trade potentialities are well documented by the data on intratrade flows, which are of the magnitude of 25 to 30 percent of total world trade flows and rising. Intraindustrial trade flows are extremely high in manufacturing industries. Reformistic develop-ment strategy should be targeted at intensifying the social structures and infrastructures of developing countries through a reorientation of their production apparatus according to international and domestic network structures, with current emphasis upon their domestic net-working structures. A common critical voice heard from trade officials from developing countries is that the necessary forward and backward linkages vital to any industrialization are largely lacking.

In the search for an effective development policy strategy the important question arises: Can intraindustrial trade flows (i.e., trade in similar differentiated products of subindustrial classification groups) and networking structures (i.e., the prime relational or linkage ties necessary for an optimal organizational system that exist alongside of hierarchical and bureaucratic structures) be applied strategically to promote indigeneous growth? As higher levels of intraindustrial trade flows and complementary networking structures emerge within LDCs, their net barter terms of trade will improve allowing them to take part more equally in the distribution of the fruits of progress. These developments deserve close attention since intraindustrial trade flows and networking represent a viable alternative in which developing countries can participate in as well as contribute to world prosperity without being perpetually locked into a pattern of low-skilled labor-intensive industrial development (see Erzan and Laird 1984; UNCTAD 1980; Broll and Gilroy 1985a, b).

Intraindustry trade flow among developing countries as well as industrialized countries enhances an international division of labor, which does not imply that nations have to negatively compete for high export quotas. The international divison of labor must not necessarily be a zero-sum game in which developed countries win at the expense of developing countries, or vice versa. Rather, the further industrialization of newly industrializing countries, as indicated by their intraindustrial trade flows, contributes to the volume of world trade, permitting higher integration levels in world markets as they move up on the income escalator and as their patterns of comparative advantage evolve along this path (Krugman 1982; Broll and Gilroy 1985a, b, 1989). As Ohmae (1990, 6) puts it, "In an interlinked borderless economy, the old zero-sum logic does not hold. If South Korea prospers, there are greater oportunities for everyone else. If Thailand joins the $10,000 GNP per capita club, everyone benefits."

Intra-LDC investments are complementary to DC investments to the extent that they increase the demand in host countries for capital goods and other inputs supplied by the parents of DC affiliates or the demand for the DC affiliates' own products by raising national income. LDC enterprises are increasingly acting as subcontractors to DC enterprises in the host developing countries. Enterprises from poor and rich countries may further unite their efforts through collaborations in third countries (see, e.g., Kumar and McLeod 1981; Lall et al. 1983; Wells 1983; Agarwal 1985).

The process of development in LDCs is to an even greater extent than for DCs contingent upon the cumulative effects of appropriation and development of technological advancement. As Lall (1990, 16) has commented, however, "The development of national technological capability is subject to a large, diffuse set of influences, and there does not exist a corpus of economic theory that allows us to specify the precise chain of causation and attribute the contribution of different variables influencing it."

In light of the accuracy of the above statement, this chapter makes no attempt at comprehensiveness, but rather emphasizes insights as to how the obtainment of technological capability and human resource capital through networking offers a workable framework within which a wide variety of economic, political, and cultural aspects of the development process may be simultaneously regarded. After a brief examination of foreign direct investment flows to selected developing countries, the development strategy of ensuring economic viability through export-oriented manufacturing subsidiaries is discussed. The recent export-oriented strategy of various newly industrializing countries then sets the basis for a discussion of network policies for development.

FOREIGN DIRECT INVESTMENT FLOWS TO SELECTED DEVELOPING COUNTRIES

The positive contribution of foreign direct investment to development is now generally acknowledged. As a recent OECD (1989, 15) study on international direct investment and the new economic environment remarks, the "reluctance to accept multinational enterprises as partners in the development process [is] now largely a thing of the past."

Given this new awareness, the 1980s were characterized by a rapid increase of foreign direct investment in developing countries in various forms, including traditional foreign-owned subsidiaries and the rise of strategic alliances through joint ventures, nonequity, and subcontracting arrangements (Buckley 1983; Oman 1984, 1988; Franko 1987; Helleiner 1989).

Presently systematic data on foreign direct investments and network linkage arrangements in developing countries are unfortunately highly limited. As documented in Table 5.1, the various forms of foreign direct investment growth taken as a whole has been concentrated largely in a number of Southeast Asian countries (in particular Thailand, Malaysia, and Singapore). More recently Indonesia, the Republic of Korea, Taiwan Province of China, and the Philippines have increasingly become host countries of foreign capital. Taken as a whole, foreign direct investment in these countries increased by some 60 percent in 1987 as compared to the preceding year (from U.S. $8 billion to $12.4 billion, with variations ranging from 22 percent to 36 percent for the individual countries). This trend continued through the first half of 1988. Lately increases in foreign direct investment activities have also been registered for other developing countries (mainly in Sri Lanka, Turkey, Chile, and Mexico (UNCTAD 1990a, 3-4)).

Foreign direct investment in manufacturing industries of developing countries recouped its prior stagnation due to recession only since 1987. In that year it amounted to approximately 32 percent of overall foreign direct investment of Japan, 22 percent of the United States, and 38 percent of the United Kingdom (UNCTAD 1990a, 4).

Asian developing countries are currently the main beneficiaries of new sources of foreign direct investment and collaborative arrangements in manufacturing industries. This trend has also been accompanied by a parallel shift of importance of major investor countries. Foreign direct investments from the United States no longer hold their predominant position of the 1970s and early 1980s. Indeed, until 1986 they declined considerably, being approximately 60 percent below their 1980 levels. Only since 1987 have they begun to increase once again.

The findings of Franko (1987) regarding the propensity of 70 United States enterprises from five industries (automobiles, motor vehicle parts, food processing, pharmaceuticals, and computers) to apply strategic alliances in LDCs indicate that collaborative agreements were primarily a function of the interaction of competitive behavior in oligopolistic industries and the ownership and trade-protection policies of DC governments. Leading American enterprises avoided the use of strategic alliances in LDCs, whereas the propensity to collaborate increased in the smaller firms in their attempt to position themselves better. The minority of the partnerships in LDCs were found in only a few developing countries that pursued aggressive ownership policies, import substitution, and protected market "development" policies. Collaborative agreements were notably less common in the export-promoting newly industrializing countries (NICs), who are viewed as having pursued the most effective development strategies of the past two decades.

Given the data limitations for European Community countries, a less clear picture is obtained. For example, the United Kingdom and the Netherlands have recorded increases in foreign direct investment flows to developing countries, whereas France has registered de-

Table 5.1

Foreign Direct Investment Flows to Selected Developing Countries

	1986		1987		1988 Jan.-June 1987 Jan.-June
	Million $	Increase rate 86/85 in %	Million $	Increase rate 87/86 in %	Increase rate in %
South East Asia					
Thailand[1]	1.358	+67	6.505	+360	+190
Indonesia	826	- 4	1.484	+80	+318
Taiwan	770	+10	1.419	+84	- 24
South Korea	354	-34	1.060	+199	+51
Singapore[1]	547	+34	725	+22	+ 1
Malaysia[1]	202	+61	301	+43	+205
Philippines[1]	78	-35	165	+14	+404
Latin America					
Mexico	2.421	+29	3.877	+60	+37
Chile	565	+22	1.237	+119	+214
Colombia	441	-10	321	-27	+19

[1] Indicates increase rates based on national currency.

Source: 1989 JETRO White Paper on World Direct Investments. Japan External
    Trade Organization, March 1989, cited according to UNCTAD/ITP/32, 10
    May (1990), page 31.

creases. Traditionally, Japan has always been more extensively in-volved in foreign direct investment flows to developing countries. As early as the mid-1970s approximately 80 percent of Japanese multinational enterprise ventures in LDCs were 50-50 or minority joint ventures (UNCTAD 1990a, 7). Since 1985 Japanese investors have consistently invested more than U.S. investors in Asian regions (UNCTAD 1990a, 4).

The more advanced developing countries such as the Republic of Korea, Hong Kong, Singapore, and Taiwan Province of China have also greatly increased their foreign direct investments in the manufacturing industries of other LDCs (UNCTAD 1990a, Agarwal 1985). Although the amount of foreign direct investment of these four countries in other developing economies is still very modest, it has become significant for various partners and is growing faster than flows from developed countries. Taiwan and Hong Kong already rank third and fifth in cumulative foreign direct investment in Thailand. Singapore ranked third amongst all foreign investors in Malaysia, and Hong Kong second in Indonesia. A number of Brazilian and Argentinian enterprises have also made significant investments in other developing countries. These developments are fostering eco-nomic cooperation of developing countries among themselves. This has enhanced their experience of managing foreign investment pro-motion policies in line with their developmental priorities (UNCTAD 1990a, b).

Multinationals from LDCs generally invest in and collaborate with neighboring countries with similar populations, and ethnic and cultural backgrounds. Ethnic and cultural similarity is correlated with the similarity of demand structures of home and host countries. Eth-nic and cultural similarity further promotes an elastic local supply of adequate personnel from the foreign investor perspective that can be trained for managerial and technical jobs. Foreign investment in countries at great distances—geographically, culturally, economically, and politically—brings about higher information and management costs (Agarwal 1985).

Table 5.2 shows that there has also been a tendency toward significant alterations in the sectoral composition of foreign direct investment over time. Traditionally, multinational enterprise invest-ments in developing countries were concentrated in the trade and primary sectors. Currently the significance of foreign direct invest-ment in the manufacturing and other services sectors has become important. The composition of U.S. foreign direct investment in de-veloping countries in the 1970s illustrates that although primary pro-

Table 5.2:

U.S. Flows of Direct Foreign Investment to Developing Countries,

By Sector, 1970-72 and 1979-81

	1970-72		1979-81	
	$ billions	%	$ billions	%
Primary	3.1	46	7.9	50
Manufacturing	1.5	22	5.1	32
Services	2.1	32	2.3	15
Other	-	-	0.4	2
Total	6.8	100	15.7	100

Source: United Nations (1983, page 293)

duction is still dominant, manufacturing investments are rising and services declining.

ENSURING ECONOMIC VIABILITY THROUGH EXPORT-ORIENTED MANUFACTURING SUBSIDIARIES

LDCs account for approximately one-fourth of world trade, both as suppliers of exports and as importers of other countries' exports (see Table 5.3). The share of LDCs in world trade is approximately the same as their share of world income. There has been a general shift toward more export oriented policies in LDCs instead of import-substitution policies. The structure and destination of LDCs' exports has also been changing. Institutional factors, changing investment strategies and investment patterns, as well as outward-oriented policy adjustments, of many developing countries have intensified cooperation between enterprises of developed and developing countries.

In the 1980s, developing countries exhibited high growth rates of their exports of manufactures. Total world exports were still dominated by industrialized countries, with 71 percent in 1960; by 1980 this had decreased to 66 percent, indicating that the growth for other

Table 5.3: Share of LDC's in World Exports							
To	World				LCD's			
From	1955	1960	1970	1980	1955	1960	1970	1980
World					24.4	22.4	18.7	18.8
LCD's	24.2	21.6	17.8	27.4	5.8	4.8	3.6	7.0
Africa	5.2	4.7	3.9	4.5	0.7	0.6	0.4	0.6
Latin America	8.3	6.8	5.4	5.4	1.5	1.2	1.1	1.4
Middle East	3.9	4.0	3.8	10.4	1.0	0.9	0.7	2.6
Asia	6.8	5.9	4.7	6.9	2.6	2.1	1.4	2.2

Source: Agarwal (1988), page 316.

countries was even more rapid. Developing countries have taken part in the growth in both income and trade over the last forty years (Stern 1989, 636).

The four newly industrializing countries (NICs) of East Asia— South Korea, Hong Kong, Taiwan, and Singapore—often serve as examples of successfully applied development strategies. During the last twenty-five years these economies have performed very well, earning them the names "Four Dragons" or the "Gang of Four." They have excelled in growth rates of income and consumption per capita, in low unemployment and inflation rates, and in various social welfare indicators such as literacy and life expectancy (Carbaugh 1989, 163). Korea and Taiwan possess a much deeper and broader industrial competence than the more specialized island economies, Hong Kong and Singapore (Lall 1990, 12). Their GDPs now double or exceed that of Hong Kong and Singapore. Korea's economy is currently even larger than Belgium's, Austria's, or Denmark's, and approaching that of Switzerland. Since 1987 Singapore and Hong Kong have had GDPs above Spain and Ireland (Lall 1990, 32).

Economic growth rates of these countries have accelerated, ranging between 6 to 8 percent per year over the past two decades. Such growth rates have been tightly associated with a rapid expansion of exports, as presented in Table 5.4.

Table 5.4: Exports as a Share of Domestic Output: Japan and the East Asian NICs, 1985	
Country	Ratio of exports of goods and services to gross domestic product*
Japan	13%
South Korea	40%
Hong Kong	106%
Singapore	168%
Taiwan	58%

* These figures include reexports, which account for about 40 percent of merchandise exports in Hong Kong and 33 percent in Singapore.

Source: Balassa and Williamson (1987), page 4.

Table 5.5 illustrates that from the mid-1960s to 1980 the performance of the middle-income countries was superior in both output and export growth to the low-income countries. Exports of manufactured goods by developing countries have grown much more rapidly than exports as a whole. In the 1960s and early 1970s this tendency characterized the growth from the middle-income countries. More recently, however, the low-income countries also are participating actively.

The informal empiricism of the above tables is leading to a growing recognition of the importance of network externalities, or "economies of cooperation," in the areas of information processing and learning and acquisition of technological capability, which belong to the core of the development process (e.g., Bardhan 1990, 4). Increased exports generate a source of demand for home-produced inputs and, through higher incomes, for domestic consumer goods. Furthermore, exports generate a source of foreign exchange needed

Table 5.5: Growth Rates of Income and Exports for Developing Countries			
	1963-73	1973-80	1980-86
Real GDP	6.5	5.4	3.6
Low-income countries	5.5	4.6	7.4
Middle-income countries	7.0	5.7	2.0
Exports	4.9	4.7	4.4
Low-income countries	2.0	4.7	5.4
Middle-income countries	5.3	4.8	4.2
Exports of manufactures	11.6	13.8	8.4
Low-income countries	2.4	8.2	8.4
Middle-income countries	14.9	14.8	8.4

Source: World Development Report, (1988),
cited according to Stern (1989, page 637).

to finance imports of inputs and capital goods for manufacturing and development. The share of exports of DCs and NICs is still moderate. All the same, the stunning success of East Asian NICs in industries such as steel, textiles, computers, and automobiles does demonstrate that it is possible for developing countries to break out of their simple subcontractor status and produce products with higher value-added, thereby setting the seeds of growth and development. While export-oriented strategies contribute strong incentives for industrial development, the ability to react to those incentives depends on the degree of network skills present.

NETWORKING FOR DEVELOPMENT

A necessary condition for development is that existing resources have a potential for economic utilization (Casson 1990b, 130). Traditional economic theory and the "neoclassical litany about getting the prices right" (Bardhan 1990, 4) underestimate the obstacles inhibiting the development of any given potential.

The spread of new technologies is one of the main forces determining today's world patterns of trade, competition, and industrial development. Essentially, development is founded to a large extent upon what Lall (1990) has termed "technological capability," that is, the entire complex of human skills such as entrepreneurial, managerial, and technical competency. Technological capability is basically a learning process. Learning entails arranging knowledge and activities in particular sequences, training and education, search and experimentation. Consequently, "learning to learn" can itself be learned, thereby enhancing any initial comparative advantages or aiding in overcoming disadvantages (Stiglitz 1987; Lall 1990).

In any given instance the learning process of technological development will largely be determined by the organizational, institutional, and network environment present. As Helleiner (1989, 1443) writes, "From the standpoint of the host country and the analysis of economic development, then, what is at issue is the acquisition of scarce inputs and complementary services, e.g. export marketing, from external sources on the best terms."

This does not immediately mean that developing countries must rely totally on the "extended hand" of technology transfers from multinational enterprises from developed countries. Multinationals from LDCs have increasingly taken on an important intermediary role by exporting technology that was initially imported from industrially more advanced countries. The ownership advantages created by such LDC multinationals commonly arise from the scaling down of technologies imported from developed countries (e.g., Lall 1983; Dahlman 1984; Katz 1984; UNIDO 1984; Rabelloti 1990). Enterprises from LDCs manufacture commodities at the mature end of the product cycle applying standardized technologies adapted for local market conditions. Adjusting the value-added chain to the market environment factilitates the obtainment of a competitive positional advantage over the original producers of these techniques in these markets while simultaneously lessening the technological gap (Agarwal 1985).[2]

---

2. For an interesting critical viewpoint on the issue of technology imports see Katrak (1988), who argues under application of a theoretical model that imports of technology may reduce an enterprise's need (or incentive) to develop its own technologies. Technology imports become substitutes for indigenous technological development.

Given that such adapted firm-specific assets and not simply scale economies are the foundation of a LDC's enterprise advantage, there is no reason why small firms might not go transnational at relatively early stages in their growth. As pointed out in the collection of papers in Agmon and Kindleberger (1977), there is potential for smaller and medium-sized multinational enterprises from small or developing countries to become more active in the process of development. It may reasonably be assumed that such enterprises will be more sensitive to the developmental needs of the respective markets than the large OECD-based multinational enterprises. Intensifying the activities of small and developing country multinationals would have the further effect of enhancing global competition at the individual industry level. Buyers' markets for technology and information would loosen up. The availability of adapted technologies would increase, improving future prospects of development via strategic alliances (Helleiner 1989), 1473).

Multinationals from DCs are more labor intensive than their northern counterparts. They usually produce standardized products on smaller-scale operations, depending heavily upon cheap local inputs. Their Third World experience along with these factors have often enabled them to establish profitable market niches. For example, LDC multinationals have been successful, without necessarily undertaking foreign direct investment, in construction, consultancy, and a variety of consumer and capital goods of a more capital-intensive and technological nature (Lall et al. 1983, 16–7, 259–62; Helleiner 1989, 1473).

Any development process is inherently intertwined with levels of total manufacturing value-added (MVA), as summarized in Table 5.6. In 1985 the three largest developing countries (India, Brazil, and Mexico) achieved levels of MVA of $36–58 billion. Korea and Taiwan together had levels of $22–25 billion. Singapore, Hong Kong, Malaysia, and Thailand had MVAs ranging from $4.3 to 7.7 billion. Kenya, being one of the least developed countries, only obtained an MVA of $0.6 billion.

A different developmental picture arises if one measures the degree of industrialization by MVA as a proportion of GDP or by MVA per capita. Measured by MVA as a proportion of GDP, Taiwan is the most highly industrialized, not only in this group but in the world as a whole, with some 40 percent of GDP originating in manufacturing. Korea follows with 30 percent. Singapore, Hong Kong, Brazil, Mexico, and Thailand achieve levels ranging from 20 to 30 percent. India and Malaysia register 19 percent and Kenya 12 per-

Table 5.6: Industry In Selected Countries						
	Mfg. % GDP 1986	MVA (US$m) 1985	Mfg. empl. ('000) 1983	VA/ emp. ($)[2]	Growth in MVA (1980 prices)		Per capita MVA ($) 1985
					1963-73	1973-85	
South Korea	30	24 466	2 165	11 301	20.0	11.0	595
Taiwan	39	22 213	2 047	10 851	16.4	12.9	1 151
Singapore	27	4 311	277	15 563	17.0	7.0	1 658
Hong Kong	21	6 739	855	7 882	8.5	8.0	1 248
Malaysia	19[1]	6 770	559	12 111	6.6	8.8	434
Thailand	21	7 696	2 227	3 456	13.0	7.5	149
India	19	35 597	6 253	5 693	3.0	7.0	47
Brazil	28	58 089	5 313	10 933	9.0	7.9	428
Mexico	26	43 613	1 691	25 791	12.5	5.7	553
Kenya	12	631	186	3 392	14.0	8.0	31

MVA: Manufactured value added

VA/Emp.: Value added per employee

[1] 1984

[2] MVA in 1985 divided by maufacturing employment in 1983.

Source: Lall (1990), page 33.

cent. As shown in the last column of Table 5.6, Singapore, Hong Kong, and Taiwan are the most industrialized according to per capita MVA in 1985, approximately twice the levels of Korea, Brazil, or Mexico. India and Kenya reach approximately 3 to 4 percent of the levels obtained by the first three, and under 10 percent of Korea or Mexico.

Measuring the average MVA per employee, Table 5.6 offers a rudimentary indicator of the complexity, capital intensity, and productivity of industry. Along these lines Mexico is the most advanced and capital-intensive industrial country. This result is largely due to Mexico's large petroleum refining and petrochemical industries. Singapore follows, based upon its petrochemical sector and high technology sectors. The ranking continues with Taiwan, Korea, Malaysia, Brazil, and Hong Kong. At the bottom of the ranking one finds India, Thailand, and Kenya. The growth rates in MVA presented in Table 5.6 illustrate the enduring success of Korea and Taiwan, as well as the somewhat more limited success of the other countries.

Table 5.7 illustrates the structure of industry and the distribution of MVA across selected groups of activities over time. The table portrays the present stage of development as well as achievement of transforming the structure over time away from traditional low value-added activities.

The process of industrialization commonly begins with the simplest consumer goods industries—food, beverages, tobacco, textiles, and clothing.[3] The role of these traditional activities is shown in the first two columns of the table for the years 1975 and 1985. The least-developed country of the sample, Kenya, has the anticipated highest weight.

During the decade observed, Kenya even increased its industrial activities in the traditional sector. Hong Kong has grown largely by specializing in low-tech industry. Between 1975 and 1985 Hong Kong decreased its activities in the traditional sector while simultaneously upgrading the remaining activities. The other countries have generally also decreased their endeavors in this area. Singapore, with only 10 percent of MVA coming from food and textiles in 1985, has diversified the most away from traditional manufacturing.

Singapore emerges as the most advanced in the manufacture of capital goods, producing approximately half of its MVA in machinery and equipment. As Lall (1990) notes, however, the high magnitude

_____

3. See further the interesting approach to the development sequence in Casson (1990b, ch. 6).

Table 5.7: Evolving Structure of Industrial Activity

Percent of MVA

	Traditional[1]		Capital goods[2]		Low skill[3]		High skill[4]	
	1975	1985	1975	1985	1973	1983	1973	1983
South Korea	40.3	32.0	13.5	22.8	49.0	40.5	33.4	40.4
Taiwan	38.4	30.6	17.0	23.8	45.6	38.1	35.4	38.8
Singapore	12.8	10.2	40.7	46.5	30.5	20.0	51.6	38.7
Hong Kong	53.1	43.2	15.1	20.3	63.0	53.4	25.2	27.5
Malaysia	34.8	27.5	19.0	23.0	49.2	43.4	31.4	29.8
Thailand	56.4	39.2	9.6	14.9	68.0	24.3	29.6	21.6
India	30.3	25.9	22.7	27.4	40.9	30.2	42.1	47.0
Brazil	25.7	26.8	23.6	25.4	42.4	36.9	36.0	40.4
Mexico	30.3	22.8	17.6	14.6	14.6	36.9	31.1	45.2
Kenya	44.2	50.5	14.2	13.4	13.4	50.4	64.4	34.9

MVA. Manufactured Value Added

1. "Traditional" industries are food processing, beverages, tobacco, textiles and clothing

2. "Capital Goods" include machinery and transport equipment.

3. "Low Skill" activites include traditional industries plus wood and paper products and "other" manufactures

4. "High Skill" activities include chemicals, petroleum products, basic metals and transport equipment. The distinction is based on average wages and saleries paid in these countries in the US in 1980.

Source: Lall (1990), page 34.

of Singapore's MVA is somewhat misleading. Although Singapore is a major producer of electronic products, it is not a broad-based machinery producer in the normal sense. Rather, Singapore has specialized in making components for foreign equipment producers. Similarly, Hong Kong is also a primary producer of electronic goods but a marginal producer of machinery.

Korea, Taiwan, India, and Brazil are distinguished by much broader industrial structures. For example, during the 1970s Korea invested successfully in heavy engineering, shipbuilding, electronics, and transport equipment through its chaebol networks.

After China, Brazil is the largest equipment manufacturer in the developing world. Yet it still lacks a degree of sophistication in local design and product development capabilities. Mexico is a moderate manufacturer of capital goods with a well-developed automobile sector—which is, however, entirely foreign owned.

Malaysia's and Thailand's industrial structures are still largely characterized by offshore electronics assembly plants. Kenya is currently at an even lower stage of industrial development, lacking the necessary mechanical engineering experience needed to upgrade its industrial structure.

With the exception of Mexico and Kenya, Table 5.7 demonstrates for all countries a reduction in the share of MVA arising from low-skill activities during the period 1973–83. Singapore has the lowest share of MVA in low-skilled activities, whereas Hong Kong, due to its specialization in textiles and garments, achieves half of its MVA from low-skill activities. In general Table 5.7 substantiates the "graduation" of industry across skill categories with time and growth.

As seen in column 4 of Table 5.7, Mexico is the leader in the high-skill category. This is due to Mexico's large petrochemical industry. The remaining countries are at levels of approximately 40 percent. Hong Kong, Malaysia, and Thailand rank lower, within the 25 to 30 percent range.

Along the lines of the above discussion, recent additional empirical observation (e.g., Erzan and Laird 1984) shows that countries that previously belonged to the group of LDCs but have now made the transition to NICs all exhibit increased levels of intraindustrial trade. Through the intensification of (human) capital-intensive production methods and an upgrading of MVA through international networks in important export sectors, these countries were able to either increase output levels or stand firm against international competitors, thus avoiding to a large extent the common balance of payments dilemma facing many LDCs.

In the process of international competition, only those economies capable of adapting continuously to technical developments will be in a position not to fall too much behind their competitors, permitting them to penetrate the various product markets in which purchasing power exists. As exemplified by the rising index level of intraindustrial trade flows for the NICs and the corresponding structural changes in manufactured value-added, these developments may be interpreted as an indicator that these nations were in a position to internalize the advantages of intraindustrial trade and international collaborations in such a manner as to promote their own economical development as well as to simultaneously strengthen world trade flows.

SUMMARY

This chapter has highlighted developmental issues of networking as illustrated by the experience of countries in East Asia and Latin America. During the 1980s enterprise strategies of major multinationals have shifted due to a major shift of competitive positions on global markets. Cooperative arrangements among enterprises throughout the world are increasing. The general insight obtained is that the superior industrial performance and development of the East Asian NICs is not founded simply in the general superiority of export-oriented industrialization strategies over import-substitution strategies. Much more essential than naïve export promotion is a network strategy of promoting stronger linkages between economic agents within the domestic economy as well as between DCs and LDCs and among LDC themselves.

Technological capability of developing countries depends upon "long-term effort to build systematically on externally generated physical, organizational and social imputs and internally on accumulated experience. Industrial capability can therefore be defined as the capability to undertake the entrepreneurial, managerial, productive and technological functions, and selection of the right mix between external and internal inputs" (Rabellotti 1990, 77).

In conclusion, as emphasized above in chapter 4, networking is not simply the process of technology transfer; it also implies a transfer of entrepreneurial and management skills. A development strategy based upon the logic of networks of interfirm linkages implies additional benefits based upon the reduction of risks and costs of investments, the adoption of appropriate technologies and products, the utilization of local assets, learning effects, and ultimately a leveling of bargaining power and control over local industry.

As Lewis (1978, 74) wrote: "The engine of growth should be technological change, with international trade serving as a lubricating oil and not as fuel. The gateway to technological change is through agricultural and industrial revolutions, which are mutually dependent."

CHAPTER 6

Networking and Public Policy

> The most difficult challenge of all for U.S. poli-
> cymakers may be to define the role that the United
> States will play in constructing the new arrange-
> ments. The country's ideology, built on a century of
> economic growth in relative isolation from Europe,
> still radiates a basic assurance regarding the superi-
> ority of the U.S. economic system. The three dec-
> ades of economic leadership that followed World
> War II have only served to reaffirm among Ameri-
> cans the superiority of U.S. economic values. The
> doubts and misgivings that some Americans have
> been expressing in the 1980s regarding U.S. foreign
> economic policies have not yet fostered much toler-
> ance for the disparate views of other governments
> on international economic relations. A capacity for
> listening and learning has still to be developed."
> —Vernon and Spar, *Beyond Globalism*

The theories outlined above in chapter 2, as well as the economic
rationale and management aspects of strategic alliances for DCs and
LDCs discussed in the preceding chapters, have largely focused upon
the more economic explanations for the growth of multinational network expansion. However, a fuller appreciation of the process of
networking compels an examination of political and public policy aspects in order to explain the rise of or limits to network structures
and their communication chain as contrasted to the value-added chain
of our previous analysis.

The challenge to any analysis of networks and public policy is
that government and industry are not guided by tightly drawn boundaries. Neither the nation-state nor multinational enterprises have su-
perseded the other (Gill and Law 1988; Wilks and Wright 1989).
Rather, as technology has evolved, the fortunes and misfortunes of
governments, producers, and consumers worldwide have become
ever more closely linked.

Networks of multinational enterprises are the most visible link
of the world's functional dependencies. Foreign direct investment
flows and the magnitude of sales and purchases of foreign-owned
enterprises in host countries have surpassed simple import and export cross-border sales, representing a new dominant link worldwide.
A doubling of current levels in real terms of foreign direct investment
by 1995 is likely to occur. States have become interdependent. Many

182

links along diverse dimensional levels significantly shape the modes of international business that may be implemented (Julius 1990). Indeed, it is because of the network interconnections among nation-states that it is possible to speak of a global market or global system (Jacobson 1984, 6).

Optimal economic policy of sovereign states entails establishing a policy instrument mix that relates directly to multinational enterprises' allocations. The traditional goal of public policy from a national perspective is to maximize real income and ultimately per capita domestic utility. Unfortunately, a fundamental assignment dilemma exists since the policies that maximize the incomes of source countries, host countries, and the world as a whole are not interchangeable. Situations of conflict are predestined to arise in policy areas of national and international welfare, corporate taxation, natural resource rents, extensive subventions and preferential capital allocations, government procurement, government inspired cartels or guaranteed riskless investments, industrial and technological targeting, and regulation, to cite just a few.[1]

The effects of public policy on business are often little understood, as well as far reaching. "In seeking to understand and evolve theories to explain the mechanisms and outcomes of exchanges between government and industry, we are operating within a context of substantial ignorance" (Wilks and Wright 1989, 2). Much evidence exists to support such a view.

Perhaps one of the most paradoxical examples of the effects of public policy upon enterprises were the American antitrust laws enacted to prevent monopoly power. Due to the manner in which these laws are enforced, the result has been to make American enterprises both larger and more efficient than their global counterparts, since in America, unlike in Europe and Japan, the establishment of cartels is illegal as a means of reducing competition.

In Japan, for example, the number of legal cartels mounted to 162 in 1955 and soared to some 1,000 by the end of the late 1970s. The figures have fallen since then, but MITI continues to count on their usage to stabilize business, principally for small and medium-size enterprises (Okimoto 1989, 7).

Was American antitrust policy a main catalyst in the upsurge of rapid expansion of American multinational enterprises? Jorde and Teece (1989) have recently suggested that U.S. antitrust laws encour-

---

1. For an overview see Caves 1982; OECD 1983; Waterson 1984; Tirole 1988; Schmalensee and Willig 1989; Behrman and Grosse 1990; Best 1990.

age foreign network linkages rather than domestic linkages. They raise the important question of whether laws that accommodate alliances between, for example, a Korean or Japanese automobile manufacturer on easier terms than applied under collaborations among American enterprises are healthly for the U.S. economy.

The upsurge of networks is becoming increasingly important to any understanding of public policy analysis as enterprises react upon their public policy environment (Auster 1990, 84). Public policy concerning American defense spending is an often cited example. The goal of the Department of Defense spending is to sustain and promote the nation's security. Of course, one of the main consequences of the large military budget and bias for domestic procurement has been to give American enterprises important competitive advantages in many fields of high technology. Similarly, the commercial impact of the American space program has enhanced the competitive positioning of American enterprises in an important future market (Vogel 1989).

The role of government in fostering competitiveness is now a major issue in public policy debates.[2] Can and should countries generate network organizational comparative advantages via industrial policy? The United States is largely reliant on NASA and Pentagon procurements. France subsidizes high technology (especially telecommunications). Europe in general relies on import quotas and tariffs to protect its industries (Boyd 1989). Japan is characterized by networks of social structures intertwined with business interests. Since foreign direct investment is now a more important linkage than simple trade flows, competition policy has the potential to overtake trade policy as the most contentious area of international relations (Julius 1990). In fact, the increased politicization of business represents one of the most significant changes in business—government relations over the last two decades (Vogel 1989).

At first glance one might expect that restrictive governmental policies will depress the formation of international collaborative arrangements, whereas more pronounced policy formulation should enhance international network building. The world is, however, often much more complex than such simple logic would indicate. A recent illustration of this is the U.S. antitrust case of 1984 which resulted in

---

2. For a concise critical overview of the evolution of competition policy in the United States see Langenfeld and Scheffman (1988). Further see the discussions in Badarrocco and Yoffie (1982), Schultze (1983), Krugman (1987a, b), Vogel (1989), Porter (1990a), and Reich (1982, 1983, 1991).

the breakup of AT&T. Two major effects have ensued. First, the AT&T case has served as a model and catalyst for countries such as the United Kingdom and Japan to also attempt to stimulate a sector that was historically a public monopoly. Second, the remnant AT&T company has been activated into becoming a strong global player by building strategic alliances with competitors throughout the world. Telecommunications monopolies elsewhere are now being challenged by the new fact of global competition. Consequently they too have been confronted with the task of designing international alliance strategies to keep up with the underlying forces now shaping the industry (Julius 1990, 31).

Nation-states were the original units within which the division of labor evolved, and their corresponding public policies have commonly enhanced economic growth. They have promoted essential transportation and communication networks, supporting legal systems as well as networks of human resource development through public education (Jacobson, 1984). Interdependencies, as illustrated by the AT&T case, have made states increasingly aware of policy prescriptions beyond their borders. Sometimes this policy awareness is founded upon mutual and symmetrical convictions. More often, however, it is asymmetrical and may influence states differently based upon their size and factor endowments.

There are numerous justifications to study government–industry relationships and their network structures. A serious deficiency of research exists when it comes to taking into consideration the existence of collaborative arrangements in the theory of industrial organization and public policy. As pointed out by Mariti and Smiley (1983, 439), neglecting the existence of networks of strategic alliances and partnerships can lead to incorrect theoretical results and policy prescriptions. For example, Baumol and Fischer (1978) derive the standard result that the optimal number of firms in an industry depends on the size of the market and knowledge of economies of scale in the production process. Of course, through collaborative agreements enterprises can take advantage of economies of scale in one or more of their manufacturing processes while remaining separate entities. As a consequence, a greater number of enterprises in the industry is predicted than is the case in the traditional analysis. The inclusion of collaborative arrangements in theoretical industrial organization analysis may change many of our previous traditional insights.

The aim of this chapter is, however, not as ambitious as endeavoring to reexamine common theoretical public policy insights from conventional industrial organization literature. Rather, our primary interest is to complement previous work by focusing upon network *processes* of government–industry relations. Levels of interstate co-operation and the currently observed intensification of regional trade and investment blocks are examined. We then look at first lessons from recent financial market integration. Finally we turn to a comparative "organizational mapping" of American and Japanese public policy regimes based upon their network structures.

LEVELS OF INTERSTATE COOPERATION

Table 6.1 presents a theoretical typology of five conceptually different levels of economic cooperation expressing the degree of interstate collaboration. The economic interactions among states cover the spectrum, from what might be termed regional economic disarmament—the elimination of trade barriers among member states by means of a free trade area—to increasingly complex cooperation schemes, e.g. in areas of technology development (Jacobson 1984; Wilks and Wright 1989).

The main characteristic of the customs union in Table 6.1 is a common external tariff applied to nonparticipating states. A common market permits additionally the free flow of factors among member states. In an economic union diverse public policies such as social security, transporation, and monetary concerns are harmonized. The final stage of cooperation—full economic integration—implies that the member states have become one for all economic purposes.

Due to recent regional trade developments such as the Canada–United States Free Trade Area (Rugman 1990), the European Community Common Market 1992 (Cecchini et al. 1988), and the various intergovernmental cooperative agreements among Asian and developing countries (UNCTAD 1990b) public policy attention is once again directed toward trade and investment and the economic theory of integration. To a large extent the emergence of these regional trade and investment blocs may be interpreted in light of the defensive positionalist strategy of the partner and rivals model presented above in chapter 3, as nations endeavor to maintain their relative trade and investment capabilities vis-à-vis their potential rivals.

As pointed out by Jacobson (1984) among others, these five levels of cooperation provide useful benchmarks of analysis. In practice, however, sovereign nation-states have refused to be constrained by such a stringent categorization. "When groups of states have decided to cooperate, they have simply picked those devices that seemed

Table 6.1: Levels of Economic Cooperation Among States

	No Tariffs or Quotas Internally	Common External Tariff	Free Flow of Factors	Harmonization of Economic Policies	Unification of Policies and Institutions
1. Free Trade Area	X				
2. Customs Union	X	X			
3. Common Market	X	X	X		
4. Economic Union	X	X	X	X	
5. Total Economic Integration	X	X	X	X	X

Source: Drawn from Bela Balassa (1961) and Nye (1971). Cited according to Jacobson (1984), page 209.

suitable, whether or not they fitted this logical categorization" (Jacobson 1984, 219).

FIRST LESSONS FROM GLOBAL FINANCIAL MARKET INTEGRATION

Julius's (1990) analysis of financial market integration offers a useful starting point to consider the basic implications for public policy of increased integration and world network structures. Three major issues arise. First, the integration of the world's global finance market has demonstrated how the ability of domestic policies to control the structure of the market or the behavior of market participants has been vastly reduced. Public policy often breeds induced effects of side-channels. Novel slippages and lags develop between a change of policy and market reaction. For example, policies of high tax environments may promote increased use of internal transfer pricing systems of multinational enterprises that undermine, at least to some extent, any domestic policy autonomy.

Second, financial market integration has demonstrated that a vigorous internal dynamic emerges for global policy convergence. Regulations may benefit or penalize enterprises and other interest groups. As international competition intensifies, enterprises and interest groups will turn to political pressure as a means of improving their situation. Countries commonly compete for foreign direct investment flows, the transmission channel being the link to the international market for public policy regimes. Any threat of policy retaliation in today's interdependent world of two-way cross-investment flows is quite real and credible. Market-led forces will bring about convergence toward harmonization of policies in the long run. Illustrative of such a tendency is the convergence of corporate tax rates across OECD countries.

Market forces induce regulated parties to adapt to the net burdens that regulation endeavors to dictate. Furthermore, the decisions established by regulators are themselves contingent upon the interplay of market forces and political, bureaucratic, and economic networks of interrelationships (Kane 1991). Public policy is not exogeneous, but rather an endogenous variable, for which a clear distinction regarding the manner of causality may often be controversial.

Finally, the question of systematic stability of integrated markets arises. Does policy convergence possibly drive the level of regulation so low that the foundations of the market itself are undermined? In areas such as banking, public safety, or environment, systemic instabilities may emerge requiring tight and focused international policy coordination.

AMERICAN PUBLIC POLICY AND NETWORKING

At a simple conceptual level of analysis, government and industry relationships require an "organizational map" of both public and private organizations, their functions, personnel, and resources im-

plemented in the process of establishing public policy. As noted by
Wilks and Wright (1989, 1):

> Perhaps the unifying theme underlying all study of govern-
> ment and industry in capitalist economies is an awareness of
> the ever present tension between the two "sides." Easton's
> (1965) classic definition of politics as "the authoritative alloca-
> tion of values for a society" can be contrasted with the logic
> of industry which represents "the profitable allocation of val-
> ues for a society." If government is about "who gets what,
> when and how" (Lasswell 1958) so also is industry. But the
> distribution of benefits within society produced by the unre-
> stricted operation of industry is unlikely to square with the
> choices selected by any given government. While industry is
> ruled by the logic of the market, government is ruled by the
> logic of the [democratic] political process.

The relationships between key players of the policy-making process
are often complex and, due to their sometimes informal nature, not
apparent to the outside observer. Relational bonds and linkages may
be established, sustained, and discontinued corresponding to congru-
ous advantage of agents' short-term welfare payoffs and long-term
positional payoffs. Public policy issues kindle relationships as agents
attempt to influence the outcomes of the political process. These
interactions or network linkages need to be the focus of intensified
future research.

Players of the public policy game face a situation similar to that
of enterprises considering entering into a strategic alliance—as described in chapter 3 above under "Traditional Microeconomic Analysis of Networks." Any attempt to reach a point on a political network
contract curve depends upon the material and intellectual factor en-
dowment allocations of the respective agents. The process of political
exchange will be mandated by the formal and informal rules of the
game which regulate their conduct and performance. A substantial
new element, however, is that the number of transactional players
has increased enormously. Consequently, the levels of interaction are
magnified, making the search for a dominant strategy difficult and
costly.

Public policy networks may take many forms: between an enterprise and a government agency; between a group of enterprises or a
representative association and government agencies or several government agencies, etc. The structures of these relationships are thus
manifold, ranging from formally institutionalized to loosely structured

interactions. Public policy structures also have a life cycle of their own, changing and adapting throughout time as the political popularity of policy issues changes. Several policy networks may simultaneously exist within any one industrial branch.

In America (as well as in other nations) a process of osmosis exists which promotes a consistent circulation of political and business leaders to and from the American executive branch and the corporate sector (Dye 1979). As Gill and Law (1988, 206) tell us, the U.S. government has even devolved regulating power to large corporate interests, in effect extending the economic authority of private business into political authority.

Figure 6.1 presents a schematic picture of enterprise influence in the American policy-making process as documented by Dye (1979). Although it is rather simple in its graphical structure, the complexity of the interdependencies given is self-evident.

The cabinet of the Carter Administration, for example, contained three members who had been on the board of IBM. Public policy interests of American blue-chip enterprise capital are represented on the private Conference Board. This powerful organization not only provides advice and policy recommendations to the U.S. government, but also many of its members (who are top CEOs of American enterprises) carry high government office. Reagan's second Secretary of State, George Schulz, had been dean of the University of Chicago School of Business and vice-president of the world's largest private company, the Californian-based Bechtal Corporation. Reagan's first Secretary of Defense, Caspar Weinberger, was also a vice-president at Bechtel at the same time as Schultz (Gill and Law 1988, 206).

Based upon these "personified" linkages as well as other linkages (e.g., trade associations, research foundations, policy planning groups, etc.) between the American state and enterprise capital, business interests are favorably represented in the executive branch, in Congress, and among the governmental bureaucracies. Naturally, this does not imply that economic interests ultimately shape American public policy, particularly when national security issues are at stake. But it does document the usage of networks to promote information and political transactions relevant to American multinational enterprise.

In 1961 only 130 enterprises were represented by registered lobbyists in Washington, and of these only 50 had their own Washington staffs. By 1979, 650 enterprises had their own registered lobbyists and 247 had full-time employees in Washington. In 1970 a small

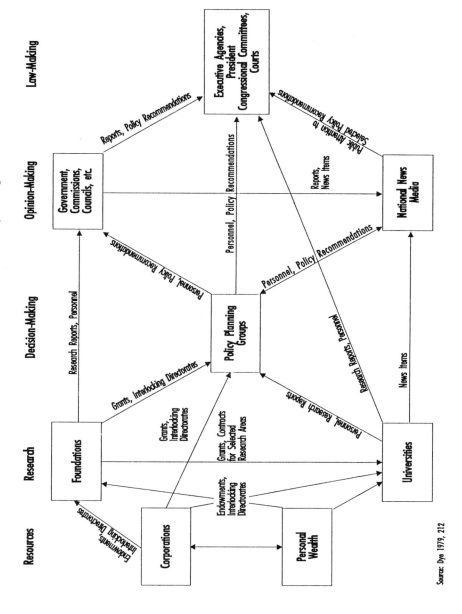

Figure 6.1 Corporate Influence in the U.S. Policy-Making Process

Source: Dye 1979, 212

minority of the *Fortune* 500 companies had public affairs offices; as of 1980, 80 percent now maintain public affairs offices. In 1974 there were 89 corporate political action committees; by 1982 the number exploded to some 1,555. Enterprise public relations programs and attempts to create grass roots support among employees, stockholders, and community groups were generally unheard of prior to 1970. Nowadays such programs are an important element of essentially every exertion on the part of the business community network to influence the public policy network. Furthermore, American enterprises have devoted enormous resources toward influencing intellectual ambience by sponsorship of conferences, publications, and academic research (Vogel 1989, 110).

At the community level American consortia networks have emerged since the passage of the National Cooperative Research Act in 1984. The Microelectronics and Computer Technology Corporation (MCC) and Semiconductor Manufacturing Technology (SEMATECH), both based in Austin, Texas, are the two most publicized examples. MCC consists of 21 enterprises collaborating in areas of advanced computer technology, computer-aided design, semiconductor packaging/interconnect, software technology, and superconductivity with an annual research budget of some $65 million (Gibbson and Rogers 1988; Auster 1990). Founded in 1987, SEMATECH consists of 14 American enterprises working together in an attempt to gain back market shares from the Japanese in the dynamic random-access memory market. Both MCC and SEMATECH are illustrative of the new industrial boundaries being created due to the collective goal of pursuing global market shares (Auster 1990).[3]

The current common interpretation of the public policy debate as two polar positions, contrasting between assertive interventionist states and noninterventionist states, is largely missing the point. The widening of the gap between the rhetoric of these debates and observed political practice is inhibiting our understanding of world network structures. As argued by Vogel (1989, 95), "To understand business—government relations in America, we need to pay less attention to what American economists and politicians contend govern-

---

3. At the international community level, a recent illustration of the public policy aspects of the emerging American–Japanese network is the July 1987 U.S. Senate vote to forbid imports of Toshiba products to castigate them for their subsidiary having sold superquiet submarine propellers to the Russians. The extent of Toshiba's interdependencies with U.S. enterprises caused an unanticipated repercussion of lobbying from Toshiba's American partners (Auster 1990, 84).

ment can and cannot do, and examine more closely what the American goverment has actually done."

THE MYTH OF JAPAN INCORPORATED

Why have the Japanese been so successful in fields such as steel, automobiles, and shipbuilding? Are computers, banking, and biotechnology the future areas of Japanese supremacy? The list of such questions could go on and on. The Japanese public policy of "administrative guidance" has led to the myth or stereotype of "Japan Incorporated" (Okimoto 1989). It is commonly believed that the Ministry of International Trade and Industry (MITI) and other agencies such as the Ministry of Finance (MOF) manage the Japanese economy by remote control. The Japanese model of public policy is only now beginning to be adequately understood on a broader basis. However, as Richmond and Kahan (1983, 26) correctly assert: "Frankly, too few Americans—even those with a deep interest in forcing Japan to come to terms with us—really understand the closely interwoven monolith that rules Japan. This is not the phantom 'Japan Inc.,' which is only a distorted attempt to 'name the beast' that confronts us. The actual monolith is part and parcel of Japan's tradition—that is, prewar ruling elite."

Japanese managers and enterprises are motivated by the same fundamental economic rationale as their Western counterparts. "If, then, a manager or enterprise is predisposed to collaborate with government, it is not because he is patriotic or typically Japanese (although he may well be both), but because he or his company or industry association has learnt that such collaboration can be of material benefit" (Boyd 1989, 64)."

As seen above, American public policy is also characterized by many linkages at all levels of public policy making (Figure 6.1). In comparing American and Japanese policy making, perhaps the most distinctive difference between the two systems is the more extensive use of direct collaborative linkages by the Japanese founded upon a social history of collectivity, mutual interdependencies, and an imperative search for consensus and harmonious resolution of conflict (Boyd 1989; Casson 1990b).

In Japan close government–industry relationships are not generally opposed, enabling collaborations based upon extensive channels of information, communication, trust, and mutual dependence. Formal and informal networks of consultation exist which are further facilitated by the practice of elite recruitment from Tokyo University (see Figure 6.2). The reins of current networks in Japan are held strongly in the hands of the historically dominant Liberal Democratic Party (LDP). Advisory councils and policy clubs (more factually, dinner clubs) bring together officials, politicians, and industrialists on a regular nonaccountable basis. The communication chain is further enforced by trade and industry associations. Interfirm groups or keiretsu linkages integrate the industrial constituency and provide a "transmission belt for ideas in both directions: from and to the key bureaucratic agencies" (Boyd 1989).

The bureacracy's penetration and control of these networks has raised the question of bureaucratic dominance. The practice of amakudari, which moves retired bureaucrats from MITI and MOF into the administration of the Liberal Democratic Party where many become ministers and even prime ministers,[4] into public enterprises, the Bank of Japan, commercial banks, and into trade and industry associations is said to ensure articulation and a receptive ear in the range of relationships that fabricate the policy network community (Boyd 1989; Okimoto 1989).

The complex relationships are ones of interdependency and reciprocity. The bureaucracy cannot act without the legitimating seal of the Diet (Parliament), and is, in consequence, constrained to cooperate with the Liberal Democratic Party which controls the Diet (Okimoto 1989, 5). This three-way relationship permits the "depoliticization" of the industrial policy-making process: the goal or "mission" of Japanese economic growth is beyond question and public debate. "The business of keeping the industrial policy process out of politics is intensely political" (Boyd 1989, 70).

The congruence of policy directives which originate from the interests of the business world or Zaikai, is illustrated in Figure 6.3. "Zaikai" is shorthand for the main associations of Japanese enterprise such as the Federation of Economic Organizations (Keidanren), the Federation of Employers Associations (Nikkeiren), the Committee for Economic Development (Keizai-Dōyūkai), and the Japan Chambers of Commerce and Industry.

Keidanren is the ruling institutional referent for Zaikai. More than one hundred industrywide associations (trade, finance, transportation, manufacturing, mining, etc.) and some eight hundred large corporations are organized in thirty "basic" agenda-setting commit-

---

4. Ex-bureaucrats constitute at least 30 percent of the membership of the LDP membership in both houses of the Diet—Japan's parliament (Boyd 1989). As Yamamura (1987, 188) suggests, "Japanese politics too have caught up with the West in its essential characteristics."

Figure 6.2 Japanese Government-Industry Relations of Dependence and Interdependence

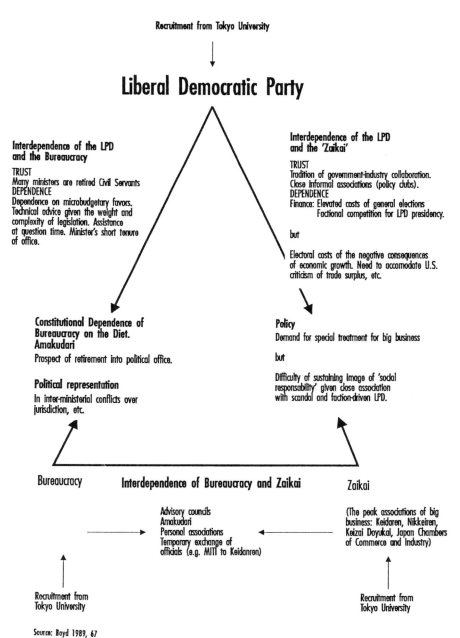

Recruitment from Tokyo University

Liberal Democratic Party

**Interdependence of the LPD
and the Bureaucracy**

TRUST
Many ministers are retired Civil Servants
DEPENDENCE
Dependence on microbudgetary favors.
Technical advice given the weight and
complexity of legislation. Assistance
at question time. Minister's short tenure
of office.

**Interdependence of the LPD
and the 'Zaikai'**

TRUST
Tradition of government-industry collaboration.
Close informal associations (policy clubs).
DEPENDENCE
Finance: Elevated costs of general elections
          Factional competition for LPD presidency.

but

Electoral costs of the negative consequences
of economic growth. Need to accomodate U.S.
criticism of trade surplus, etc.

**Constitutional Dependence of
Bureaucracy on the Diet.
Amakudari**

Prospect of retirement into political office.

Political representation

In inter-ministerial conflicts over
jurisdiction, etc.

Policy

Demand for special treatment for big business

but

Difficulty of sustaining image of 'social
responsability' given close association
with scandal and faction-driven LPD.

Bureaucracy   **Interdependence of Bureaucracy and Zaikai**   Zaikai

Advisory councils
Amakudari
Personal associations
Temporary exchange of
officials (e.g. MITI to Keidanren)

(The peak associations of big
business: Keidaren, Nikkeiren,
Keizai Doyukai, Japan Chambers
of Commerce and Industry)

Recruitment from
Tokyo University

Recruitment from
Tokyo University

Source: Boyd 1989, 67

Figure 6.3 Horizontal and Vertical
Communications in Japanese Industry

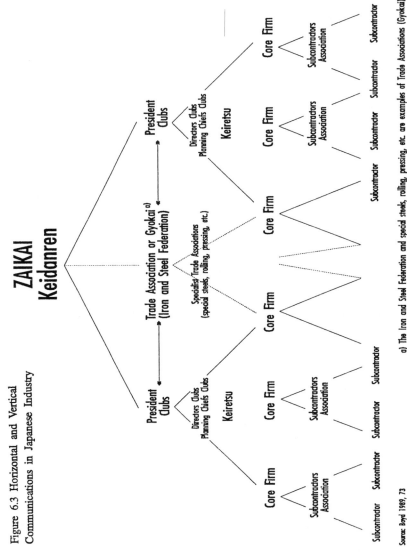

Source: Boyd 1989, 73

a) The Iron and Steel Federation and special steels, rolling, pressing, etc. are examples of Trade Associations (Gyokai) and Specialist Trade Associations respectively. The pattern of communication is of general significance.

tees within the Keidanren. Keidanren acts to mediate disputes and secure agreement among members and to make policy recommendations to the government. The industrial structure in Japan promotes horizontal and vertical communication and coordination (Boyd 1989). As mentioned in chapter 1, these relationships between a group of firms are further consolidated by their close relationship to a mutual "house" bank.

The next level of Japanese industrial organization are the keiretsus. The interfirm group member is itself at the center of a group of small and medium-size enterprises, enhancing vertical communication flows. Ninety-eight percent of manufacturing enterprises in Japan employ less than a hundred employees. Finally, at the lowest level the subcontractors are organized in their own associations (Yamamura 1987; Boyd 1989; Okimoto 1989).

SUMMARY

Today's multinational enterprises are characterized by their intimate relationships with government. These relationships are often "dependent, symbiotic, and sometimes suborning" (Galbraith 1978, 86). Multinationals seek legitimately, just as large national corporations do, to influence the public policy-making process.

Public policy recommendations touching areas of multinational enterprise are very complex, discouraging any inclination to treat them in simple terms. The issues raised by international strategic alliances exemplify the effects of collaborative agreements upon the process of competition. A conclusive analysis of the final impact of networking upon public policy is still outstanding.[5]

The answers to the questions are basically to be found in the now evolving concept of dynamic competitive advantage. Much of our conventional knowledge concerning public policy regarding costs and benefits of multinational enterprises needs to be revised to include the interactive comparative intergovernment, business, and enterprise network relationships. The expected future pressures of escalating levels of world interdependencies will challenge policy makers and enterprise executives alike. Network analysis will

---

5. That this state of affairs is to continue is reflected by Yamamura (1987, 200): "Industrial policy has much in common with religion. Avowed supporters of industrial policy include true believers and those who confuse their own greed with national interest. The market-trusting critics of industrial policy, on the other hand, call it a hocus-pocus having no 'rational' basis and often accuse it of being detrimental to economic efficiency. As in the debate on the existence of God, neither side really has infallible means to prove their case."

strengthen traditional policy wisdom by increasing the transparency of the government–business interactions.

Part of what public policy is about, then, is maintaining and promoting inter-government and interfirm networks such that a guided balance between cooperation and competition emerges. The policy makers' task is now one of setting out the prerequisites for sustaining competitive prosperity.

Any endeavor to evaluate the success of national industrial policy systems must take into account the significance of the levels of vertical and horizontal communication between government and industry. The effectiveness of any public policy strategy is conditional upon the existence of a chain of network linkages and privileged points of access between government and industry. The consequence of networks is the "quasi-integration" of the industrial policy community, which expedites economic and political transactions (Boyd 1989).

Suggestions for Further Research

> The basic task for organizations is to create the mutual trust and understanding that underpin successful networks and to find mechanisms for improving the flow of information. —*Kevin Barham*

We have explored the phenomena of multinational enterprise and strategic alliances from the perspective of networking. The 1980s and the early 1990s have been characterized by a striking increase in world network structures and alliances, politically as well as economically. Multinational enterprises are one of the most visible forces in the creation of enhanced global networks of interdependencies.

A wide range of strategic alliances and network structures are evolving because international partners need to:

(1) collaborate in order to spread and lower the development costs of high-risk, technology intensive production;

(2) obtain global economies of scale and scope in value-adding activities;

(3) learn about a partner's technology and proprietary processes or to seek access to new distribution channels;

(4) participate in shaping the evolution of competitive activity in the industry;

(5) collaborate in order to meet consumer demands for high variety and low cost.

To a large extent these activities all consist of exchanges of information and collective goal setting while maintaining high levels of competition. Substantial research has been conducted concerning multinational enterprises and industrial organization over the years. Very broadly, common to almost all of this research is the emphasis placed upon hierarchical structures and the potential for conflict. The purpose of this book is not to suggest that a hierarchical interpretation of multinational enterprise is necessarily wrong. But as Dunning (1988a, b) among others foresaw, a step-by-step interweaving of the approaches of the economist, business analyst, and organizational theorist is emerging based upon an understanding that networks do not replace hierarchies per se but that they do make them more effective.

199

As transactional relationships evolve on a global level, the effectiveness of any multinational enterprise or national public policy will depend upon an awareness of the economic logic of networks. The multinational enterprise manager is now confronted with a search for an optimal portfolio of interorganizational transactional relationships that serve long-run enterprise survival and excellence. It is not simply a question of obtaining the optimal value-added chain linkages; equally important is the development of efficient organizational communication chains based upon mutual dependency and reciprocity.

As Casson (1990b, 207) correctly argues, future research in this area will require a diversity of professional skills to address it. Multidisciplinary research has, however, commonly been inhibited by an overextension of the intellectual division of labor. This problem is further complicated by the fact that multiple levels of analysis are germane to any inquiry from a network perspective.

From a pragmatic viewpoint, however, a future research agenda should contain a minimum of at least the following four key levels of analysis as proposed by Auster (1990): (1) the individual level, (2) the organizational level, (3) the population/grouping level, and (4) the community/organizational field level. How do people influence interorganizational relations and what are the effects of interorganizational relations on individuals? What are the relevant organizational characteristics that affect the creation, management, maintenance, and stability of interorganizational relations? What range of various network linkages, as well as the configuration of organization sets and the structure of networks within a grouping/population, are observable? In what manner are environmental and industry characteristics correlated with the establishment and stability of network linkages and the formation of distinctive organization sets and networks over time? At the community/organizational field level, the focus of analysis is on consortia, trade associations, and strategic alliances that cut across multiple populations and institutions as they attempt to expedite collective interests.

To what extent these questions will be researched and answered in the future depends largely upon the interaction of academic networks and their pursuit of open and plentiful communication linkages through mutually cooperative efforts.

References

Abegglen, J. C. 1982. U.S.–Japan Technological Exchange in Perspective, 1946–1981. In *Technological Exchange: The U.S.–Japanese Experience,* ed. C. Vehara. New York: New York University Press.

Abegglen, J. C., and George Stalk, Jr. 1985. *Kaisha: The Japanese Corporation.* New York: Basic Books.

Agarwal, J. P. 1985. Intra-LDCs Foreign Direct Investment: A Comparative Analysis of Third World Multinationals. *The Developing Economies* 23.3: 236–53.

Agarwal, Manmohan. 1988. South–South Trade: Its Role in Development. In *Challenges of South—South Co-Operation,* ed. H. W. Singer, N. Hatti, and R. Tandon, 313–42. New Delhi: Ashishi Publishing House.

Agmon, Tamir, and Charles P. Kindleberger, eds. 1977. *Multinationals from Small Countries.* Cambridge, MA: MIT Press.

Aharoni, Yair. 1966. *The Foreign Investment Decision Process.* Boston: Division of Research, Graduate School of Business Administration, Harvard University.

———. 1971. On the Definition of a Multinational Corporation. *Quarterly Review of Economics and Business* 11: 27–37.

Alchian, A. A., and Demsetz, H. 1972. Production, Information Costs, and Economic Organization. *American Economic Review* 62: 777–95.

Aldrich, Howard E., and David A. Whetten. 1981. Organization-Sets, Action-Sets, and Networks: Making the Most of Simplicity. In *Handbook of Organizational Design,* ed. Paul C. Nystrom and William H. Starbuck, 385–408. London: Oxford University Press.

Anderson, E., and D. C. Schmittlein. 1984. Integration of the Sales Force: An Empirical Examination. *Rand Journal of Economics* 15: 385–95.

Ansoff, H. I. 1965. *Corporate Strategy.* London: Penguin.

Arndt, Sven W., and Lawrence Bouton. 1987. *Competitiveness: The United States in World Trade.* Washington: American Enterprise Institute for Public Policy Research.

Arora, Ashish, and Alfonso Gambardella. 1990. Complementary and External Linkages: The Strategies of the Large Firms in Biotechnology. *Journal of Industrial Economics* 38: 361–79.

201

Arrow, K. J. 1962. The Economic Implications of Learning by Doing. *Review of Economic Studies* 29: 155–73.

———. 1969. *The Organization of Economic Activity: Issues Pertinent to the Choice of Market versus Nonmarket Allocation.* U.S. Congress Joint Economic Committee 1: 47–64.

———. 1975. Vertical Integration and Communication (Symposium on the Economics of Internal Organization). *Bell Journal of Economics* 6: 173–84.

Auster, Ellen R. 1990. The Interorganizational Environment: Network Theory, Tools and Applications. In *Technology Transfer: A Communication Perspective,* ed. Frederick Williams and David Gibson, 171–91. Newbury Park, CA: Sage Publications.

Axelrod, R. 1984. *The Evolution of Cooperation.* New York: Basic Books.

Axelrod, R., and William D. Hamilton. 1981. The Evolution of Cooperation. *Science* 211: 1390–96.

Bacharach, S. B., and M. Aiken. 1976. Structural and Process Constraints on Influence in Organizations. *Administrative Science Quarterly* 21: 623–42.

Badaracco, Joseph L., Jr. 1988. Changing Forms of Corporation. In *The U.S. Business Corporation: An Institution in Transition,* ed. John R. Meyer and James M. Gustafson, 67–93. Cambridge, MA: Ballinger.

Badaracco, J. L., Jr., and D. B. Yoffie. 1982. Industrial Policy: It Can't Happen Here. *Harvard Business Review* Nov./Dec.: 96–175.

Balassa, Bela, and John Williamson. 1987. *Adjusting to Success: Balance of Payments Policy in the East Asian NICs.* Washington: Institute for International Economics.

Baranson, Jack. 1990. Transnational Strategic Alliances: Why, What, Where and How. *Multinational Business* 2: 54–61.

Bardhan, Pranab. 1990. Symposium on the State and Economic Development. *Journal of Economic Perspectives* 4: 3–9.

Barham, Kevin. 1991. Networking—The Corporate Way round International Discord. *Multinational Business* 4: 1–11.

Bartlett, Christopher, and Sumantra Ghoshal. 1988. Organizing for Worldwide Effectiveness: The Transnational Solution. *California Management Review* 31: 1–21.

———. 1989. *Managing across Borders.* Cambridge, MA: Harvard Business School Press.

Bartolomé, Fernando. 1989. Nobody Trusts the Boss Completely—Now What? *Harvard Business Review* Mar./Apr.: 135–42.

Baumol, W. J. 1977. On the Proper Cost Test for Natural Monopoly in a Multiproduct Industry. *American Economic Review* 67: 809–22.

Baumol, W. J., and D. Fischer. 1978. The Cost Minimizing Number of Firms and the Determination of Industry Structure. *Quarterly Journal of Economics,* 92: 439–68.

Behrman, Jack N. 1962. Foreign Associates and Their Financing. In

U.S. Private and Government Investment Abroad, ed. Raymond F. Mikesell, 77–113. Eugene, OR.

Behrman, Jack N., and Robert E. Grosse. 1990. *International Business and Governments: Issues and Institutions.* Columbia: University of South Carolina Press.

Bellon, B. 1983. La Chimie. In *L'Industrie en France,* ed. B. Bellon and J. M. Chevalier, 157–97. Paris: Flammarion.

Benson, J. K. 1975. The Interorganizational Network as a Political Economy. *Administrative Science Quarterly* 20: 229–49.

Best, Michael H. 1990. *The New Competition: Institutions of Industrial Restructuring.* Cambridge, MA: Polity Press.

Birley, Sue. 1985. The Role of Networks in the Entrepreneurial Process. *Journal of Business Venturing* 1: 107–17.

Blair, Roger D., and David L. Kaserman. 1978. Uncertainty and the Incentive for Vertical Integration. *Southern Economic Journal* 45: 266–72.

Boddewyn, J. J. 1985. Theories of Foreign Direct Investment and Divestment: A Classificatory Note. *Management International Review* 25: 57–66.

Bonanno, Giacomo. 1990. General Equilibrium Theory with Imperfect Competition. *Journal of Economic Surveys* 4: 297–329.

Borner, Silvio. 1983. *Die Wettbewerbsfähigkeit im Internationalen Markt: Theoretische Verknüpfung von Weltwirtschafts-und Unternehmungsebene.* Diskussionspapier Nr. 5 des Instituts für angewandte Wirtschaftsforschung. Basel: University of Basel.

———. 1985. *New Forms of Internationalization: An Assessment in the Light of Swiss Experience,* Forschungsbericht Nr. 11 des NFP 9. Zurich: University of Zurich.

———. 1986. *Internationalization of Industry: An Assessment in the Light of a Small Open Economy (Switzerland).* New York: Springer Verlag.

Borrus, M., L. D. Tyson, and J. Zysman. 1987. Creating Advantage: International Trade in Semiconductor Industry. In *Strategic Trade Policy and the New International Economics,* ed. P. R. Krugman, 91–115. Cambridge, MA: MIT Press.

Boyd, Richard. 1989. Government–Industry Relations in Japan: Access, Communication, and Competitive Collaboration. In *Comparative Government–Industry Relations: Western Europe, the United States, and Japan,* ed. Stephen Wilks and Maurice Wright, 61–90. Oxford: Clarendon Press.

Brenner, Reuven. 1990. *Rivalry in Business, Science, among Nations,* Cambridge: Cambridge University Press.

Broll, Udo, and B. Michael Gilroy. 1985a. International Division of Labor and Intra-Trade. *Economica Internazionale* 37: 161–67.

———. 1985b. Developing Countries in Light of Intra-Trade. *Asian Economies* 55: 20–28.

———. 1988. Intra-Industry Trade and Differences in Technology. *Scottish Journal of Political Economy* 35: 398–403.

————. 1989. *Aussenwirtschaftstheorie: Einführung und Neuere Ansätze*. Munich: Oldenbourg Verlag.

Brown, W. 1984. Firm-Like Behavior in Markets: The Administered Channel. *International Journal of Industrial Organization* 2: 263–76.

Brown, W. B. 1976. Islands of Conscious Power: MNCs in the Theory of the Firm. *MSU Business Topics* Summer: 37–45.

Buchanan, J. 1965. An Economic Theory of Clubs. *Economica* 32: 1–14.

Buckley, Peter J. 1981. A Critical Review of Theories of the Multinational Enterprise. *Aussenwirtschaft* 36: 70–87.

————. 1983. New Forms of International Cooperation: A Survey of the Literature with Special Reference to North–South Technology Transfer. *Aussenwirtschaft* 38: 195–222.

————. 1985. The Economic Analysis of the Multinational Enterprise: Reading versus Japan? *Hitsubashi Journal of Economics* Dec. 2: 117–24.

————. 1987. *The Theory of the Multinational Enterprise*. Uppsala Lectures in Business Vol. 26. Uppsala: Uppsala University.

————. 1988. The Limits of Explanation: Testing the Internalization Theory of the Multinational Enterprise. *Journal of International Business Studies* 19: 181–93.

————, ed. 1990. *International Investment*. Brookfield, VT: Elgar Publishing.

Buckley, Peter J., and Patrick Artisien. 1987. Policy Issues of Intra-EC Direct Investment: British, French and German Multinationals in Greece, Portugal and Spain, with Special Reference to Employment Effects. *Journal of Common Market Studies* 26: 207–31.

Buckley, Peter J., and Mark Casson. 1991. *The Future of the Multinational Enterprise*, 2nd ed. London: Macmillan.

————. 1988. A Theory of Co-operation in International Business. *Management International Review* 28: 19–39.

————. 1985. *The Economic Theory of the Multinational Enterprise*. London: Macmillan.

Buckley, Peter J., and H. Davies. 1981. Foreign Licensing in Overseas Operations: Theory and Evidence from the UK. In *Research in International Business and Finance*, Vol. 2, ed. R. G. Hawkins and A. D. Prasad, 75–89. Greenwich, CT: JAI Press.

Buckley, Peter J. Christopher L. Pass, and Kate Prescott. 1988. Measures of International Competitiveness: A Critical Survey. *Journal of Marketing Management* 4: 175–200.

Business International. 1990. *Making Alliances Work: Lessons from Companies' Successes and Mistakes*. London: Business International, A Member of the Economist Group.

Calvet, A. L. 1981. A Synthesis of Foreign Direct Investment Theories and Theories of the Multinational Firm. *Journal of International Business Studies* Spring/Summer: 43–59.

Canadian Council of Professional Engineers. 1983. *Brief on Research and Development in Canada*. Ottawa: CCPE.

Cantwell, John. 1987. The Reorganisation of European Industries after Integration. *Journal of Common Market Studies* 26: 127–53.

———. 1989. *Technological Innovation and Multinational Corporations.* Oxford: Basil Blackwell.

Carbaugh, Robert J. 1989. *International Economics*, 3rd ed. Belmont, CA: Wadsworth Publishing Company.

Carlsson, Bo. 1987. Reflections on "Industrial Dynamics": The Challenges Ahead. *International Journal of Industrial Organization* 5.

———, ed. 1989. *Industrial Dynamics: Technological, Organizational, and Structural Changes in Industries and Firms.* Boston: Kluwer Academic Publishers.

Cascio, Wayne F., and Manuel G. Serapio, Jr. 1991. Human Resources Systems in an International Alliance: The Undoing of a Done Deal? *Organizational Dynamics* Winter: 63–76.

Casson, Mark. 1979. *Alternatives to the Multinational Enterprise.* London: Macmillan.

———. 1985. Transaction Costs and the Theory of the Multinational Enterprise. In Buckley, P. J. and Casson, M. C., *The Economic Theory of the Multinational Enterprise,* ed. Buckley and Casson, 20–28. London, Macmillan.

———. 1987. *The Firm and the Market: Studies on Multinational Enterprise and the Scope of the Firm.* Oxford: Basil Blackwell.

———. 1990a. *Internalization Theory and Beyond,* University of Reading, Department of Economics, Discussion Papers in International Investment and Business Studies, series B, vol. 3.

———. 1990b. *Enterprise and Competitiveness: A Systems View of International Business.* Oxford: Clarendon Press.

———, ed. 1990c. *Multinational Corporations.* Brookfield, VT: Elgar Publishing.

Casson, Mark, with David Barry, James Foreman-Peck, Jean-Francois Hennart, Dennis Horner, Robert A. Read, Bernard M. Wolf. 1986. *Multinationals and World Trade: Vertical Integration and the Division of Labour in World Industries,* London: Allen & Unwin.

Caves, R. E. 1960. *Trade and Economic Structure,* Cambridge, MA: Harvard University Press.

———. 1971a. International Corporations: The Industrial Economics of Foreign Investment. *Economica* 38: 1–27.

———. 1971b. Industrial Economics of Foreign Direct Investment: The Case of the International Corporation. *Journal of World Trade and Law* 5: 303–14.

———. 1974a. Multinational Firms, Competition, and Productivity in Host-Country Markets. *Economica* 41: 176–93.

———. 1974b. Causes of Direct Investment: Foreign Firms' Shares in Canadian and United Kingdom Manufacturing Industries. *Review of Economics and Statistics* 56: 279–93.

———. 1974c. Industrial Organization. In *Economic Analysis and the*

Multinational Enterprise, ed. J. H. Dunning, 115–46. London: Allen & Unwin.

———. 1980. Investment and Location Policies of Multinational Enterprises. *Zeitschrift für Volkswirtschaft und Statistik* 116: 327–38.

———. 1982. *Multinational Enterprises and Economic Analysis.* Cambridge: Cambridge University Press.

———. 1985. International Trade and Industrial Organization: Problems, Solved and Unsolved. *European Economic Review* 28: 377–95.

Caves, R. E., H. Crookell, and J. P. Killing. 1982. *The Imperfect Market for Technology.* Cambridge, MA: Harvard Institute of Economic Research, Discussion Paper No. 903.

Caves, R. E., and R. Jones. 1985. *World Trade and Payments,* 4th ed. Boston: Little, Brown.

Caves, R. E., and William F. Murphy. 1976. Franchising: Firms, Markets, and Intangible Assets. *Southern Economic Journal* 43: 572–86.

Caves, R. E., and P. J. Williamson. 1985. What Is Product Differentiation Really? *Journal of Industrial Economics* 34: 113–32.

Cecchini, Paolo, with Michel Catinat and Alexis Jacquemin. 1988. *Europa '92: Der Vorteil des Binnenmarkts.* Lenkungsausschuss für d. Forschungsprogramm "Kosten d. Nichtverwicklichung Europas". Baden-Baden: Nomos Verlag.

Chandler, Alfred D., Jr. 1977. *The Visible Hand.* Cambridge, MA: Harvard University Press.

———. 1987. Technology and the Transformation of Industrial Organization. In *Technology, the Economy, and Society: The American Experience,* ed. Joel Colton and Stuart Bruchey, 56–82. New York: Columbia University Press.

Cheung, Steven N. S. 1969. Transaction Costs, Risk Aversion, and the Choice of Contractual Arrangements. *Journal of Law and Economics* 12: 23–42.

Clegg, Jeremy. 1988. *Multinational Enterprise and World Competition: A Comparative Study of the USA, Japan, the UK, Sweden and West Germany.* London: Macmillan.

Coase, R. H. 1937. The Nature of the Firm. *Economica,* n.s. 4: 386–405.

———. 1960. The Problem of Social Cost. *Journal of Law and Economics* 1: 1–44.

———. 1972. Industrial Organization: A Proposal for Research. In *Policy Issues in Research Opportunities in Industrial Organization,* ed. V. R. Fuchs, New York: National Bureau of Economic Research.

———. 1988. The Nature of the Firm: Influence. *Journal of Law, Economics, and Organization* 4: 33–47.

Contractor, F. J. 1985. *Licensing in International Strategy: A Guide for Planning and Negotiations.* Westport, CT: Greenwood Press.

Contractor, F. J., and Peter Lorange, eds. 1988a. *Cooperative Strategies in International Business.* Lexington, MA: Lexington Books.

————. 1988b. Competition vs. Cooperation: A Benefit/Cost Framework for Choosing Between Fully-Owned Investments and Cooperative Relationships. *Management International Review,* 28: 5–17.

Cordon, W. M. 1967. Monopoly, Tariffs and Subsidies. *Economica* 34: 50–58.

————. 1974. The Theory of International Trade. In *Economic Analysis and the Multinational Enterprise,* ed. J. H. Dunning, 184–210. London: Allen & Unwin.

Cornwall, R. 1977. The Concept of General Equilibrium in a Market Economy with Imperfectly Competitive Producers. *Metroeconomica* 29: 57–72.

Dahlman, C. J. 1984. Foreign Technology and Indigenous Technological Capability in Brazil. In *Technological Capability in the Third World,* ed. M. Fransman and K. King, London, Macmillan.

Davidson, William H. 1991. The Role of Global Scanning in Business Planning. *Organizational Dynamics* Winter: 4–17.

Davidson, W. W., and D. G. McFetridge. 1984. International Technology Transactions and the Theory of the Firm. *Journal of Industrial Economics* 32: 253–64.

Dean, Robert D., and Thomas M. Carroll. 1977. Plant Location under Uncertainty. *Land Economics* 53: 423–44.

Deardorff, A. V. 1984. Testing Trade Theories and Predicting Trade Flows. In *Handbook of International Economics,* Vol. 1, ed. R. Jones and P. Kennen, ch. 10. Amsterdam: North-Holland.

De Jong, Henk Wouter. 1981. Competition and Economic Power in the Pharmaceutical Industry. In *The Structure of European Industry,* ed. H. W. De Jong, 209–35. Boston: Martinus Nijhoff.

Delapierre, M., and J. B. Zimmerman. 1984. *L'industrie du traitement del'information. Note de travail pour GEST,* Grappe technologique et strategie industrielle. Paris.

DeMeza, David, and Frederick Van Der Ploeg. 1987. Production Flexibility as a Motive for Multinationality. *Journal of Industrial Economics* 35: 343–53.

Demsetz, Harold. 1988. The Theory of the Firm Revisited. *Journal of Law, Economics and Organization* 4: 141–62.

Dolles, H., and H. F. Jung. 1990. *Subcontracting in Japan,* Discussion Paper. FRG: University of Erlang-Nürnberg.

Dosi, G. 1988. Sources, Procedures, and Microeconomic Effects of Innovation. *Journal of Economic Literature* 1120–71.

Doz, Yves L. 1986. *Strategic Management in Multinational Companies.* New York: Pergamon Press.

————. 1988. Value Creation Through Technology Collaboration. In *Technology and Public Policy,* ed. Heinz Hauser, 175–91. Grüsch: Rüegger.

Doz, Yves, L., and C. K. Prahalad. 1988. Quality of Management: An Emerging Source of Competitive Advantage? In *Strategies in Global Competition,* ed. Neil Hood and Jan-Erik Vahlne, 345–70. New York: Croom Helm.

Drucker, Peter. 1954. *The Practice of Management.* New York: Harper & Row.

Dunning, J. H. 1958. *American Investment in British Manufacturing Industry.* London: Allen & Unwin.

————. 1973. The Determinants of International Production. *Oxford Economics Papers,* Vol. 25: 289–336.

————. 1974a. Comment. In *On the Economics of Intra-Industry Trade,* ed. H. Giersch, Tübingen: J. B. B. Mohr.

————, ed. 1974b. *Economic Analysis and the Multinational Enterprise,* London: Allen & Unwin.

————. 1977. Trade, Location of Economic Activity and Multinational Enterprise: A Search for an Eclectic Approach. In *The International Allocation of Economic Activity,* ed. B. Ohlin, P. O. Hesselborn, and P. M. Wijkman, London: Macmillan.

————. 1979a. The UK's International Direct Investment Position in the mid-1970s. *Lloyds Bank Review* 132: 1–21.

————. 1979b. Explaining Changing Patterns of International Production: In Defense of the Eclectic Theory. *Oxford Bulletin of Economics and Statistics* 41: 255–67.

————. 1980. Toward an Eclectic Theory of International Production: Some Empirical Tests. *Journal of International Business Studies* Spring/Summer: 9–31.

————. 1981a. *International Production and the Multinational Enterprise,* London: Allen & Unwin.

————. 1981b. Alternative Channels and Modes of International Resource Transmission. In *Controlling International Technology Transfer,* ed. R. W. Sagafi-nejad, R. W. Moxon, and H. V. Perlmutter, 3–26. New York: Pergamon Press.

————. 1981c. Explaining the International Direct Investment Position of Countries: Towards a Dynamic of Developmental Approach. *Weltwirtschaftliches Archiv* 117: 30–64.

————. 1982. *Non-Equity Forms of Foreign Economic Involvement and the Theory of International Production.* University of Reading Discussion Papers in International Investment and Business Studies No. 59.

————. 1987. *Multinational Enterprises and the Growth of Services: Some Conceptual and Theoretical Issues.* University of Reading Discussion Papers in International Investment and Business Studies No. 114.

————. 1988a. The Eclectic Paradigm of International Production: A Restatement and Some Possible Extensions. *Journal of International Business* 19: 1–31.

————. 1988b. *Explaining International Production.* London: Unwin Hyman.

————. 1989. *The Study of International Business: A Plea for a More Interdisciplinary Approach.* University of Reading Discussion Papers in International Investment and Business Studies No. 127.

Dunning, J. H., and M. McQueen. 1982. The Eclectic Theory of the

Multinational Enterprise and the International Hotel Industry. In *New Theories of the Multinational Enterprise*, ed. A. M. Rugman, 76–106. Beckenham, Kent: Croom Helm.

Dunning, J. H., and George Norman. 1986. Intra-Industry Investment. In *Research in International Business and Finance*, vol. 5, ed. Peter H. Gray, 73–95. Greenwich, CT: JAI Press.

Dunning, J. H., and R. D. Pearce. 1981. *The World's Largest Industrial Enterprises*. Farnborough: Gower.

Dunning, J. H. and Peter Robson. 1987. Multinational Corporation Integration and Regional Economic Integration. *Journal of Common Market Studies* 26: 103–27.

Dye, Thomas. 1979. *Who's Running America?* Englewood Cliffs, NJ: Prentice-Hall.

Easton, D. 1965. *A Framework for Political Analysis*. Englewood Cliffs, N.J.: Prentice-Hall.

Eliasson, Gunnar. 1987. Industrial Targeting: Defensive of Offensive Strategies in a Neo-Schumpeterian Perspective. In *Free Trade in the World Economy: Towards An Opening of Markets*, ed. Herbert Giersch, 333–61. Tübingen: J. C. B. (Paul Siebeck).

Erzan, R., and S. Laird. 1984. *Intra-Industry Trade of Developing Countries and Some Policy Issues*. Seminar Paper No. 289, Institute for International Economic Studies, Stockholm.

Ethier, W. 1986. The Multinational Firm. *Quarterly Journal of Economics* 101: 805–33.

Etzkowitz, H. 1983. Entrepreneurial Scientists and Entrepreneurial Universities in American Academic Science. *Minerva* 21: 198–233.

Evan, William. 1966. The Organization-Set: Toward a Theory of Interorganizational Relations. In *Approaches to Organizational Design*, ed. J. D. Thompson, Pittsburgh: University of Pittsburgh Press.

Feller, Irwin. 1990. Universities as Engines of R & D–Based Economic Growth: They Think They Can. *Research Policy* 19: 335–48.

Fennema, M. 1982. *International Networks of Banks and Industry*. Boston: Martinus Nijhoff.

Ferguson, Charles H. 1990. Computers and the Coming of the U.S. Keiretsu. *Harvard Business Review*, July-Aug.

Forbis, J. C., and N. Mehta. 1981. Value-based Strategies for Industrial Products. *Business Horizons*, 24: 3.

Forsgren, Mats. 1989. *Managing the Internalization Process: The Swedish Case*. London: Routledge.

Franko, Lawrence G. 1976. *The European Multinationals: A Renewed Challenge for American and British Big Business*. New York: Harper & Row.

———. 1987. New Forms of Investment in Developing Countries by US Companies: A Five Industry Comparison. *Columbia Journal of World Business*, 22.

Fusfeld, Herbert. 1988. Technology and Public Policy. In: *Technology and Public Policy*, ed. Heinz Hauser. Grüsch: Rüegger.

Gabszewicz, J. J., and J. P. Vial. 1972. Oligopoly 'a la Cournot' in General Equilibrium Analysis. *Journal of Economic Theory* 4: 381–400.

Galbraith, Craig S., and Neil M. Kay. 1986. Towards a Theory of Multinational Enterprise. *Journal of Economic Behavior and Organization* 7: 3–22.

Galbraith, John Kenneth. 1978. The Defense of the Multinational Enterprise. *Harvard Business Review* Mar.–Apr.: 83–93.

Gandolfo, Giancarlo. 1987. *International Economics*. Heidelberg: Springer Verlag.

Gardner, David. 1987. The Product Life Cycle "Its Role in Marketing Strategy." *Die Unternehmung: Schweizerische Zeitschrift für betriebwirtschaftliche Forschung und Praxis* 3: 219–31.

Gerlach, M. 1987. Business Alliances and the Strategy of the Japanese Firm. In *Organizational Approaches to Business Strategy,* ed. G. Caroll and D. Vogel, 27–143. Cambridge, MA: Ballinger.

Ghoshal, Sumantra, and Christopher A. Bartlett. 1990. The MNC as an Interorganizational Network. *Academy of Management Review* 15: 603–26.

Gibson, D., and E. Rogers. 1988. The MCC Comes to Texas. In *Measuring the Information Society,* ed. F. Williams. Newbury Park, CA, Sage Publications.

Giddy, Ian H. 1978. The Demise of the Product Cycle Model in International Business Theory. *Columbia Journal of World Business* 13: 90–97.

Giddy, Ian, and Alan M. Rugman. 1979. *A Model of Trade, Foreign Direct Investment and Licensing.* Graduate School of Business, Columbia University. Mimeo.

Gill, Stephen, and David Law. 1988. *The Global Political Economy: Perspectives, Problems, and Policies.* NY: Harvester, Wheatsheaf.

Gilroy, Bernard Michael. 1989. Intra-Firm Trade: Evidence and Theoretical Aspects. *Journal of Economic Surveys* 3: 325–43.

Gottinger, Hans W. 1982. The Economics of Organizational Design. *Journal of Economic Behavior and Organization* 3: 261–76.

Grabowski, Henry G., and Dennis C. Mueller. 1975. Life-Cycle Effects on Corporate Returns on Retentions. *Review of Economics and Statistics* 57: 400–416.

Gray, Barbara. 1989. *Collaborating: Finding Common Ground for Multiparty Problems.* San Francisco: Jossey-Bass.

Gray, H. J. 1983. Technology's Global Role in Industrial Transition. *High Technology* Dec: 12–14.

Greenaway, David. 1983. Intra-Industry and Inter-Industry Trade in Switzerland. *Weltwirtschaftliches Archiv* 119: 109–21.

———. 1986. *International Trade Policy: From Tariffs to the New Protectionism.* London: Macmillan.

———. 1987. Intra-Industry Trade, Intra-Firm Trade and European Integration. *Journal of Common Market Studies* 26: 153–73.

Grosse, Robert E. 1985. An Imperfect Competition Theory of the MNE. *Journal of International Business Studies* 16: 37–57.

Grosse, Robert E., and Duane Kujawa. 1988. *International Business: Theory and Managerial Applications*. Homewood, IL: Irwin.

Gruber, W., D. Mehta, and R. Vernon. 1967. The R & D Factor in International Trade and International Investment of United States Industries. *Journal of Political Economy* 75: 20–37.

Hadley, Eleanor. 1970. *Antitrust in Japan*. Princeton: Princeton University Press.

Hagedoorn, John and Jos Schakenraad. 1990. Strategic Partnering and Technological Co-operation. In *Perspectives in Industrial Organization*, ed. B. Dankbaar, J. Groenewegen, and H. Schenk, 171–95. Boston: Kluwer Academic Publishers.

Hahn, F., and T. Negishi. 1962. A Theorem on Non-Tatonnement Stability. *Econometrica* July.

Haklisch, C. S. 1986. *Technical Alliances in the Semiconductor Industry*. Mimeo.

Hall, R. H., et al. 1972. Patterns of Interorganizational Relationships. *Administrative Science Quarterly* 22: 457–74.

Hall, W. K. 1980. Survival Strategies in a Hostile Environment. *Harvard Business Review* 58: 75–85.

Hamel, Gary, Yves L. Doz, and C. K. Prahalad. 1986. *Strategic Partnerships: Success or Surrender?* Paper presented at the Rutgers/Wharton Colloquium on Cooperative Strategies in International Business, October.

———. 1989. Collaborate with Your Competitors and Win. *Harvard Business Review* Jan.-Feb.

Hammonds, Keith H. 1991. Corning's Class Act: How Jamie Houghton Reinvented the Company. *Business Week* May 13: 38–43.

Harrigan, Kathryn Rudie, and William H. Newman. 1990. Bases of Interorganization Cooperation: Propensity, Power, Persistence. *Journal of Management Studies* 27: 417–34.

Hart, O. D. 1985. Imperfect Competition in General Equilibrium: An Overview of Recent Work. In *Frontiers of Economics*, ed. K. J. Arrow and S. Honkapohja, 100–149. Oxford: Basil Blackwell.

———. 1987. Incomplete Contracts. In *The New Palgrave: A Dictionary of Economics*, ed. John Eatwell, Murray Milgrate, and Peter Newman, 752–58. London: Macmillan.

Hartley, Keith. 1983. *NATO Arms Co-operation: A Study in Economics and Politics*. London: Allen & Unwin.

Hauser, Heinz. 1981a. Joint-Ventures: Sonderlösungen für Einzelfälle oder allgemein verwendbare Instrumente zur internationalen Kooperation. *Aussenwirtschaft* 2: 176–94.

———. 1981b. Zur ökonomischen Theorie von Institutionen. In *Nationalökonomie Morgen*, ed. M. Timmermann, 59–84. Stuttgart: W. Kohlhammer.

———. 1986. Alternative Forms of International Cooperation and Technology Transfer: a Transactional Framework. In *Technology, Politics and*

Economics, ed. C. Keller, H. Matejla, and K. Sz.-Zborovàri, 45–55. Geneva: Graduate Institute of International Studies.

————, ed. 1988. *Technology and Public Policy.* Grüsch: Rüegger.

Havrylshyn, O., and E. Civan. 1983. Intra-Industry Trade and the Stage of Development: A Regression Analysis of Industrial and Developing Countries. In *Intra-Industry Trade: Empirical and Methodological Aspects,* ed. P. K. M. Tharakan, 111–40. Amsterdam: Elsevier Science Publishers.

Hax, A. C., and N. S. Majluf. 1984. *Strategic Management: An Integrative Perspective.* Engelwood Cliffs, NJ: Prentice-Hall.

Hayek, Friedrich A. 1945. The Use of Knowledge in Society. *American Economic Review,* 35: 519–30.

————. 1968. *Der Wettbewerb als Entdeckungsverfahren.* Kiel.

Haynes, Stephen E. 1988. Identification of Interest Rates and International Capital Flows. *Review of Economics and Statistics* 70: 103–11.

Helleiner, G. K. 1989. Transnational Corporations and Direct Foreign Investment. In *Handbook of Development Economics,* Vol. 2, ed. H. Chenery and T. N. Srinivasan, 1442–80.

Helpman, E. 1981. International Trade in the Presence of Product Differentiation, Economics of Scale and Monopolistic Competition: A Chamberlin–Heckscher–Ohlin Approach. *Journal of International Economics* 11: 305–40.

————. 1983. *The Multiproduct Firm: Horizontal and Vertical Integration.* Massachusetts Institute of Technology Department of Economics Working Paper No. 332.

————. 1984a. A Simple Theory of International Trade with Multinational Corporations. *Journal of Political Economy* 92: 451–71.

————. 1984b. *Imperfect Competition and International Trade: Evidence from Fourteen Industrial Countries.* The Foerder Institute for Economic Research, Tel Aviv University, Working Paper No. 35–84.

————. 1985a. Multinational Corporations and Trade Structure. *Review of Economic Studies* 52: 443–57.

————. 1985b. International Trade in Differentiated Middle Products. In *Structural Adjustment in Developed Open Economies,* ed. Karl Jungenfelt and Douglas Hague, 3–24. London: Macmillan.

————. 1987a. Imperfect Competition and International Trade: Evidence from Fourteen Industrial Countries. Journal of the Japanese and International Economies 1: 62–81.

————. 1987b. Imperfect Competition and International Trade: Opening Remarks. *European Economic Review* 31: 71–82.

Helpman, E., and P. R. Krugman. 1985. *Market Structure and Foreign Trade, Increasing Returns, Imperfect Competition, and the International Economy.* Cambridge, MA: MIT Press.

Hennart, J. F. 1982. *A Theory of Multinational Enterprise,* Ann Arbor: University of Michigan Press.

————. 1986. What Is Internalization? *Weltwirtschaftliches Archiv* 122: 791–804.

————. 1988. A Transaction Costs Theory of Equity Joint Ventures. *Strategic Management Journal* 9: 361–74.

————. 1989. Can The "New Forms of Investment" Substitute for the "Old Forms?" A Transactions Cost Perspective. *Journal of International Business Studies* 20: 211–35.

Hill, Charles W. L. 1988. Differentiation versus Low Cost or Differentiation and Low Cost: A Contingency Framework. *Academy of Management Review* 13: 401–12.

Hirsch, Seev. 1967. *Location of Industry and International Competitiveness*. Oxford: Clarendon Press.

————. 1975. The Product Cycle Model of International Trade—A Multi-Country Cross Section Analysis. *Oxford Bulletin of Economics and Statistics* 37: 305–17.

————. 1976. An International Trade and Investment Theory of the Firm. *Oxford Economic Papers* 28: 258–70.

Hirschleifer, J. 1967. Investment Decision under Uncertainty: Choice-Theoretic Approaches. *Quarterly Journal of Economics* 79: 509–36.

Hood, N., and J. Young. 1979. *The Economics of Multinational Enterprise*. London: Allen and Unwin.

Hufbauer, Gary C. 1966. *Synthetic Materials and the Theory of International Trade*. Cambridge, MA: Harvard University Press.

————. 1970. The Impact of National Characteristics and Technology on the Commodity Composition of Trade in Manufactured Goods. In *The Technology Factor in International Trade*, ed. Raymond Vernon. New York: National Bureau of Economic Research.

————. 1975. The Multinational Corporation and Direct Investment. In *International Trade and Finance: Frontiers for Research*, ed. P. B. Kenen, 253–319. Cambridge: Cambridge University Press.

Hymer, Stephen 1968. The Large Multinational Corporation. *Revue Economique* 19: 949–73. Rpt. *Multinational Corporations*, ed. Mark C. Casson.

————. 1970. The Efficiency (Contradictions) of Multinational Corporations. *American Economic Review, Papers and Proceedings* 60: 441–48.

————. 1971. The Multinational Corporation and the Law of Uneven Development. In *Economics and World Order*, ed. J. Bhagwati, 113–40. New York: Macmillan.

————. 1976. *The International Operations of National Firms: A Study of Direct Investment*, Cambridge, MA: MIT Press.

Iacocca, Lee, and William Novak. 1984. *Iacocca—Eine amerikanische Karriere*. Berlin: Ullstein Sachbuch.

Imai, Ken-ichi. 1989. Evolution of Japan's Corporate and Industrial Networks. In *Industrial Dynamics: Technological, Organizational, and Structural Changes in Industries and Firms*, ed. Bo Carlsson, Boston: Kluwer Academic Publishers.

Imai, Ken-ichi, and Hiroyuki Itami. 1984. Interpenetration of Organization and Market: Japan's Firm and Market in Comparison with the U.S. *International Journal of Industrial Organization* 2: 285–310.

Imai, Ken-ichi, Ikujiro Nonaka, and Hirotaka Takeuchi. 1985. Managing the New Product Development Process. In *The Uneasy Alliance,* ed. Kim Clark, Robert Hayes, and Christopher Lorenz, Cambridge, MA: Harvard Business School Press.

Imai, Masaaki. 1986. *Kaizen: The Key to Japan's Competitive Success.* New York: McGraw-Hill.

Ireland, Thomas R. 1990. The Formation of Organizations, Networks, and Markets. *Journal of Behavioral Economics* 19: 103–124.

Issak, Robert A. 1991. *International Political Economy: Managing World Economic Change.* Englewood Cliffs, NJ: Prentice-Hall.

Ishihara, Shintaro. 1991. *The Japan That Can Say No.* New York: Simon & Schuster.

Jacobson, Harold K. 1984. *Networks of Interdependence: International Organizations and the Global Political System,* 2nd ed. New York: McGraw-Hill.

Jaikumar, Ramchandran. 1986. Postindustrial Manufacturing. *Harvard Business Review,* 64: 69–76.

Jarillo, J. Carlos. 1988. On Strategic Networks. *Strategic Management Journal* 9: 31–41.

———. 1989. Entrepreneurship and Growth: The Strategic Use of External Resources. *Journal of Business Venturing* 4: 133–47.

Johanson, Jan, and Lars-Gunnar Mattson. 1987. Interorganizational Relations in Industrial Systems: A Network Approach Compared with the Transaction-Cost Approach. *International Studies of Management and Organization* 17: 34–48.

———. 1988. Internationalisation in Industrial Systems—A Network Approach. In *Strategies in Global Competition,* ed. Neil Hood and Jan-Erik Vahlne, 287–315. London: Croom Helm.

Johnston, Russell, and Paul R. Lawrence. 1988. Beyond Vertical Integration—the Rise of the Value-Adding Partnership. *Harvard Business Review* July-Aug.: 94–101.

Jones, Gareth R., and Charles W. L. Hill. 1988. Transaction Cost Analysis of Strategy–Structure Choice. *Strategic Management Journal* 9: 159–72.

Jones, Ronald W. 1967. International Capital Movements and the Theory of Tariffs and Trade. *Quarterly Journal of Economics* 81: 1–38.

———. 1971. A Three-Factor Model in Theory, Trade and History. In *Trade, Balance of Payments and Growth,* ed. J. N. Bhagwati et al., 3–21. Amsterdam: North-Holland.

Jones, Ronald W., and Fumio Dei. 1983. International Trade and Foreign Investment: A Simple Model. *Economic Inquiry* Oct: 449–64.

Jones, Ronald W., J. Peter Neary, and Frances P. Ruane. 1983. Two-Way Capital Flows: Cross-hauling in a Model of Foreign Investment. *Journal of International Economics* 14: 357–66.

Jorde, T., and D. Teece. 1989. Antitrust Law's Drag on Innovation. *The Wall Street Journal* June 18: 17.

Julius, DeAnne. 1990. *Global Companies and Public Policy: The Growing Challenge of Foreign Direct Investment.* London: Pinter.

Kaldor, N. 1934. The Equilibrium of the Firm. *Economic Journal* 44: 60–76.

Kane, Edward. 1991. Financial Regulation and Market Forces. *Schweizerische Zeitschrift für Volkswirtschaft und Statistik* Sept. 127: 325–42.

Kang, T. W. 1989. *Is Korea the Next Japan?* New York: The Free Press.

Katayama, Osamu. 1991. Company Strategy: Mitsubishi Corporation, Green Thumb. *Look Japan* May: 20–21.

Katrak, Homi. 1988. Payments for Imported Technologies, Market-Rivalry and Adaptive Activity in the Newly Industrialising Countries. *Journal of Development Studies* 25: 43–54.

Katz, J. M. 1984. Domestic Technological Innovations and Dynamic Comparative Advantage: Further Reflections on a Comparative Case-Study Program. *Journal of Development Economics* 16: 13–38.

Kay, N. M. 1983a. *The Evolving Firm.* London: Macmillan.

———. 1983b. Multinational Enterprise, A Review Article. *Scottish Journal of Political Economy* 30: 304–09.

Keesing, D. B. 1966. Labor Skills and Comparative Advantage. *American Economic Review, Papers and Proceedings* May 56: 249–58.

Kemp, M. C. 1964. *The Pure Theory of International Trade.* Englewood Cliffs, NJ: Prentice-Hall.

———. 1966. The Gain from International Trade and Investment: A Neo-Heckscher-Ohlin Approach. *American Economic Review* 56: 788–809.

Kennan, John, and Raymond Riezman. 1988. Do Big Countries Win Tariff Wars? *International Economic Review* 29: 81–84.

Kharan, A. 1985. A Note on the Dynamic Aspects of the Heckscher-Ohlin Model: Some Empirical Evidence. *World Development* 13: 1171–75.

Killing, Peter J. 1983. *Strategies for Joint Venture Success.* New York: Praeger.

———. 1988. Understanding Alliances: The Role of Task and Organizational Complexity. In *Cooperative Strategies in International Business,* ed. Farok Contractor and Peter Lorange, 55–69. Lexington, MA: Lexington Books.

Kindleberger, C. P. 1969. *American Business Abroad: Six Lectures on Direct Investment.* New Haven: Yale University Press.

———, ed. 1970. *The International Corporation,* Cambridge, MA: MIT Press.

———. 1973. *International Economics,* 5th ed. Homewood, IL: Richard D. Irwin.

Klein, B., R. G. Crawford, and A. A. Alchian. 1978. Vertical Integration, Appropriable Rents and the Competitive Contracting Process. *Journal of Law and Economics* 21: 297–326.

Knight, F. H. 1921. *Risk Uncertainty and Profit,* ed. G. J. Stigler. Chicago: University of Chicago Press.

Kogut, Bruce. 1983. Foreign Direct Investment as a Sequential Process. In *The Multinational Corporation in the 1980s,* ed. Charles P. Kindleberger and David B. Audretsch, 38–69. Cambridge, MA: MIT Press.

———. 1984. Normative Observations on the International Value-added Chain and Strategic Groups. *Journal of International Business Studies* Fall: 151–67.

———. 1985. Designing Global Strategies: Profiting from Operational Flexibility. *Sloan Management Review* Fall: 27–38.

———. 1988. A Study of the Life Cycle of Joint Ventures. *Management International Review* 28: 39–53.

———. 1989a. Research Notes and Communications: A Note on Global Strategies. *Strategic Management Journal* 10: 383–89.

———. 1989b. The Stability of Joint Ventures: Reciprocity and Competitive Rivalry. *Journal of Industrial Economics* 38: 183–98.

Kotha, Suresh, and Daniel Orne. 1989. Generic Manufacturing Strategies: A Conceptual Synthesis. *Strategic Management Journal* 10: 211–31.

Koutsoyiannis, A. 1982. *Non-Price Decisions: The Firm in a Modern Context.* London: Macmillan.

Kravis, I. B. 1956. "Availability" and Other Influences on the Commodity Composition of Trade. *Journal of Political Economy* 64: 143–55.

Krugman, P. 1979a. Increasing Returns, Monopolistic Competition, and International Trade. *Journal of International Economics* 9: 469–79.

———. 1979b. A Model of Innovation, Technology Transfer, and the World Distribution of Income. *Journal of Political Economics* 87: 253–66.

———. 1980. Scale Economies, Product Differentiation, and the Pattern of Trade. *American Economic Review* 70: 950–59.

———. 1981. Intraindustry Specialization and the Gains from Trade. *Journal of Political Economy* 89: 959–73.

———. 1982. Trade in Differentiated Products and the Political Economy of Trade Liberalization. In *Import Competition and Response,* ed. J. N. Bhagwati, Chicago: NBER.

———. 1983a. New Theories of Trade among Industrial Countries. *American Economic Review, Papers and Proceedings:* 343–47.

———. 1983b. The "New Theories" of International Trade and the Multinational Enterprise. In *The Multinational Corporation in the 1980's,* ed. Charles P. Kindleberger and David B. Audretsch, 57–73. Cambridge, MA: MIT Press.

———. 1985. A "Technology Gap" Model of International Trade. In *Structural Adjustment in Developed Open Economies,* ed. Karl Jungenfelt and Douglas Hague, 35–50. London: Macmillan.

———. 1987a. Is Free Trade Passé? *Economic Perspectives* 1: 131–44.

———, ed. 1987b. *Strategic Trade Policy and the New International Economics.* Cambridge, MA: MIT Press.

———. 1988. Multistage International Competition. In *International*

Competitiveness, ed. M. Spence and H. Hazard, 289–99. Cambridge, MA: Ballinger.

Kruskal, J. K., and M. Wish. 1978. *Multidimensional Scaling*. Beverly Hills, CA: Sage Publishing.

Kulatilaka, Nalin, and Stephen Gary Marks. 1988. The Strategic Value of Flexibility: Reducing the Ability to Compromise. *American Economic Review* 78: 574–81.

Kumar, K., and M. G. McLeod, eds. 1981. *Multinationals from Developing Countries*. Lexington, MA: Lexington Books.

Lall, S. 1980. Monopolistic Advantages and Foreign Involvement by US Manufacturing Industry. *Oxford Economic Papers* 32: 105–22. Rpt. Lall, *The Multinational Corporation*, London: Macmillan, 1980.

———. 1983. Determinants of R & D in an LDC: The Indian Engineering Industry. *Economic Letters*. 13: 379–83.

———. *Multinationale Konzerne aus der Dritten Welt*. Frankfurt: Campus.

———. 1990. *Building Industrial Competitiveness in Developing Countries*. Paris: Development Centre of the Organisation for Economic Co-Operation and Development.

Lall, S., et al. 1983. *The New Multinationals: The Spread of Third World Enterprises*. New York: Wiley.

Langenfeld, James, and David Scheffman. 1988. Innovation and U.S. Competition Policy. In *Technology and Public Policy*, ed. Heinz Hauser, 45–95. Grüsch: Rüegger.

Langlois, Richard N. 1989. Economic Change and the Boundaries of the Firm. In *Industrial Dynamics: Technological, Organizational, and Structural Changes in Industries and Firms*, ed. Bo Carlsson, 85–107. Boston: Kluwer Academic Publishers.

LAREA/CEREM. 1986. *Les Strategies d'accords des groupes européens entre la cohésion et l'éclatement*. Nanterre: University of Paris-X.

Larson, Andrea. 1991. Partner Networks: Leveraging External Ties to Improve Entrepreneurial Performance. *Journal of Business Venturing* 6: 173–89.

Lasswell, H. 1958. *Politics: Who Gets What, When, How?* New York: Meridan.

Lei, David, and John W. Slocum, Jr. 1991. Global Strategic Alliances: Payoffs and Pitfalls. *Organizational Dynamics* Winter: 44–63.

Leijonhufvud, Axel. 1986. Capitalism and the Factory System. In *Economics as a Process: Essays in the New Institutional Economics*, ed. R. N. Langlois, New York: Cambridge University Press.

Levine, Sol, and Paul E. White. 1961. Exchange as a Conceptual Framework for the Study of Interorganizational Relations. *Administrative Science Quarterly* 5: 583–601.

Levitt, Theodore. 1965. Exploit the Product Life Cycle. *Harvard Business Review*, Nov./Dec.

Lewis, W. A. 1978. *The Evolution of the International Economic Order.* Princeton: Princeton University Press.

Linder, Staffan Burenstam. 1961. *An Essay on Trade and Transformation.* New York.

Lipson, Charles. 1984. International Collaboration in Economics and Security Affairs. *World Politics* 37.

Loertscher, R., and F. Wolter. 1980. Determinants of Intra-Industry Trade among Countries and across Industries. *Weltwirtschaftliches Archiv* 116: 280–93.

Lorange, P. 1988. Co-Operative Strategies: Planning and Control Considerations. In *Strategies in Global Competition,* ed. Neil Hood and Jan-Erik Vahlne, 370–90. New York: Croom Helm.

Luce, R. Duncan, and Howard Raiffa. 1957. *Games and Decisions: Introduction and Critical Survey.* New York: Wiley.

Lundgren, N. 1975. *International koncerner i idustrilander (International Enterprises in Industrial Countries).* Stockholm, National Central Bureau of Statistics.

Lyles, Majorie A. 1988. Learning among Joint Ventures—Sophisticated Firms. In *Cooperative Strategies in International Business,* ed. Farok Contractor and Peter Lorange, 301–16. Lexington, MA: Lexington Books.

———. 1990. A Research Agenda for Strategic Management in the 1990s. *Journal of Management Studies* 27: 363–76.

MacDougall, G. D. A. 1960. The Benefits and Costs of Private Investment from Abroad: A Theoretical Approach. *Economic Record* 36: 13–35.

MacMillan, K. and D. Farmer. 1976. Redefining the Boundaries of the Firm. *Journal of Industrial Economics* 27: 277–85.

Madeuf, B., and C. Ominami. 1983. Crise et investissement international. *Revue Economique* 34: 926–70.

Magee, S. P. 1977a. Information and the Multinational Corporation: An Appropriability Theory of Direct Foreign Investment. In *The New International Order,* ed. J. N. Bhagwati, 317–40.

———. 1977b. Multinational Corporations, Industry Technology Cycle and Development. *Journal of World Trade Law* 11: 278–321.

Malinvaud, E. 1976. *Lectures on Microeconomic Theory,* 4th ed. Amsterdam: North-Holland.

Mallampally, Padma. 1990. Professional Services. In *The Uruguay Round: Services in the World Economy,* ed. Patrick A. Messerlin and Karl P. Sauvant, 84–94. New York: The World Bank and The United Nations Centre on Transnational Corporations.

Marcati, Alberto. 1989. Configuration and Coordination—The Role of US Subsidiaries in the International Network of Italian Multinationals. *Management International Review* 29: 35–50.

Mariti, P., and R. H. Smiley. 1983. Co-operative Agreements and the Organization of Industry. *Journal of Industrial Economics* 31: 437–51.

Markusen, J. R. 1984. Multinationals, Multi-Plant Economies, and the Gains from Trade. *Journal of International Economics* 16: 205–26.

Markusen, J. R., and J. Melvin. 1984. The Gains-from-Trade Theorem with Increasing Returns to Scale. In *Monopolistic Competition and International Trade*, ed. H. Kierzsowki, 10–34. Oxford: Clarendon.

—. 1988. *The Theory of International Trade*. New York: Harper & Row.

Marshall, A. 1940. *Principles of Economics*, 8th ed. London: Macmillan.

Masten, Scott E. 1982. Transaction Costs, Institutional Choice and the Theory of the Firm. PhD. Dissertation, University of Pennsylvania.

—. 1984. The Organization of Production: Evidence from the Aerospace Industry. *Journal of Law and Economics*, 27: 403–17.

—. 1986. Institutional Choice and the Organization of Production: The Make-or-Buy Decision. *Zeitschrift für die Gesamte Staatswissenschaft* 142: 493–510.

—. 1988. Equity, Opportunism, and the Design of Contractual Relations. *Journal of Institutional and Theoretical Economics* 144: 180–96.

Masten, Scott, James W. Meehan, and Edward A. Synder. 1989. Vertical Integration in the U.S. Auto Industry: A Note on the Influence of Transaction Specific Assets. *Journal of Economic Behavior and Organization* 12: 265–74.

McManus, J. 1972. The Theory of the International Firm. In *The Multinational Firm and the Nation State*, ed. G. Paquet, Ontario: Collier-Macmillan.

Michalet, C. A., M. Delapierre, B. Madeuf, and C. Ominami. 1983. *Nationalisations et internationalisations: strategies des multinationales françaises dans la crise*. Paris: Maspero.

Miles, Raymond, and Charles Snow. 1984. Fit, Failure and the Hall of Fame. *California Management Review* 26: 10–28.

—. 1986. Organizations: New Concepts for New Forms. *California Management Review* 28: 62–73.

Milgrom, Paul, and John Roberts. 1990. The Economics of Modern Manufacturing: Technology, Strategy, and Organization. *American Economic Review* 80: 511–28.

Modigliani, Franco, and M. H. Miller. 1958. The Cost of Capital, Corporation Finance and the Theory of Investment. *American Economic Review* 48: 261–97.

Monkiewicz, Jan. 1985. Internalization of Production Processes of Developing Countries: Some Empirical Evidence. *Vierteljahresberichte* 102: 333–48.

Monteverde, K., and D. J. Teece. 1982. Supplier Switching Costs and Vertical Integration in the Automobile Industry. *Bell Journal of Economics* 13: 206–13.

Morrison, Allen J., David A. Ricks, and Kendall Roth. 1991. Globalization versus Regionalization: Which Way for the Multinational? *Organizational Dynamics* Winter: 17–30.

Moxon, R. W. 1974. Offshore Production in the Less Developed Countries. *The Bulletin*, July, Institute of Finance, New York University.

Moxon, R. W., T. W. Roehl, and J. F. Truitt. 1988. International Cooperative Ventures in the Commercial Aircraft Industry: Gains, Sure, But What's My Share? In *Cooperative Strategies in International Business,* ed. Farok Contractor and Peter Lorange, 255–79. Lexington, MA: Lexington Books.

Mueller, Robert K. 1986. *Corporate Networking: Building Channels for Information and Influence.* New York: The Free Press.

Mullor-Sebastian, Alicia. 1983. The Product Life Cycle Theory: Empirical Evidence. *Journal of International Business Studies* Winter: 95–105.

Mytelka, Lynn Krieger. 1987. Knowledge-Intensive Production and the Changing Internalization Strategies of Multinational Firms. In *A Changing International Division of Labor,* ed. James A. Caporaso, 43–71. Boulder, CO: Lynne Rienner.

Mytelka, Lynn Krieger, and Michael Delapierre. 1987. The Alliance Strategies of European Firms and the Role of ESPRIT. *Journal of Common Market Studies* 26: 231–55.

Mytelka, Lynn Krieger, and R. Mahon. 1983. Industry, the State and the New Protectionism: Textiles in Canada and France. *International Organization* 37: 551–82.

Nayak, P. Ranganath, and John M. Ketteringham. 1986. *Breakthroughs.* New York: Rawson.

Nelson, R. R. 1959. The Simple Economics of Basic Research. *Journal of Political Economy* 3: 297–305.

Niosi, Jorge. 1985. *Canadian Multinationals.* Toronto: Between the Lines.

Noyelle, Thierry, and Anna B. Dutka. 1987. *International Trade in Business Services.* Cambridge, MA: Ballinger.

O'Brien, Peter, and Melissa Tullis. 1989. Strategic Alliances: The Shifting Boundaries between Collaboration and Competition. *Multinational Business* 4: 10–17.

OECD. 1983. *Transparency for Positive Adjustment: Identifying and Evaluating Government Intervention.* Paris: OECD.

———. 1986a. *Technical Co-operation Agreements Between Firms: Some Initial Data and Analysis,* Part I. Paris: OECD.

———. 1986b. *Technical Co-operation Agreements Between Firms: Some Initial Data and Analysis,* Part II. Paris: OECD.

———. 1987a. *Interdependence and Co-operation in Tomorrow's World.* Paris: OECD.

———. 1987b. *International Investment and Multinational Enterprises (Recent Trends in International Direct Investment).* Paris: OECD.

———. 1989. *International Direct Investment and the New Economic Environment.* Paris: OECD.

Ohmae, Kenichi. 1985. *Triad Power.* New York: The Free Press.

———. 1989a. *The Borderless World.* New York: The Free Press.

———. 1989b. The Global Logic of Alliances. *Harvard Business Review,* Mar.-Apr.: 143–54.

————. 1990. The Borderless World. *McKinsey Quarterly* 3: 3–20.

Ohno, T. 1984. "How the Toyota Production System Was Created." In *The Anatomy of Japanese Business,* ed. K. Sato and Y. Hoshino. London: Croom Helm.

Okimoto, Daniel I. 1989. *Between MITI and the Market: Japanese Industrial Policy for High Technology.* Stanford: Stanford University Press.

Oman, Charles. 1984. *New Forms of International Investment in Developing Countries.* Paris: OECD.

————. 1988. Cooperative Strategies in Developing Countries: The New Forms of Investment. In *Cooperative Strategies in International Business,* ed. Farok Contractor and Peter Lorange, 383–403. Lexington, MA: Lexington Books.

Omestad, Thomas. 1989. Selling Off America. *Foreign Policy* 76: 135–36.

Ouchi, W. G. 1980. Markets, Bureaucracies and Clans. *Administrative Science Quarterly* 25: 206–13.

Oye, Kenneth A., ed. 1986. *Cooperation under Anarchy.* Princeton: Princeton University Press.

Pearce, Robert D. 1988. *World Product Mandates and MNE Specialisation.* University of Reading Department of Economics Discussion Paper No. 121.

Penrose, Edith. 1956. Foreign Investment and the Growth of the Firm. *Economic Journal* 66: 220–35.

————. 1959. *The Theory of the Growth of the Firm.* Oxford: Basil Blackwell.

————. 1987. Multinational Corporations. In *The New Palgrave: A Dictionary of Economics,* Vol. 2, ed. J. Eatwell, M. Milgate, and P. Newman, 562–64. London: Macmillan.

Perlmutter, Howard, and David Heenan. 1986. Cooperate to Compete Globally. *Harvard Business Review* Mar.-Apr. 86: 136–52.

Peters, Thomas J., and Robert H. Waterman. 1983. *In Search of Excellence: Lessons from America's Best Run Companies.* New York: The Free Press.

Pfeffer, J., and P. Nowak. 1976. Joint Ventures and Interorganizational Interdependence. *Administrative Science Quarterly* 21: 398–418.

Pfeffer, J., and G. R. Salancik. 1974. The Bases and Use of Power in Organizational Decision Making: The Case of a University. *Administrative Science Quarterly* 19: 453–73.

Polanyi, Michael. 1967. *The Tacit Dimension.* Garden City, NY: Doubleday.

Porter, Michael E. 1980. *Competitive Strategy.* New York: The Free Press.

————. 1981. The Contributions of Industrial Organization to Strategic Management. *Academy of Management Review* 6: 609–20.

————. 1985. *Competitive Advantage.* New York: The Free Press.

————, ed. 1986. *Competition in Global Industries.* Cambridge, MA: Harvard Business School Press.

————. 1986. Changing Patterns of International Competition. *California Management Review* 28: 9–40.

————. 1990a. The Competitive Advantage of Nations. *Harvard Business Review* Mar.-Apr.: 73–93.

————. 1990b. Europe's Companies After 1992. *The Economist* June 9: 17–21.

————. 1991. *The Competitive Advantage of Nations.* New York: The Free Press.

Porter, Michael, and V. E. Milar. 1985. How Information Gives You Competitive Advantage. *Harvard Business Review* July-Aug.: 149–60.

Posner, M. V. 1961. Technical Change and International Trade. *Oxford Economic Papers* 3: 323–41.

Powell, Walter W. 1987. Hybrid Organizational Arrangements. *California Management Review* 30: 67–87.

Poynter, T., and A. Rugman. 1982. World Product Mandates: How Will Multinationals Respond? *Business Quarterly* Autumn: 54–61.

Preusse, Heinz Gert. 1985. Inter- and Intra-Industrial Division of Labour and the Gains from Trade. *Aussenwirtschaft* 40: 389–405.

Pruijm, Rudd A. M. 1990. *Corporate Strategy and Strategic Information Systems.* Deurne: Samson.

Rabelloti, Roberta. 1990. The Organization Variable in Developing Countries. In *Technological Change in a Spatial Context: Theory, Empirical Evidence and Policy,* ed. E. Ciciotti, N. Alderman, and A. Thwaites, 67–84. New York: Springer-Verlag.

Raffer, Kunibert. 1986. Siphoning Off Resources from the Periphery: The Relevance of Raul Prebisch's Thinking for the Eighties. *Development and South-South Cooperation* 2: 100–121.

————. 1987. *Unequal Exchange and the Evolution of the World System.* London: Macmillan.

Reich, Robert B. 1982. Making Industrial Policy. *Foreign Affairs* Sept.: 852–97.

————. 1983. An Industrial Policy of the Right. *Public Interest* Fall: 3–17.

————. 1991. *The Work of Nations: Preparing Ourselves for 21st-Century Competition.* New York: Knopf.

Reich, Robert, and Eric Mankin. 1986. Joint Ventures with Japan Give Away Our Future. *Harvard Business Review,* July–Aug.

Richardson, G. B. 1972. The Organisation of Industry. *Economic Journal* 82: 883–96.

Richmond, F. W., and M. Kahan. 1983. *How to Beat the Japanese at Their Own Game.* Englewood Cliffs, NJ: Prentice-Hall.

Robinson, E. A. G. 1931. *The Structure of Competitive Industry.* London: Nisbet.

———. 1934. The Problem of Management and the Size of the Firm. *Economic Journal* 44: 242–57.

Robinson, Richard D. 1988. *The International Transfer of Technology: Theory, Issues, and Practice*. Cambridge, MA: Ballinger.

Robinson, Richard B., Jr. and John A. Pearce II. 1986. Product Life Cycle Considerations of Strategic Activities in Entrepreneurial Firms. *Journal of Business Venturing* 1: 207–24.

Roehl, T., and J. F. Truitt. 1987. Stormy, Open Marriages Are Better: Evidence from U.S. Japanese and French Cooperative Ventures in Commercial Aircraft. *Columbia Journal of World Business* 21: 87–96.

Rubner, Uli. 1990. Unternehmer Aller Länder Vereinigt Euch! *Politik und Wirtschaft* 5: 60–70.

Ruffin, R. J. 1984. International Factor Movements. In: *Handbook of International Economics*, Vol. 1, ed. R. Jones and P. Kenan, 238–86. Amsterdam: North-Holland.

Ruffin, Roy J. and Farhad Rassekh. 1986. The Role of Foreign Direct Investment in U.S. Capital Outflows. *American Economic Review* 76: 1126–30.

Ruggie, John Gerard. 1972. Collective Goods and Future International Cooperation. *American Political Science Review* Sept. 66.

Rugman, A. M. 1980a. A New Theory of the Multinational Enterprise: Internalization versus Internationalization. *Columbia Journal of World Business* 15: 23–29.

———. 1980b. Internalization as a General Theory of Foreign Direct Investment: A Re-Appraisal of the Literature. *Weltwirtschaftliches Archiv* 114: 365–79.

———. 1981. *Inside the Multinationals: The Economics of Internal Markets*. New York: Columbia University Press.

———. 1982. *New Theories of the Multinational Enterprise*. London: Croom Helm.

———. 1986. New Theories of the Multinational Enterprise: An Assessment of Internationalization Theory. *Bulletin of Economic Research* 38: 101–18.

———. 1990. *Multinationals and Canada–United States Free Trade*. Columbia: University of South Carolina Press.

Rugman, A. M., and John McIlveen. 1985. *Megafirms: Strategies for Canadian Multinationals*. Toronto: Methuen.

Rutenberg, D. 1982. International Operations Management: Global Product Mandating. In *International Business: A Canadian Perspective*, ed. K. C. Dhwan, H. Etemad, and R. Wright, 588–98. Ont.: Addison-Wesley.

Schelling, T. C. 1960. *The Strategy of Conflict*. Cambridge, MA: Harvard University Press.

Schmalensee, Richard, and Robert D. Willig, eds. 1989. *Handbook of Industrial Organization*. Amsterdam: North-Holland.

Schulze, Charles. 1983. Industrial Policy: A Dissent. *Brookings Review* Fall.

Schumacher, D. 1983. Intra-Industry Trade Between the Federal Republic of Germany and Developing Countries. In *Intra-Industry Trade: Empirical and Methodological Aspects,* ed. P. K. M. Tharakan. Amsterdam: North-Holland.

Shachar, Joseph, and Ehud Zuscovitch. 1990. Learning Patterns within A Technological Network: The Case of the European Space Program. In *Perspectives in Industrial Organization,* ed. Ben Dankbaar, John Groenewegen, and Hans Schenk, 133–50. Dordrecht: Kluwer Academic Publishers.

Singer, H. W., N. Hatti, and R. Tandon, eds. 1988. *Challenges of South-South Co-operation.* New Delhi: Ashishi Publishing House.

Smith, Adam. 1970. *The Wealth of Nations,* ed. Andrew Skinner. Harmondsworth: Penguin. Originally published 1776.

Sonnenberg, Frank K. 1990. How to Reap the Benefits of Networking. *Journal of Business Strategy* Jan./Feb.: 59–62.

Stalk, Georg Jr. 1988. Time–The Next Source of Competitive Advantage. *Harvard Business Review.* July-Aug.: 41–51.

Starreveld, R. W. 1962. *Leer van de administratieve organisatie (Bestuurlijke Informatieverzorging deel I en II).* Alphen: Samsom.

Starreveld, R. W., E. J. Joels, and H. B. De Mare. 1985. *Bestuurlijke Informatieverzorging deel I en II.* Alphen: Samsom.

Steers, Richard M., Yoo Keun Shin, and Gerado R. Ungon. 1989. *The Chaebol: Korea's Next Industrial Might.* Cambridge, MA: Ballinger.

Stern, N. 1989. The Economics of Development: A Survey. *Economic Journal* 99: 597–686.

Stiglitz, Joseph E. 1987. Learning to Learn: Localized Learning and Technological Progress. In *Economic Policy and Technological Development,* ed. P. Dasgupta and P. Stoneman. Cambridge: Cambridge University Press.

Stopford, J. M., and J. H. Dunning, eds. 1982. *The World Directory of Multinational Enterprises.* London: Macmillan.

Sylos-Labini, P. 1984. *The Forces of Economic Growth and Decline.* Cambridge, MA: MIT Press.

Tallman, Stephen B., and Oded Shenkar. 1990. International Cooperative Venture Strategies: Outward Investment and Small Firms from NICs. *Management International Review* 30: 299–315.

Taylor, Michael. 1976. *Anarchy and Cooperation.* New York: Wiley.

Teece, D. J. 1977. Technology Transfer by Multinational Firms: The Resource Cost of Transferring Technological Knowledge. *Economic Journal* 87.

———. 1980. Economies of Scope and the Scope of the Enterprise. *Journal of Economic Behavior and Organization* 1: 223–47.

———. 1981. *Markets in Microcosm: Some Efficiency Properties of Vertical Integration.* Discussion Papers, Wissenschaftszentrum Berlin, IIM/IP-81-29.

———. 1982. Towards An Economic Theory of the Multiproduct Firm. *Journal of Economic Behavior and Organization* 3: 39–64.

———. 1983. Technological and Organizational Factors in the Theory of the Multinational Enterprise. In *Growth of International Business*, ed. M. C. Casson. London: Allen & Unwin.

————. 1985. Multinational Enterprises, Internal Governance, and Industrial Organization. *American Economic Review, Papers and Proceedings* 233–38.

————. 1986. Transaction Cost Economics and the Multinational Enterprise: An Assessment. *Journal of Economic Behavior and Organization* 7: 21–47.

Telser, L. G. 1980. A Theory of Self-Enforcing Contracts. *Journal of Business* 22: 27–44.

Thorelli, H. B. 1986. Networks: Between Markets and Hierarchies. *Strategic Management Journal* 7: 37–51.

Tirole, J. 1988. *The Theory of Industrial Organization*. Cambridge, MA: MIT Press.

Topkis, Donald. 1978. Maximizing a Submodular Function on a Lattice. *Operations Research* 26: 305–21.

Toyne, Brian 1989. International Exchange: A Foundation for Theory Building in International Business. *Journal of International Business* 20: 1–17.

Traxler, Franz, and Brigitte Unger. 1990. Institutionelle Erfolgsbedingungen wirtschaftlichen Strukturwandels. Zum Verhältnis von Effizienz und regulierung aus theoretischer und empirischer Sicht. *Wirtschaft und Gesellschaft* 16: 189–225.

Tucker, Jonathan B. 1991. Partners and Rivals: A Model of International Collaboration in Advanced Technology. *International Organization* 45: 83–121.

Tung, Rosalie L. 1991. Handshakes across the Sea: Cross-Cultural Negotiating for Business Success. *Organizational Dynamics* Winter: 30–44.

UNCTAD. 1980. *Intra-Industry Trade and International Subcontracting*. Report by the UNCTAD Secretariat (TD/B/805/Supages2).

————. 1990a. *Trade Expansion among Developing Countries: Constraints and Measures to Overcome Them*. Report by the UNCTAD Secretariat (TD/B/1260).

————. 1990b. *The Role of International Collaboration Arrangements in Developing Countries' Exports of Manufactures*. Study Prepared by the UNCTAD Secretariat. (ITP/32).

UNCTC. 1987. *Transnational Corporations and Technology Transfer: Effects and Policy Issues*. New York: United Nations.

————. 1989. *Foreign Direct Investment and Transnational Corporations in Services*. New York: United Nations.

UNIDO. 1981. *Intra-Firm Trade and International Industrial Restructuring*. UNIDO Working Papers On Structural Changes, No. 20.

————. 1984. *Case Studies in the Acquisition of Technology (II)*. Development and Transfer of Technology Series No. 14. New York: United Nations.

United Nations. 1983. *Transnational Corporations in World Development.* Third Survey. New York: United Nations.

Van de Ven, A. H. 1976. On the Nature, Formation, and Maintenance of Relations among Organizations. *Academy of Management Review* 1: 24–36.

Van de Ven, A. H. and D. L. Ferry. 1980. *Measuring and Assessing Organizations.* New York: Wiley.

Van de Ven, A. H. and G. Walker. 1984. The Dynamics of Interorganizational Coordination. *Administrative Science Quarterly* 29: 598–621.

Van Dierdonck, R., K. Debackere, and B. Engelen. 1990. University–Industry Relationship: How Does the Belgium Academic Community Feel about It? *Research Policy* 19: 551–66.

Varian, Hal R. 1978. *Microeconomic Analysis.* New York: W. W. Norton.

———. 1987a. The Arbitrage Principle in Financial Economic. *Economic Perspectives* 1: 55–72.

———. 1987b. *Intermediate Microeconomics: A Modern Approach.* New York: W. W. Norton.

Vernon, Raymond. 1966. International Investment and International Trade in the Product Cycle. *Quarterly Journal of Economics* May: 190–207.

———. 1971. *Sovereignty at Bay.* London: Pelican.

———. 1977a. The Location of Economic Activity. In *Economic Analysis and the Multinational Enterprise,* ed. J. H. Dunning. London: Allen & Unwin.

———. 1977b. *Storm over the Multinationals: The Real Issues.* London: Macmillan.

———. 1979. The Product Cycle Hypothesis in a New International Environment. *Oxford Bulletin of Economics and Statistics* 41: 255–67.

———. 1987a. Product Cycle. In *The New Palgrave: A Dictionary of Economics,* Vol. 2, ed. J. Eatwell, M. Milgate, and P. Newman, 986–87. London: Macmillan.

———. 1987b. Global Interdependence in a Historical Perspective. In *Interdependence and Co-operation in Tomorrow's World,* 22–36. Paris: OECD.

Vernon, Raymond, and W. H. Davidson. 1979. *Foreign Production of Technology-Intensive Products by U.S.–Based Multinational Enterprises.* Working Paper 79-5, Harvard Business School.

Vernon, Raymond, and Debora L. Spar. 1989. *Beyond Globalism: Remaking American Foreign Economic Policy.* New York: The Free Press.

Vernon, Raymond, and Louis T. Wells, Jr. 1981. *Manager in the International Economy.* Englewood Cliffs, NJ: Prentice-Hall.

Vogel, David. 1989. Government-Industry Relations in the United States: an Overview. In *Comparative Government-Industry Relations: Western Europe, the United States, and Japan,* ed. Stephen Wilks and Maurice Wright, 91–115. Oxford: Clarendon Press.

Von Hippel, E. 1985. *User Innovation: An Analysis of the Functional Sources of Innovation.* Cambridge, MA: Sloan School of Management, MIT.

————. 1986. Lead Users: A Source of Novel Product Concepts. *Management Science* 32: 791–805.

————. 1989. Cooperation Between Rivals: Informal Knowhow-Trading. In *Industrial Dynamics: Technological, Organizational and Structural Changes in Industries and Firms*, ed. Bo Carlsson, 157–75. Boston: Kluwer Academic Publishers.

Walker, G. 1988. Network Analysis for Cooperative Interfirm Relationships. In *Cooperative Strategies in International Business*, ed. Farok Contractor and Peter Lorange, 227–40. Lexington, MA: Lexington Books.

Waterson, Michael. 1984. *Economic Theory of the Industry*. Cambridge: Cambridge University Press.

Wells, L. T., Jr., ed. 1972. *The Product Life Cycle and International Trade*. Boston: Harvard University Press.

————. 1983. *Third World Multinationals: The Rise of Foreign Investment from Developing Countries*. Cambridge, MA: MIT Press.

White, R. E. 1986. Generic Business Strategies, Organizational Text and Performance: An Empirical Investigation. *Strategic Management Journal* 7: 217–31.

Wilks, Stephen, and Maurice Wright, eds. 1989. *Comparative Government–Industry Relations: Western Europe, the United States, and Japan*. Oxford: Clarendon Press.

Williamson, O. E. 1971. The Vertical Integration of Production: Market Failure Considerations. *American Economic Review* 61: 112–23.

————. 1975. *Markets and Hierarchies*. New York: The Free Press.

————. 1979. Transaction-Cost Economics: The Governance of Contractual Relations. *Journal of Law and Economics* 22: 233–47.

————. 1981. The Modern Corporation: Origins, Evolution, Attributes. *Journal of Economic Literature* 19: 1537–68.

————. 1983. Credible Commitments: Using Hostages to Support Exchange. *American Economic Review* 73: 519–40.

————. 1985a. *The Economic Institutions of Capitalism: Firms, Markets, Relational Contracting*. New York: The Free Press.

————. 1985b. Reflections on the New Institutional Economics. *Journal of Institutional and Theoretical Economics* 141: 187–95.

————. 1986. The Economics of Governance: Framework and Implications. In *Economics as a Process: Essays in the New Institutional Economics*, ed. R. N. Langlois, 171–99. Cambridge: Cambridge University Press.

————. 1987. Transaction Cost Economics: The Comparative Contracting Perspective. *Journal of Economic Behavior and Organization* 8: 617–25.

————. 1991. Comparative Economic Organization: The Analysis of Discrete Structural Alternatives. *Administrative Science Quarterly* 36: 269–96.

Williamson, O. E., M. L. Wachter, and J. E. Harris. 1975. Understanding the Employment Relation: The Analysis of Idiosyncratic Exchange. *Bell Journal of Economics* 6: 250–60.

Williamson, O. E., and Sidney Winter, eds. 1991. *The Nature of the Firm: Origins, Evolution, and Development.* New York: Oxford University Press.

Willig, R. D. 1979. Multiproduct Technology and Market Structure. *American Economic Review, Papers and Proceedings:* 346–50.

Yamamura, Kozo. 1987. Caveat Emptor: The Industrial Policy of Japan. In *Strategic Trade Policy and the New International Economics,* ed. P. Krugman, 169–211. Cambridge, MA: MIT Press.

Yasumuro, Ken'ichi. 1979. The Contribution of Sogo Shosha to the Multinationalization of Japanese Industrial Enterprises in Historical Perspective. In *International Investment,* ed. Peter J. Buckley, 297–325. Brookfield, VT: Elgar.

Yoo, Sangjin, and Sang M. Lee. 1987. Management Style and Practice of Korean Chaebols. *California Management Review* Summer.

Young, A. K. 1979. *The Sogo Shosha: Japan's Multinational Trading Companies.* Boulder, CO: Westview Press.

Name Index

229

Company Index